The State of Recorded Sound Preservation in the United States:

A National Legacy at Risk in the Digital Age

August 2010

Commissioned for and sponsored by the

National Recording Preservation Board
OF THE LIBRARY OF CONGRESS

Council on Library and Information Resources
and The Library of Congress
Washington, D.C.

The National Recording Preservation Board

The National Recording Preservation Board was established at the Library of Congress by the National Recording Preservation Act of 2000. Among the provisions of the law are a directive to the Board to study and report on the state of sound recording preservation in the United States. More information about the National Recording Preservation Board can be found at http://www.loc.gov/rr/record/nrpb/.

ISBN 978-1-932326-36-9
CLIR Publication No. 148

Copublished by:

Council on Library and Information Resources
1752 N Street NW, Suite 800
Washington, DC 20036
Web site at http://www.clir.org

and

The Library of Congress
101 Independence Avenue, SE
Washington, DC 20540
Web site at http://www.loc.gov

Additional copies are available for $30 each. Orders must be placed through CLIR's Web site.
This publication is also available online at no charge at http://www.clir.org/pubs/abstract/pub148abst.html.

The paper in this publication meets the minimum requirements of the American National Standard for Information Sciences—Permanence of Paper for Printed Library Materials ANSI Z39.48-1984.

Cover image: Drawings submitted by Thomas A. Edison in support of the patent application for his Phonograph, filed December 24, 1877. Reproduced from a copy held in the Library of Congress Recorded Sound Reference Center.

Library of Congress Cataloging-in-Publication Data

The state of recorded sound preservation in the United States : a national legacy at risk in the digital age / commissioned for and sponsored by the National Recording Preservation Board of the Library of Congress.
p. cm. -- (CLIR publication ; no. 148)
"This study was written by Rob Bamberger and Sam Brylawski on behalf of the National Recording Preservation Board"--P. iv.
"August 2010."
Includes bibliographical references.
ISBN 978-1-932326-36-9 (alk. paper)
1. Sound recordings--Conservation and restoration--United States. 2. Sound recordings--Digitization--United States. 3. Digital preservation--United States. 4. Sound recording libraries--United States. 5. Sound archives--United States. 6. Copyright--Sound recordings--United States. 7. Copyright and digital preservation--United States. 8. Fair use (Copyright)--United States. I. Bamberger, Robert. II. Brylawski, Samuel. III. National Recording Preservation Board (U.S.) IV. Title. V. Series.

Z701.3.S68S73 2010
025.8'4--dc22

2010032200

Contents

Acknowledgments v
Foreword vi
Introduction and Summary 1

1. Sound Recording Collections: An Overview of Preservation and Public Access in the Twenty-first Century 9

2. Technical Issues in Digital Audio Preservation. 66

3. Development of Curricula in Recorded Sound Preservation and Archives Management 99

4. Preservation, Access, and Copyright: A Tangled Web 108

Appendix A. National Recorded Sound Preservation Study: Announcement of Study and Public Hearing (November 2006) 138

Appendix B. Report of a Task Force Discussion to Define Prerequisites, Core Knowledge, and Graduate Educational Directions for Sound Preservation Professionals, and to Review an Annotated Bibliography of Audio Preservation Resources. 144

Appendix C. Obstacles to Access and Preservation of Recorded Sound. . . . 156

Appendix D. *Folk Collections in Crisis* Report: Concluding Discussion and Recommendations 165

Bibliography available at **http://www.loc.gov/rr/record/nrpb/**

This study was written by Rob Bamberger and Sam Brylawski on behalf of the National Recording Preservation Board.

Members of the Library of Congress National Recording Preservation Board

Acknowledgments

The writers of this report would like to thank those who submitted statements and participated in the hearings and roundtable discussions, and colleagues at the Library of Congress who provided essential support and valuable suggestions.

Authors of published studies that supplement this report
June Besek
Tim Brooks
Ellen Cunningham Kruppa
Nancy Davenport
Peter Jaszi
Paul Kingsbury

Library of Congress staff
Peter Alyea
Larry Appelbaum
Matthew Barton
James H. Billington
Daniel Boomhower
Bryan Cornell
Eugene DeAnna
Karen Fishman
Carl Fleischhauer
Steven Leggett
Patrick Loughney
Gregory Lukow
Janet McKee
Laura Maddox
Marsha Maguire
Deanna Marcum
Jennifer Murray
Cary O'Dell
Donna Ross

Special thanks for assistance
David Randal Allen
Karen Allen
Don Andes
Christine Bamberger
George Blood
Jill Breedon
Sarah Cunningham
Kelly Darr
Peter Hirtle
Marc Kirkeby
Brian Leney
Roger Mayer
Annette Melville
Brenda Nelson-Strauss
Abby Smith Rumsey
Bill Schurk
Kathlin Smith
Steven Smolian
Gail Sonnemann
Konrad Strauss
Richard Warren
Paul West

Foreword

Sound recordings have existed as one of the most salient features of America's cultural landscape for more than 130 years. As a nation, we have good reason to be proud of our historical record of creativity in the sound recording arts and sciences. However, our collective energy in creating and consuming sound recordings in all genres has not been matched by an equal level of interest, over the same period of time, in preserving them for posterity.

During the closing years of the twentieth century, the Library of Congress staff began collecting an increasing amount of disturbing anecdotal evidence on a number of problem areas affecting the survival and preservation of sound recordings produced in America since the nineteenth century. That evidence resulted, in part, from the Library's own efforts over more than 85 years to build and maintain a nationally representative recorded sound collection; it also came from information reported by other cultural institutions, professional archivists, record companies, broadcasters, collectors, researchers, and interested members of the general public. Over time it became clear to the recorded sound community that an array of obstacles faced by institutions and individuals dedicated to preserving historic sound recordings had become a serious national problem.

In response, the U.S. Congress passed *The National Recording Preservation Act of 2000 (Public Law 106-474)*. That legislation affirmed the nation's collective interest in preserving sound recordings for posterity; and, to promote greater public awareness of the issues involved, established the Library of Congress National Recording Preservation Board and the National Recording Registry.

The National Recording Preservation Act of 2000 also directed that I, in my capacity as Librarian of Congress, "...implement a comprehensive national sound recording preservation program..." with a specific responsibility to "...undertake studies and investigations of sound recording preservation activities as needed, including the efficacy of new technologies, and recommend solutions to improve these practices." One of the earliest activities of the new National Recording Preservation Board was to advise me on the importance of conducting a national study and the range of issues to be investigated.

I am glad to report that the study of the state of recorded sound preservation on the United States has been completed. This is the first comprehensive, national-level study of the state of sound recording preservation ever conducted in the U.S.—through extensive research and analysis performed over a period of five years. The National Recording Preservation Board commissioned four ancillary studies, enlisting specialists in law and history. Three of those studies address copyright and related issues central to the protection and preservation of commercial and unpublished sound recordings, as well as public access; the fourth study investigated the poor survival rates in the marketplace of recordings of historic significance, dating back to the nineteenth century. These subsidiary studies developed reliable supporting and statistical information where none previously existed. All of these documents are included in *The State of Recorded Sound Preservation in the United States: A National Legacy at Risk in the Digital Age.*

The publication of *The State of Recorded Sound Preservation in the United States* is a landmark achievement in the history of the archival preservation of audiovisual materials. The authors, Rob Bamberger and Sam Brylawski, have produced a study outlining the web of interlocking issues that now threaten the long-term survival of our sound recording history. This study tells us that major areas of America's recorded sound heritage have already been destroyed or remain inaccessible to the public. It suggests that the lack of conformity between federal and state laws may adversely affect the long-term survival of pre-1972-era sound recordings in particular. And, it warns that the continued lack of national coordination among interested parties in the public and private sectors, in addressing the challenges in preservation, professional education and public access, may not yet be arresting permanent loss of irreplaceable sound recordings in all genres.

This study lays the groundwork for the *National Recording Preservation Plan* that was also mandated under the National Recording Preservation Act of 2000 and will be published by the Library of Congress later this year. The *National Recording Preservation Plan* will make specific recommendations for addressing the complex problems revealed by *The State of Recorded Sound Preservation in the United States.*

The Library of Congress has witnessed substantial progress during the past decade in preparing for the national effort called for in *The State of Recorded Sound Preservation in the United States*. Most significant is the complete transformation of the Library's facilities for storing and preserving its recorded sound and audiovisual collections that was made possible by the unprecedented gift of the $200 million Packard Campus for Audio Visual Conservation by the Packard Humanities Institute in 2007. The Packard Campus, located in Culpeper, Virginia, is now staffed and operating. After more than 85 years of collecting sound recordings, the Library of Congress now has a facility worthy of its mission to preserve and make maximally accessible a comprehensive record of the nation's recorded sound, movie, and broadcast heritage. The Packard Campus has brought together in a single facility almost all of the Library's staff and resources at this critical time when our statutory responsibilities for national leadership in recorded sound and moving image preservation are expanding in order to implement the multiple mandates of the National Recording Preservation Act of 2000.

For all those who cherish the importance of sound recordings to the cultural history of the United States, the findings and conclusions of *The State of Recorded Sound Preservation in the United States*, in the areas of copyright, collections, technology and education, will be recognized as profound and far-ranging. The national study has articulated the issues to be addressed in a national plan to provide direction and momentum to public policy decisions affecting recorded sound preservation for generations to come. America's recorded sound heritage has in many ways transformed the soundscape of the modern world. The public and private sectors should now work together to define and preserve this important and creative part of our patrimony.

—James. H. Billington
Librarian of Congress

Introduction and Summary

It is roughly 10 seconds in length: a human voice singing a recognizable fragment of "Au Clair de la Lune." Recorded on April 9, 1860, it is the earliest identifiable sound recording of the human voice. The recording was made by Parisian inventor Edouard-Leon Scott de Martinville on an instrument he called a phonautograph.[1] Scott's invention was prompted by his interest in seeing the physical characteristics of sound waves.[2] His machine scratched sound waves on paper Scott had blackened using smoke from an oil lamp. Nearly 150 years later, through the use of a digital imaging workstation commissioned by the Library of Congress and designed by Lawrence Berkeley National Laboratory, the waves appearing on Scott's phonautogram were translated into sound.

When the Scott phonautogram was unveiled in March 2008 at the annual conference of the Association for Recorded Sound Collections in Palo Alto, California, it drew worldwide attention. The hunt for the Scott phonautograms is nothing less than a recorded sound equivalent of an archaeological dig to locate and secure the permissions to make them available for study. Hearing the recognizable sound that lay in the wavy lines on that smoked paper is a profound experience—an encounter with real time and space in the mid-nineteenth century.

Recorded sound is captivating. It is a technology that has enabled us to physically etch, magnetically transcribe, or translate into

[1] The discovery and interpretation of Scott's phonautogram was the work of First Sounds [www.firstsounds.org], in collaboration with the Lawrence Berkeley National Laboratory. The earliest of Scott's phonautograms can be dated to 1853. First Sounds has discovered additional phonautograms, documented on their Web site and in the spring 2010 issue of the *ARSC Journal*.

[2] In his last years, Scott railed against Thomas Edison for usurping credit due to him; however, it was never Scott's intention to reproduce sound, which was ultimately Edison's purpose.

bytes a core part of the lived experience not only of this nation but also of the entire world. Recorded sound is more than music and entertainment; it encompasses the sounds of the streets, of nature, and of the vanished folk heritage of indigenous and transplanted cultures, as well as of important national events and precious moments in our own personal lives.

It is relatively easy to recognize the importance of recorded sound from decades ago. What is not so evident is that older recordings actually have better prospects to survive another 150 years than recordings made last week using digital technologies. In short, where recorded sound is concerned, age is no arbiter of what is endangered or what might be lost to future generations.

Many important recordings have been lost or have become unplayable since the introduction of recorded sound in the late-nineteenth century. Many others are at risk of becoming lost. It is unclear how large a universe of recordings will remain undocumented and allowed to deteriorate before additional resources are invested in their preservation.

Today's digital formats are not inherently safe harbors of preservation. Protecting and maintaining digital audio recordings poses problems that go beyond those associated with the preservation of analog recordings, and it requires that a totally new set of preservation techniques be developed. For example, successive releases of software programs may no longer be compatible with earlier files. Even without abuse, hard drives and servers crash. At worst, phonautograms float to the floor.

Study Background

Two critical needs—the need to recognize the risk to a literal and metaphorical recording of our society, culture, and heritage, and the need to fashion a coordinated response to save and preserve sound recordings—underlie this study. The National Recording Preservation Act of 2000 (P.L. 106-474) established, under the purview of the Library of Congress, the National Recording Preservation Board (NRPB) and a National Recording Registry to maintain and preserve sound recordings that are "culturally, historically, or aesthetically significant." The recordings are selected by the Librarian of Congress.[3]

The act also authorized that a study on sound recording preservation and restoration be prepared for Congress that reports on the following issues:

(1) The current state of sound recording archiving, preservation and restoration activities.

(2) Taking into account the research and other activities carried out by or on behalf of the National Audio-Visual Conservation Center[4] at Culpeper, Virginia—

(A) the methodology and standards needed to make the

[3] Sec. 124.

[4] Subsequently designated in 2005 as the Packard Campus for Audio Visual Conservation.

transition from analog "open reel" preservation of sound recordings to digital preservation of sound recordings; and
(B) standards for access to preserved sound recordings by researchers, educators, and other interested parties.

(3) The establishment of clear standards for copying old sound recordings (including equipment specifications and equalization guidelines).

(4) Current laws and restrictions regarding the use of archives of sound recordings, including recommendations for changes in such laws and restrictions to enable the Library of Congress and other nonprofit institutions in the field of sound recording preservation to make their collections available to researchers in a digital format.

(5) Copyright and other laws applicable to the preservation of sound recordings.

The 10 years between the enactment of P.L. 106-474 and the publication of this study have seen sweeping changes in digital technologies that have democratized the ability of individuals to make recordings and to manipulate sound in digital formats. A succession of new platforms enabling distribution of sound recordings have been introduced. During the past decade, the century-old business model for retail distribution of (largely) music recordings has imploded. Consequently, some of the technology and other details noted in this study may be mere snapshots of something that is in constant motion. Yet despite the pace of change, strengthening support for recorded sound preservation will require a continuing process, rather than fragmented solutions.

This study has been informed by a number of reports commissioned by the National Recording Preservation Board as well as by public hearings in Los Angeles and New York City, roundtables, written submissions from practitioners and other experts, and a bibliography of the literature on recorded sound preservation prepared specifically for this project. Several formal interviews were conducted to gather expert observations; many other encounters were informal yet equally productive.[5]

Scope of the Problem

The story of the state of recorded sound preservation begins with recognizing how little is known about the universe of existing sound recordings. This is reflected in key findings from chapter 1:

- Public institutions, libraries, and archives hold an estimated 46 million recordings, but few institutions know the full extent of their holdings or their physical condition.
- There is no correlation between the risk to sound recordings and their age. Recordings created in digital formats are at particular

[5] The reports, as well as transcripts of the hearings and submissions, are available at http://www.loc.gov/rr/record/nrpb/nrpb-clir.html.

risk. Current programs to systematically preserve these recordings are inadequate.

- Many record companies have undertaken preservation programs. However, it is uncertain whether master recordings are being retained and preserved when there is no prospect for their reissue or for monetary gain from their digital distribution.
- Master recordings are now more often in the possession of the original artists than they used to be. Many of these recordings are at risk because they are not being properly stored.
- Few institutions have the facilities, playback hardware, and staff resources to preserve recordings. Of the many recorded sound formats that have fallen into obsolescence, some are more fragile than others. Specialized equipment is required to reproduce and preserve them.
- Many recordings believed to have been made of radio broadcasts are untraceable, and numerous transcription discs of national and local broadcasts have been destroyed. Little is known of what still exists, where it is stored, and in what condition. From the mid-1920s until well into the 1950s, radio was the nation's major source for entertainment and news, as well as a mirror of the times. Threatened here is more than the loss of sound recordings—it is the loss of an irreplaceable piece of our sociocultural heritage.
- Digital recordings distributed over the Internet, including radio, are not systematically collected for preservation.
- Privately held recording collections are often more comprehensive than publicly available collections held by institutions. Record and sound collectors often have sharply focused interests, defined by genre of music, specific performer, or both. It is important to help private collectors appreciate the importance of planning for placement of their collections, at the appropriate time, with archives where they can be protected and preserved.
- Funding and advocacy for recorded sound preservation is decentralized and inadequate. Recorded sound preservation has been declared a national objective; however, without greater support as a matter of public policy, this objective will not be realized.
- Resources must be invested not only in rescuing specific collections but also in developing techniques and methodologies that will enable more institutions to afford to assume a share of the work.

Complex Technical Landscape

The recorded sound story continues with the multiple formats that have served as sound carriers since the first voice and music recordings were made. These formats include cylinders and flat discs made of different materials, some of which hold up better than others against the passage of time, neglect, and improper storage. Analog disc recordings have been made for more than a century, but some digital formats and carriers (and software designed to make the digital content available) have had the briefest of lifetimes. Many techniques can be used to stop the deterioration of sound recordings and make transfers that are as faithful as possible to the sources from which copies are struck. These techniques vary widely in scale and resource intensity, which gives rise to the need for preservation "best practices" and making the most prudent and productive use of the resources available to accomplish the work. Not every recording can be saved. What trade-offs are acceptable between hovering over a single transfer to assure a near-perfect copy, and monitoring an operation where copies of many different recordings are being created simultaneously?

Chapter 2 of this study provides an overview of the technical landscape, covering the rescue and preservation of sound recordings as well as what will be needed for maintenance and use of these digital files for decades to come. Among the findings in this chapter are:

- The capacity to adhere to current best practices for audio preservation is beyond the reach of most institutions. Preservation techniques and practices scaled for use by smaller institutions must be developed and disseminated.
- Digital preservation requires a sophisticated information technology infrastructure and an ongoing process to maintain the integrity of digital files well into the future. Most institutions lack these capacities.
- The pace of the transition to professional digital preservation is governed by many issues that are not yet resolved. These include agreement on minimal requirements for administrative and technical metadata to accompany digital preservation files and the development of tools to create metadata efficiently. Until such questions are answered, we will have no assurance that digital preservation files are being sustained for the long term.
- There is unnecessary redundancy in preservation efforts. Technical, administrative, and legal means must be developed to enable institutions to share data about recordings held in common and to locate source recordings that are in the best condition to serve as candidates for preservation. Institutions should have the means and legal sanction to share preservation files of these recordings.
- Depending on CD-Rs as a medium for storing preservation files is ill advised and has placed preservation programs at great risk. Few institutions have programs to periodically migrate audio files to new CD-Rs or to other digital storage media. Digital repositories, where files can be properly stored, kept accessible, and managed in perpetuity, are essential.

Need for Preservation Education

The curation and management of digital preservation files of sound recordings calls for implementing a process that recognizes that (1) the preservation of sound recordings demands perpetual attention, including periodic migration of preservation files to new formats, and (2) additional copies of sound recordings must be dispersed geographically to protect against loss. Implementing this process will depend upon the existence of a trained cadre of engineers and technicians who are knowledgeable about obsolete media and the hardware or software that unlocks them. Chapter 3 of this study, devoted to audio preservation education, sets forth several constructs that could be part of a curriculum devoted to recorded sound preservation. It also describes specific jobs for which such a curriculum could prepare candidates. Themes discussed in the chapter include the following:

- Degree programs to train professional audio archivists are nonexistent. Several universities offer courses that relate to audio preservation, but none offers degree programs that train professionals in audio preservation and archives management. Developing such programs must be a priority.
- Opportunities for continuing education and professional development are necessary.
- A generation of specialists with experience in making transfers from legacy media is disappearing.
- Selecting recorded sound collections to be preserved and setting priorities for their preservation will require that managers have a grounding in the history of the period of these recordings. Only with such a foundation will they be able to assess the aesthetic and cultural impact of the recordings.
- Audio archivists and curators need a blend of theoretical, managerial, and technical skills. Directors of archives will require training in organizational theory and behavior, contracting and project management, facilities planning, cost analysis, and budgeting.

The Copyright Conundrum

Copyright law and interests in protecting intellectual property are a final thread (or perhaps a seemingly unyielding tangle) in the environment affecting recorded sound preservation. At issue is how copyright law might be amended, or simple licensing mechanisms developed, to bring rightful protection of intellectual property into better balance with digital technology, thereby furthering the interests of recorded sound preservation. The availability of otherwise out-of-print commercial recordings, coupled with expectations fostered by the Internet that access should be immediate, are at the foundation of tensions between rights holders and users.

In many instances, early commercial recordings may be unavailable from rights holders. As reported in the *Survey of Reissues of U.S. Recordings*, a study commissioned by the NRPB, "ten percent or less of listed recordings have been made available by rights holders for most periods prior to World War II. For periods before 1920, the percentage approaches zero."[6] It once might have required a long and frustrating quest to acquire or hear a rare recording; today, the

[6] Tim Brooks, *Survey of Reissues of U.S. Recordings* (Washington, DC: Council on Library and Information Resources and Library of Congress, 2005), 11–14, "Summary of Key Findings and Conclusions." Available at http://www.clir.org/pubs/reports/pub133/summary.html.

Internet has made it possible to locate such a recording with a single search string or communication to a listserv. The proliferation of digital platforms and the ease with which sound recordings can be uploaded and shared are of justifiable concern to rights holders who cannot control the appropriation of their intellectual property.

There are some promising initiatives, referenced in the treatment of copyright in chapter 4 of this study, that can reconcile the demand for out-of-print recordings and the participation of, or sanction from, rights holders. The voices and opinions quoted in the chapter also clearly show, however, that advocates for competing and legitimate objectives are nowhere near any reconciliation.

The following are among the findings presented in chapter 4:

- Were copyright law followed to the letter, little audio preservation would be undertaken. Were the law strictly enforced, it would brand virtually all audio preservation as illegal. Copyright laws related to preservation are neither strictly followed nor strictly enforced. Consequently, some audio preservation is conducted.
- Libraries, archives, and other public and privately funded institutions are finding it virtually impossible to reconcile their responsibility for preserving and making accessible culturally important sound recordings with their obligation to adhere to copyright laws.
- Privileges extended by copyright law to libraries and archives to copy sound recordings are restrictive and anachronistic in the face of current technologies, and create only the narrowest of circumstances in which making copies is fully permissible.
- The perception that recordings held by institutions are unlikely to be accessible discourages private collectors from depositing their holdings with institutions.
- Collections in need of preservation may not receive funding if, once preserved, they will not be available for off-site listening.
- Copyright reform is not the sole area in which congressional action is needed, but it remains the key solution to preserving America's recorded sound history, protecting ownership rights, and providing public access.
- Revision of copyright laws will require significant compromises by all affected communities. Although achieving a consensus on copyright reform seems elusive at present, it is critical to develop innovative approaches and programs that can bring preservation and access into compliance with copyright law.
- Closer cooperation between copyright holders, intellectual property owners, and libraries is essential and could be advantageous to all parties. Efforts must be made to draw attention to the common ground on which change can be built.

The Internet and development of digital technology have unleashed a paradigm shift. At one time, support for preservation of the arts did not carry with it the expectation of access to a restored work. Today, preservation and access have become joined, locked together in the realm of sound recordings. This phenomenon has the potential to undermine efforts to attract support for preservation of sound collections, especially collections of noncommercial recordings, for which there can be no guarantee of access because the rights are unclear or do not convey with the collection. The expectation of access has not only fostered conflict between rights holders and potential users but also put rights holders into conflict on a new front, namely, with libraries and archives. Funding requests for the preservation of sound collections must compete against requests for preservation of other media to which ready access is legal. In short, however much copyright law appears at first glance to have little bearing on the prospects for recorded sound preservation, it is as central a challenge as are the challenges presented by technology and education.

Saving our Recorded Sound Heritage

The authors of this study acknowledge that a close, cover-to-cover reading of this volume is not a casual undertaking. At times, readers may feel smothered in minutiae or in concepts that can only be described as opaque. They may find themselves asking, after wading through discussions of metadata, sticky-shed syndrome, Section 108, and digital repositories, "Must this all be so complicated?" The audience for this study is diverse. Some sections will be of greatest interest to sound engineers; other sections will be relevant primarily to academics. Still others may be of value to stakeholders with interests in copyright and intellectual property law. This diversity should not, however, distract from the fundamental story presented here, which is of critical importance to policy makers, specialists, historians, and professionals of every stripe—indeed, to *anyone* who has ever been stirred by a sound recording.

As already acknowledged, we cannot save every recording. What, then, do we save? Many considerations will come to bear on those decisions. Making them wisely will require the input of people with a certain measure of cultural literacy and a knowledge of history—people who understand that it is not enough to preserve sound recordings already judged to be historically and culturally significant. Significance is too often recognized and conferred only after the passage of years. We do not have the luxury of waiting until the significance of a sound recording is apparent before its preservation begins. By then, it may be too late.

This study will be followed by publication of a national plan developed on the basis of the recommendations of task forces convened to discuss the findings presented here. The success of this effort will be assured if, at the end of this process, the discussion no longer begins with the question, Why preserve?, but with the rhetorical one, How can we not?

CHAPTER 1

Sound Recording Collections: An Overview of Preservation and Public Access in the Twenty-first Century

Introduction

Some believe that the challenge of preserving sound recording collections is narrow and easily framed—simply a matter of copying old recordings to a new medium. The preservation process, however, entails much more than transferring a recording and saving it as a digital file; indeed, these two steps fall somewhere in the middle of a lengthy chain of events.

The preservation of recorded sound collections entails a set of processes requiring careful planning and a sophisticated technical infrastructure. It comprises several steps and requires important decisions that will affect what recordings are saved and what compromises may have to be made to ensure that the greatest number of recordings will be saved.

The process of audio preservation begins with decisions about what collections should be preserved and what information, or *metadata,* about these recordings must be included as part of the digital preservation files.[7] After capture of the source audio and creation of digital files, systems must protect the files and assure their integrity, which requires periodic migration of the files to new media, validations to assure that copies of the digital files are faithful to the previous generations, and further steps to assure that these files are accessible in perpetuity. In other words, recorded sound preservation is a chain and process without end. Technical preservation practices are only a part of the preservation process. Institutions responsible for long-term care of audio collections must manage selection of

[7] Metadata is often defined as "data about data," or more specifically, information about digital files. For digital audio preservation files, metadata might describe technical attributes of the file, the audio content of the file, rights information pertaining to the file, and details about the technology or processes employed to create the file. Metadata is discussed in detail in chapter 2.

materials to be added to collections, inventory, preservation needs assessments, cataloging, access strategies, promotion, and, of course, fund-raising. These and other issues pertaining to saving recorded sound collections are explored in the pages that follow.

Scope of Recorded Sound Collections

No comprehensive survey of recorded sound holdings in the United States, let alone the world, has ever been undertaken. However, a number of recent studies outline the scope of sound recordings held in archives and libraries. In 2004, Heritage Preservation Inc., in partnership with the U.S. Institute of Museum and Library Services, conducted a survey that resulted in the Heritage Health Index.[8] The index, which measured only public institutions—libraries, archives, museums, historical societies, archaeological repositories, and scientific research collections—estimated that more than 17,000 such institutions hold sound recording collections for which they take a preservation responsibility.[9] The survey estimates the number of individual recordings for which these institutions take such responsibility at 46 million. Respondents reported that 44 percent of their audio collections were in "unknown condition," yet institutions that had conducted needs assessments reported a significantly higher percentage of collections in need of attention than did institutions that had not thoroughly assessed their holdings. In other words, it is likely that once the recordings in unknown condition are assessed, estimates of preservation needs will rise accordingly.

In 2007, the Association of Research Libraries (ARL) estimated that its 123 member libraries held more than 10 million audio recordings. The written submission by ARL in support of this study notes that these collections are "in various stages of risk."[10]

Corporate archives and privately held collections were out of scope for the Heritage Health Index survey. The *Directory of Corporate Archives in the United States and Canada*, maintained by the Society of American Archivists (SAA), lists more than 320 corporate archives in the United States, but it is by no means inclusive of all corporate archives and it does not indicate which of these archives include recorded sound.[11] No published survey includes holdings of private collectors, yet many unique copies of published and unpublished sound recordings are held in private collections not available to the public.

---

[8] Available at http://www.heritagepreservation.org/hhi/. A summary of audio-related findings submitted by Kristen Overbeck Laise of Heritage Preservation to the NRPB is available at http://www.loc.gov/rr/record/nrpb/pdf/heritage.pdf.

[9] Defined as collections that could not be replaced if lost or damaged, e.g., not current books, magazines, videotapes, or sound recordings. See http://www.heritagepreservation.org/HHI/HHIfull.pdf, page 27.

[10] Prudence S. Adler, Associate Executive Director, and Karla L. Hahn, Director, ARL. Statement submitted for the record, January 26, 2007. Available at http://www.loc.gov/rr/record/nrpb/pdf/arl.pdf.

[11] An online version of the directory, last updated May 19, 2008, is available at http://www.archivists.org/saagroups/bas/directory/corporat.asp.

Public Research Libraries and Archives

Sound recording collections held by colleges and universities are housed in libraries, archives, departmental offices, and other repositories—formal and ad hoc—located throughout the campus. A recent survey of audio and moving-image holdings at the Bloomington campus of Indiana University, summarized on p. 12 of this study, illustrates the breadth of locations of collections found on one large campus. Major research libraries often hold examples of every format of sound recording and content of a broad variety of genres, including oral history, literary spoken word, broadcasting, and natural sounds, as well as a wide variety of musical genres.

Sound recordings are commonly found in at least two locations within university library systems. General research and circulating collections include recordings that support the institution's curricula, such as spoken word as well as classical and popular music related to specific courses of study. These collections are usually in the form of compact discs (CDs) and, when older formats are retained, audiocassettes and long-playing (LP) 33⅓-rpm discs. Most rare published recordings, as well as unpublished recordings, held by public libraries, colleges, and universities are curated by specialized libraries within the institutions or are managed as special collections in departments managed by subject or format specialists. These special collections often include the recordings in greatest need of preservation attention.

In 2003, the Council on Library and Information Resources (CLIR) surveyed two groups of academic libraries to document the state of audio collections held by the institutions and to identify major barriers to preservation and access.[12] The group was composed of 18 member libraries of the ARL and 51 member libraries of the Oberlin Group, a consortium representing libraries of liberal arts colleges. Nearly every institution surveyed reported holding "significant or rare audio collections." As had those responding to the Indiana University survey, most respondents to the CLIR survey noted important audio collections held by university departments other than the libraries.

Not surprisingly, respondents to the CLIR survey "tended to identify lack of funding as the greatest barrier to access" to sound recordings in their collections. However, the survey summary noted that "the survey results tell a more complicated story." Other commonly cited barriers included the following:

- the absence of appropriate standards and tools for cost-effective inventory and bibliographical control
- the lack of effective and cost-efficient means of treating and reformatting analog originals
- the absence of clear mandates about how to provide access to valuable collections the rights to which are ambiguous or unknown

[12] Abby Smith, David Randal Allen, and Karen Allen, *Survey of the State of Audio Collections in Academic Libraries* (Washington, DC: Council on Library and Information Resources, 2004). Available at http://www.clir.org/pubs/reports/pub128/pub128.pdf.

Learning from Bloomington

In 2008–2009, Indiana University (IU) conducted a comprehensive survey of audio and moving-image holdings on its Bloomington campus to assess campus-wide preservation challenges. The *Media Preservation Survey* was conducted by a team of audiovisual media specialists under the leadership of Mike Casey, associate director for recording services at the university's Archives of Traditional Music.[1] The published survey is a significant work, not only as an analysis of the scope of challenges faced in Bloomington but also as a model of survey design, interpretation of data, presentation of useful information, and constructive recommendations for further action.

The survey, actually a census, found that more than 569,000 audio and video recordings and motion pictures are held by 80 administrative units on the Bloomington campus; nearly 365,000 (64 percent) of these are audio recordings. Additional figures are revealing and likely to be indicative of general circumstances at other university campuses throughout the United States. Of the 80 administrative units surveyed, sound recordings were reportedly held in 60—in academic department and administrative offices as well as in the various campus libraries. The audio collections comprise 23 distinct audio formats (each with its own hardware requirements for playback). Fifty percent of the audio and video holdings on campus are represented in the university's cataloging system, yet only 29 percent of the 80 units on campus that hold audio or video collections have any audiovisual collections represented in the system. The survey also reported that 95 percent of the collections are stored in "room temperature conditions." Born-digital audio and video were not included in the survey; however, it is estimated that there are 200,000 such recordings held on the Bloomington campus.

The careful and thorough design and scope of the IU study might serve as a model for other institutions. The survey goes well beyond identifying sound recordings held on campus. It also includes an inventory of playback hardware held on the campus; estimates of the number of rare and unique holdings; life expectancies of various audio and video formats; examples of uses made of the collections and the types of patrons served by major holdings on campus; and estimates of resources required to preserve existing collections. It is noteworthy that the time estimated to digitize only the collections held by the Jacobs School of Music under the current staffing level is 120 years.

The need for audio preservation is often articulated, but without surveys such as the one undertaken in Bloomington, the exact scope of the challenge will remain vague, efforts to address it will be scattered and uncoordinated, and important targets will be missed.

The Bloomington campus of Indiana University has a strong record of commitment to audio preservation and has earned recognition as a national leader in research and development of best practices in the field. Even though its needs are now documented and it is far better equipped than most universities in the country to meet them, there is no guarantee that IU can adequately preserve its collections in the near future. The survey notes that all three of IU's audiovisual digital initiatives "are entirely or in large part dependent on grant funding for their future work and development. A functioning preservation system will need to bring together and coordinate existing efforts."[2]

The Indiana University survey report concludes with several recommendations intended to support long-range planning and begin to address systematically the tasks ahead. Custodians of audio collections and preservation administrators elsewhere would be wise to consider the application of many, if not all, of the recommendations in the Indiana study. Those applicable to audio preservation planning are recommendations to:

1. Appoint a campus-wide taskforce to advise on
   - the development of priorities for preservation action,
   - the development of a campus-wide preservation plan, and
   - how units can leverage resources for the future.
2. Create a centralized media preservation and digitization center that will serve the entire campus, using international standards for preservation transfer. As part of the planning for this center, hire a media preservation specialist.
3. Develop special funding for massive and rapid digitization over the next 10 years of the recordings deemed to be the treasures of the audio collections.
4. Create a central storage space appropriate for film, video, and audio.
5. Provide archival appraisal and control across campus to
   - assure quality of digitization for preservation and
   - oversee plans for maintaining original media.
6. Develop cataloging services for special collections to improve intellectual control to
   - accelerate research opportunities and
   - improve access.

[1] Mike Casey, Patrick Feaster, and Alan R. Burdette, *Indiana University Bloomington Media Preservation Survey: A Report* (Bloomington, Ind.: Indiana University Bloomington, 2009). Available at http://research.iu.edu/resources/media_preservation/iub_media_preservation_survey_FINALwww.pdf.

[2] The three projects are the Variations Project for music reserves, the Ethnomusicological Video for Instruction and Analysis (EVIA) Digital Archive (a joint project with the University of Michigan), and the Sound Directions audio preservation project.

- the lack of staff who are sufficiently trained and conversant in the genres, formats, and rights issues unique to recorded sound collections"[13]

An appendix to the CLIR report, titled "Scan of Recorded sound Surveys," summarizes the conclusions of seven earlier surveys of special collections that include sound recordings.[14] It cites the following eight barriers to preservation:

1. There is no authoritative data set describing the content, location, and preservation status of recorded sound held in special and private collections in the United States. Furthermore, there appears to be no single approach to gathering such data.
2. Dedicated budgets for the management of recorded sound collections are limited or nonexistent.
3. Most collections lack supporting materials, such as releases or other information, necessary to resolve intellectual property and copyright questions that pertain to their holdings.
4. Proper storage conditions for recorded sound are understood, but collections are not always stored accordingly.
5. The most widely held format in the sound collections surveyed appears to be magnetic audiocassettes (compact audiocassettes).[15]
6. The range of views concerning the need, techniques, and emerging standards for preservation of recorded sound collections may be well understood by preservationists, but not always by collections managers.
7. While some formats of recorded sound media are more urgently in need of preservation than others, all formats are in some need of preservation, identification, cataloging, or reformatting.
8. The costs and requirements for preserving and offering access to a recorded sound collection may not be well understood by those responsible for creating such collections.

Written submissions to the National Recording Preservation Board (NRPB) and testimony presented at two hearings conducted in support of the study in November and December of 2006 underscored the importance of the issues outlined above and identified additional concerns related to audio preservation. The submissions and testimony provided many interesting real-world examples of challenges encountered in caring for audio collections, and contributed thoughtful recommendations to help assure the preservation and accessibility of audio collections for future users.

ARL's submission to the NRPB underlined the issue of inadequate funding for preservation: "No institution currently has sufficient resources to ensure preservation of even all the unique

[13] Smith, Allen, and Allen 2004, 10.

[14] Ibid., 54–58.

[15] The published CLIR survey noted that this does not apply to *original* sound holdings of the institutions surveyed for the report. However, another report published by CLIR, *Folk Heritage Collections in Crisis* (2001), reported that audiocassettes make up 90 percent of folk heritage collections.

materials they hold."[16] The CLIR survey of ARL and Oberlin institutions found that the average annual expenditure on audio preservation and access by the 18 ARL members represented in the survey was $51,600; Oberlin Group respondents reported average annual spending of $1,500 per institution. Sound recording-related programs were a line item in the budgets of only three of the ARL institutions, representing about 5 percent of the survey respondents. When asked how many audio engineers their institution had assigned to recorded sound collections, 30 of the 41 respondents reported that none had been assigned. Of the 11 institutions that did employ engineers, the individual full-time-equivalent (FTE) obligation was less than three-quarters. In response to a question about the number of catalogers assigned to recorded sound collections, 14 of the 49 respondents reported that none had been assigned. The average obligation of the remaining 35 institutions was .59 FTE.[17]

The Indiana University case study includes a note on audio preservation that is likely to be applicable to institutions nationwide: audio preservation is dependent on grant funding rather than on stable, line-item budgets. Major funders for audio preservation are the National Endowment for the Arts, the National Endowment for the Humanities, and the Institute of Museum and Library Services (all federal agencies); the Grammy Foundation; the Association for Recorded Sound Collections; and The Andrew W. Mellon Foundation. The Grammy Foundation has been a strong supporter of audio preservation for many years, but funding for the program is dependent upon the health of the recording industry. In 2008, Grammy Foundation audio preservation awards totaled $440,611; in 2009, they totaled $150,000.[18] The great majority of funding for the grant program of the Association for Recorded Sound Collections derives from a single, private donor. The Mellon Foundation has provided grants to support identifying materials, classifying physical condition, and setting priorities for further cataloging and preservation. The legislation that commissioned this study also established the National Recording Preservation Foundation, which is expected to begin operation in 2010. Even if Grammy Foundation grants for preservation had not been reduced in 2009 to a third of their 2008 level, the additional resources for audio preservation such as those the new foundation might provide are still essential to assure preservation of sound recordings in the United States.

Nonetheless, the authors of the CLIR survey and report note that, without the adoption of new practices and approaches, additional investments in audio preservation without will do little to rescue the most endangered materials: "New approaches to inventory control, new technologies for audio capture and automatic metadata extraction, new programs of education and training, and

[16] Adler and Hahn, January 26, 2007, 2.

[17] One institution participating in the CLIR survey reported that it had not undertaken "serious cataloguing since the 1970s. We have what we call 'a list.'" Smith, Allen, and Allen 2004, 14.

[18] Figures compiled from Grammy.com press releases.

more aggressive access policies under the fair use exemption of the copyright law for education are necessary."[19]

If archives and libraries are not wholly aware of the critical attention required for the sound recordings they hold, they do largely recognize new demands for access to their collections. Seventy-eight percent of the respondents to the CLIR survey noted that their institutions have seen an "increased demand for recorded sound in teaching." Without sufficient bibliographic access to audio collections, use of the collections at libraries and archives may never reach its potential. The problem runs the risk of becoming a vicious circle: library and archives administrators allocate resources, in part, on the basis of the potential number of patrons those resources will serve. If cataloging and collection descriptions do not exist, potential users cannot become aware of materials of research value and will not make use of the collections. Low use statistics may argue against obligation of resources to the collections by library and archives administrators, and so on. As one media preservation librarian has observed, "Many of the factors inhibiting the use and preservation of sound recordings in libraries and archives are symptomatic of a single fundamental problem: the lack of documentation and understanding about the sound recordings, their contents, and their condition."[20]

The CLIR report suggested an additional, arguably more disturbing, impediment to adequate bibliographic control of sound recordings: "If collections are hidden from the view of users because they are undescribed or otherwise hard to find, demand for access will be low. If collections are difficult or expensive to process and stabilize for service, there may be little incentive to make them available, because demand might then increase in ways that would stress the library's resources."[21] Lack of cataloging resources has a direct effect on preservation as well as on access. It is even more challenging to establish preservation priorities if knowledge is inadequate about what is in collections held by institutions. Too little is known about collections housed in archives or libraries, and less, or even nothing, is known about collections held privately. Decisions about prioritizing preservation of sound recordings are bounded by specific knowledge of the universe of recordings at risk. What is not known about existing sound recordings—their format, location, and cultural and historical value—is a more disturbing problem because without that information recordings may be lost. As Donald J. Waters, program officer for scholarly communications at The Andrew W. Mellon Foundation, observed at the NRPB hearings, it is "difficult to

---

[19] Smith, Allen, and Allen 2004, 11.

[20] Hannah Frost, "Surveying Sound Recording Collections," in Judith Matz, ed., *Sound Savings: Preserving Audio Collections*. Proceedings of a symposium sponsored by the School of Information, Preservation and Conservation Studies, University of Texas at Austin; Library of Congress; National Recording Preservation Board; and Association of Research Libraries, Austin, Texas, July 24-26, 2003 (Washington, DC: Association of Research Libraries, 2004). Available at http://www.arl.org/preserv/sound_savings_proceedings/index.shtml.

[21] Smith, Allen, and Allen 2004, 11.

mobilize resources to preserve something that you do not even know you have."[22]

There is significant duplication among the commercial recordings held by many institutions, yet it is difficult to measure the extent of redundancy when audio materials remain uncataloged. Libraries that do attempt to catalog their recording collections often benefit from compatible cataloging systems that enable sharing of data and reduce duplicate cataloging. Most cataloging systems, however, are insufficient for the purposes of cooperative preservation. Library cataloging usually treats items as artifacts or objects, for example, without regard for the fact that published recordings derived from identical master recordings can exist on a multitude of record labels and in a variety of formats. Most catalog records also ignore the physical condition of a sound recording, information that is essential for locating the best copy for reformatting. Traditional library catalog systems may not even provide any indication that the holding institution has digitally reformatted an item because that information may be tracked in internal systems that are employed only to manage the digital archive.

Ethnographic, Folklore, and Oral History Collections

The first sound recordings collected by academic institutions and libraries were those that documented oral culture. Folklife and ethnographic collections, which can include commercial and field recordings of vocal and instrumental music, folktales and storytelling, interviews, and oral history, provide audio windows into a range of cultures and geographical areas. Folklore of nearly every sort is passed orally from one generation to another, and sound recordings may be the only source for this content.[23]

Though very little collecting of commercial recordings was done at the institutional level in the early twentieth century, the academic community soon made a vital contribution to the field of recorded sound collecting by making its own recordings. Song collecting from oral traditions gained academic respectability in the nineteenth century, but was limited by the notational skills of the collector and the system of music notation itself. In March 1890, however, anthropologist Jesse Walter Fewkes journeyed to Calais, Maine, where he recorded songs and speech from Passamaquoddy

[22] Testimony of Donald J. Waters, program officer for scholarly communications, The Andrew W. Mellon Foundation, NRPB public hearings, December 19, 2006, New York. Cataloging backlogs are by no means exclusive to recorded sound collections. Addressing this problem, with funding from the Mellon Foundation, the Council on Library and Information Resources established the Cataloging Hidden Special Collections initiative (http://www.clir.org/hiddencollections/index.html) to support cataloging of "hidden special collections and archives." In the first two years of the project, 29 special collections were awarded grants. More than 50 percent of these collections include recorded sound items.

[23] Folk and ethnomusicology collections may also include (as in the case of the Archives of Traditional Music at Indiana University) original manuscripts, transcriptions, correspondence, accounts, and information documenting field material that have been provided by collectors; pamphlets; articles; piano rolls; photographs and slides; films; computer storage media; historic recording devices; and books. See http://www.indiana.edu/~libarchm/collections.html.

Indians on a portable, wind-up Edison cylinder recorder. This was a trial run for Fewkes, who was to lead an archaeological expedition to the southwestern United States later that year, which he presciently saw as an opportunity to record the Indians of that region. Fewkes made recordings of the Zuni and Hopi, and continued to make field recordings into the 1920s. His 1890 recordings, the first ethnographic field recordings, are still extant, and copies have been a vital resource not only to scholars but also to the Passamaquoddy, Zuni, and Hopi of succeeding generations. Though some recordists used the technology mainly as an aid to the transcription of music and speech, and shaved their wax cylinders for reuse, it quickly became apparent that recordings themselves could preserve cultural expressions that are likely to vanish or be dramatically altered in the near future.

The first field recordings were made on wax cylinders, a woefully fragile carrier but the only one available at the time. Cylinders were standard in field recording well into the 1930s, when portable disc cutters became available. The early disc-cutting models embossed a groove onto an aluminum base, creating a somewhat noisy but durable recording. By the late 1930s, portable machines that could record on lacquer-coated aluminum discs were available—a system that greatly reduced noise and enhanced fidelity. These discs, however, are inherently unstable over the long term. Lacquer-coating compounds exude palmitic acid, which crystallizes on the surface of the disc; the coatings are prone to cracking and separating from the disc surface. During World War II, aluminum was rationed, and glass was used to make disc blanks. Countless recordings made on glass-based discs have been lost to breakage. Some of the first preservation reformatting performed by the Library of Congress's Recording Laboratory was the copying of wax cylinders and lacquer discs to magnetic tape in the 1940s.

The preservation challenges that ethnographic and folklore archives face are similar to or even greater than those faced by all research collections that include unpublished sound recordings; at the same time, ethnographic, folklore, and oral history collections also face a special set of challenges. For example, sound recordings held by ethnographic archives are usually unique, unpublished documentation of fieldwork conducted by folklorists and ethnomusicologists. Generally, media used for unpublished audio, such as wax cylinders, instantaneous discs, audiocassettes, open-reel tapes, and digital audiotapes (DAT), are far less stable than shellac or vinyl pressings or compact discs, the most common published recording formats. If these collections are to be maintained for posterity, reformatting—copying to a new format (presumably, digital files)—is essential. Such recordings are often accompanied by field notes, content listings, and labels that may have artifactual value but that also contain information crucial to the documentation and interpretation of the audio. These materials must be scanned and associated with the digital audio files in a shared database during the preservation process.

In December 2000, the American Folklore Society and the Library of Congress American Folklife Center sponsored a conference of folklorists, ethnomusicologists, librarians, archivists, representatives of the recording industries, and recording engineers with the objectives of defining the challenges facing folklore and ethnographic archives and devising strategies for varied stakeholders to collaborate on overcoming the obstacles. In preparing for the conference, the sponsors surveyed individuals and institutions holding folklore, ethnographic, and oral history collections. One hundred seventy-eight organizations and 119 individuals responded to the survey. Introducing the survey results, the editors noted, "It was the expectation of those who designed the survey that it would result in a baseline data set about the nation's recorded folklore, something sorely needed by archivists, librarians, researchers, and communities that have been documented. Although the results are profoundly interesting and paint a vivid picture of the state of collections, not enough data were gathered to serve that purpose. Rather, this survey reveals where the state of knowledge ends and ignorance begins." Among the findings of the survey:[24]

- **Funding.** Thirty-six percent of organizational collections operate on an annual budget of less than $10,000. Thirty-seven percent operate without any annual allocations. Nine percent of individual collectors use personal funds to support maintenance of their collections.
- **Staff.** Sixty-eight percent of organizations holding folklore, ethnographic, and oral history collections have a full-time staff, and 61 percent include staff with archival or collection management background. Ten percent of private individuals holding like collections have archival or collection-management training.
- **Conservation.** Forty-nine percent of organizational collections are stored in areas in which temperature and humidity are monitored and stabilized for long-term conservation.
- **Collection assessment.** Eighteen percent of organizations and 2 percent of individuals have assessed the state of preservation of their collections.
- **Bibliographic control.** Thirty-eight percent of organizations and 80 percent of individuals manage their collections without the use of a database. Although larger organizations use a database to manage their collections, 44 percent of university archives and 50 percent of state and nonprofit agencies cannot retrieve any part of their holdings from their databases.
- **Intellectual property documentation.** Twenty-five percent of organizations reported having release forms for the bulk (76–100 percent) of their collections. Thirty-nine percent of all individuals do not have release forms for their materials; most of them hold materials recorded between 1961 and 1980, and 40 percent of these collectors are ethnomusicologists.
- **Formats.** Approximately 90 percent of the audio recordings held in organizational and individual collections are audiocassettes.

[24] Council on Library and Information Resources, *Folk Heritage Collections in Crisis* (Washington, DC: Council on Library and Information Resources, 2001), 59–63.

This survey is close to 10 years old, and the status of some collections may have progressed in the meantime. However, its findings remain instructive as a barometer of the critical circumstances of collections in 2000, and there is little evidence of major changes since that time in the amount of support provided to archives throughout the United States.

Aside from the high proportion of unpublished sound recordings held by folklore and ethnographic archives, and the additional resources required to maintain such collections, these archives face one more challenge—balancing preservation and use of collections against ethical as well as legal guidelines. Digital audio technology and the inherent potential of the World Wide Web to make audio collections accessible beyond the walls of archives and libraries to home computers and portable digital devices have placed enormous pressure on archives and libraries, as well as on individual and corporate rights holders, to distribute audio collections widely by means of all available new technologies. The complexity of legal impediments to such distribution is discussed in chapter 4 of this study. However, in managing collections of folklore and ethnographic materials, administrators must understand and adhere to appropriate ethical uses as well as uses allowable under intellectual property laws. Folklore and ethnographic collections often include recordings of sacred stories, rituals, and music. Such events are not intended as entertainment or, in some cases, to be heard at all by individuals outside the cultural communities of which they are a part. In these instances, even preservation may be ethically improper without explicit written permissions.

Challenges of ethical responsibility can be compounded by the absence of adequate documentation, such as written agreements between collectors and artists, relating to recordings in archives. As the *Folk Collections in Crisis* report notes

> access issues in the field of traditional art and knowledge are complicated by rights issues: the right to use, even the right to record, is not always clearly documented in many of the folk heritage collections most in need of preservation intervention. Too often the various intellectual property rights, moral rights, and privacy concerns of the subject, fieldworker, or repository are difficult to determine or merely ignored for the sake of convenience, yet how can an institution give priority to treating materials without accompanying documentation that would sanction use?[25]

Lack of documentation about unpublished recordings extends beyond folklore and ethnographic collections. A written submission in support of this study, in noting how the development of small, portable audiocassette recorders in the 1970s aided oral historians, observes

> Soon programs ... around the country were amassing scores, or hundreds, if not thousands of oral history interviews. Yet few

[25] Ibid., 2.

> programs knew what information the interviews contained beyond the topic or project title. Tens of thousands of these interviews were locked away in filing cabinets or languished on shelves without indices, without finding aids and therefore are virtually inaccessible and unused.[26]

The written submission to the NRPB by the Society for Ethnomusicology succinctly summarizes the challenges faced by ethnographic archives as follows:

> Those responsible for maintaining collections of ethnomusicological recordings, particularly in smaller institutions, face the additional challenges of limited staffing and technical resources, and of funding and managing digitization projects, locating and paying for reliable long-term digital file storage, and managing source recordings and accompanying metadata. Some grant support is available for the preservation of our most physically vulnerable or historically and culturally significant recorded materials, but the bulk of our collections of ethnographic recordings remain at risk unless cooperative solutions can be found.[27]

The conclusion of the *Folk Collections in Crisis* report, provided in Appendix D, includes a thoughtful and thorough set of recommendations for further work that should be undertaken to ensure the health of folklore and ethnographic archives and libraries.

Recorded Radio Collections and Archives

Commercial radio began in the early 1920s. Perhaps no other sound medium has conveyed to listeners so much of the nation's history and culture, through music, diverse entertainment programming, daily news and public affairs, and interviews. Many types of archives and collections include radio broadcast recordings. Few, if any, other forms of sound recordings are held in as wide a variety of archives and collections, both professional and amateur. Yet support for broadcasting archives has been sporadic; American radio broadcasting has never been documented systematically, and few archives have provided formal support of radio broadcast recordings.

Too little is known about the size of the broadcast-recordings universe and the whereabouts of radio recordings. The first 15 years of commercial radio in the United States are hardly documented at all by authentic off-air recordings. Recording of radio broadcasts was nearly nonexistent until the introduction of lacquer discs for instantaneous recording in the mid-1930s, more than 10 years after

[26] Written submissions of Jeffrey S. Suchanek, Director, Louie B. Nunn Center for Oral History, University of Kentucky Libraries, and Kopana L. Teny, Image Management Specialist Senior, Digital Programs, University of Kentucky Libraries, to NRPB, November 3, 2006, 4-5. Suchanek and Teny also note that the gathering of oral history has become part of many graduate programs. Available at http://www.loc.gov/rr/record/nrpb/pdf/kentucky.pdf.

[27] Laurel Sercombe and Suzanne Flandreau, [n.d.] Comments from the Society for Ethnomusicology. Available at http://www.loc.gov/rr/record/nrpb/pdf/ethnomusicology.pdf.

network broadcasting began. Until then, broadcast excerpts were occasionally captured on wax cylinders by home amateurs, and some complete programs were recorded on solid aluminum discs by broadcasters, performing artists, collectors, and, occasionally, commercial record companies. The number of extant early radio broadcast recordings is unknown. The radio broadcast archives in the Library of Congress, believed to be the largest in the United States, include fewer than 50 pre-1933 radio broadcast recordings and fewer than 1,000 made before 1936. Undoubtedly, other early broadcast archives exist, both institutional and private, but the scope of their holdings is unknown.

Commercial Radio Network Recordings

The development of lacquer-coated recording discs made it possible to incise a blank disc for instantaneous playback; commercial record-production techniques of the time, by contrast, required many stages of electroplating and molding of copies to produce a playable disc. (Solid aluminum discs could also be auditioned immediately, but the result was of lower fidelity, with more surface noise than lacquer discs.) Recording of radio broadcasts burgeoned after the development of the lacquer disc. Tens of thousands of radio broadcasts were recorded by the National Broadcasting Company (NBC) in the late 1930s and 1940s. Local stations, too, recorded radio broadcasts, both network feeds and originating programs, on lacquer disc. Sometimes performers or sponsors commissioned professional studios to record their programs, and accumulated archives of significant size.

NBC broadcast transcriptions are held by the University of Wisconsin, and possibly other archives, as well as by the Library of Congress. The history of no other major radio network is as well represented in archives as that of NBC. No extensive archive of Columbia Broadcasting System (CBS) broadcasts is known to exist. Whether one ever existed—and if so, its fate—remains a mystery to broadcasting archivists and historians. Some people believe that a large cache of transcription discs was discarded in the 1980s; others believe that a collection of entertainment broadcast recordings still exists at the network's Los Angeles studios. Both stories are unsubstantiated. The network's New York City archives include some recordings of World War II news broadcasts by the network, but the most complete collection of recordings of CBS's highly regarded World War II coverage is held at the National Archives and Records Administration facility in College Park, Maryland. That collection exists because a CBS affiliate station in Seattle, KIRO, recorded the news feeds from New York during the war, saved them, and later transferred them to the National Archives. A collection of broadcast transcription discs of the American Broadcasting Company (ABC) also is held by the National Archives. Recordings of broadcasts by the Mutual network from the 1930s through the 1950s are included in the WOR Collection at the Library of Congress.

The exact intentions of radio networks in making recordings of their broadcasts, and how they singled out specific broadcasts for recording, are not entirely known. The NBC Radio Collection at the Library of Congress includes more than 150,000 sixteen-inch lacquer discs, approximately 70,000 hours representing broadcasts (including television audio tracks) from the mid-1930s to the early 1970s.[28] However, many popular and culturally significant programs aired by the network are not represented in the collection. It is likely, but not confirmed, that the network recorded programs that its executives thought most significant, such as news broadcasts or programs it produced and owned, as opposed to those leased from sponsors or outside producers. Programs also may have been recorded and retained solely to protect against possible litigation. Compounding the issue of seemingly erratic runs of programs recorded, radio transcription collections in archives are often incomplete. Many individual radio recordings of substantial value have found their way into the hands of collectors. Collections at the Library of Congress, for example, lack valuable discs known to have been among inventories supplied by NBC. In at least two instances, gifts of recordings to the Library by private collectors have included discs that were once part of the NBC Radio Collection.

Radio programs of the era of radio's primacy, the early 1930s through early 1950s, unlike broadcasts today, enjoyed no aftermarket—i.e., repurposing for new media and markets. Until World War II, all U.S. network broadcasts were live. Network broadcast programming was not repeated in the summer months, and programs were not repackaged for retail sale. Networks had little financial incentive to record a broadcast. When preserving radio broadcast recordings and planning to make them accessible to the public, it is important to be aware that networks' contracts with performers, unions, and other parties most often encompassed live broadcasts only. Ancillary or aftermarket uses of the programs may well have required, and may continue to demand, specific descriptions of further possible uses and markets, and additional payments. The lack of such terms and the resultant limitation of network rights created a disincentive for the networks to invest in the preservation of broadcast recordings and may deter archives from publishing or providing Web access to network programming.

Archives and libraries are believed to hold several hundred thousand instantaneous discs of radio broadcasts. However, as noted earlier, lacquer-coated discs are a very unstable recording medium. Added to this risk is the fragility of discs manufactured during World War II, which employed a glass, rather than an aluminum, base. Recordings of that era with a glass base are very susceptible to breakage. Given the instability and fragility of the medium, time is running out for preservation reformatting. Tens of thousands of lacquer discs in archives in the United States remain unpreserved.

[28] It may be worth noting, even if only for the charming incongruity of technologies, that NBC recorded audio feeds of its television coverage of late 1960s and early 1970s NASA lunar missions on 16-inch lacquer discs—1930s technology.

In the very near future, custodians of these collections will have to decide whether to preserve these recordings or lose access to their content.

Radio networks were not the only parties that commissioned broadcast transcriptions. Radio artists, program sponsors, and others often hired private recording services to record their broadcasts off air. Tens of thousands of such recordings exist in archives throughout the United States. Privately made broadcast transcriptions held by the Library of Congress are included in the donated collections of such programs and people as Major Edward Bowes's *Amateur Hour*, Bob Hope, Harold Ickes, Durwood Kirby, Andre Kostelanetz, and Raymond Gram Swing. Significant collections of off-air transcription discs are also held by the Thousand Oaks Library Foundation's American Radio Archives in southern California and the Museum of Broadcast Communications in Chicago. Most privately made recordings of broadcasts made before the early 1950s exist as lacquer-coated discs or aluminum discs. However, the Library of American Broadcasting at the University of Maryland holds 3,000 spools—3,000 hours—of magnetic wire recordings of broadcasts made by Arthur Godfrey. It was the popular broadcaster's personal collection, and it includes recordings of *Arthur Godfrey Time*, *Arthur Godfrey's Talent Scouts*, audio (only) from his television series *Arthur Godfrey and His Friends*, and other programs. Wire recordings are possibly the most difficult analog recording medium to preserve. A one-hour reel of wire is more than 7,000 feet long. The medium is very thin, becomes brittle, and tangles or breaks easily. There is only one new machine known to play back wire recordings. Most preservation of wires is done with rebuilt recorders of the 1940s, 1950s, and 1960s. A rough, but conservative, estimate of the cost to reformat the Godfrey wire recordings is $700,000.

Collections are often donated to institutions without any rights for the institution to share the collection with scholars and the public. At the Library of Congress, federal funds support preservation reformatting and cataloging, yet the collections can be used only on the premises. Corporate donations of recordings without funds for support *or* the granting of rights to share the recordings are impediments to preservation. Given the assumed lack of any substantial archive of early CBS radio programming, NBC must be commended for its foresight in recording thousands of programs and for its generosity in donating them to the Library of Congress. However, no funds for preservation or cataloging accompanied the gift, and dissemination of the collection is tightly restricted, making it difficult to attract the financial resources needed to complete preservation of the collection. One potential user, a public radio station archivist, expressed his frustration at the hearing conducted for this study:

> NBC and other commercial networks have donated their materials to the Library of Congress and other archives so that scholars can easily access the material; however, public radio producers with little or no licensing budgets cannot begin to even

> get fair use access to these materials without paying exorbitant per-second charges, while [the] corporate donor gets a tax break for the donation and pays nothing for the care, cataloging, preservation, or maintenance of the collection. … history, at least for radio producers, is being held hostage."[29]

U.S. radio station programming commonly derives from three sources: radio network feeds, in-house-produced programs, and syndicated programming leased to the station. It is believed that the first syndicated radio program was *Amos 'n' Andy*. Before the series was carried by NBC, the team responsible for it created its own "network" by recording the daily comedy series and distributing it to several dozen stations on phonograph records. From the 1930s to the 1970s, hundreds of radio programs and musical recordings made especially for broadcast were distributed on discs, termed "electrical transcriptions" by the trade and on the air. For a relatively brief period, tapes replaced discs for syndicated radio series. Today, syndicated radio programs are distributed by satellite and either aired live by radio stations or recorded by the station for later broadcast. Many audio archives include transcribed radio program discs. The two largest collections in the United States are those at the Library of Congress and the University of Missouri, Kansas City.

During World War II, the U.S. government created the Armed Forces Radio Service (AFRS, later AFRTS, the Armed Forces Radio and Television Service) to provide radio programs for U.S. personnel overseas and for use on American bases and armed forces hospitals. Most AFRS programming was distributed weekly to military stations on transcription discs. (Supplementing these recorded programs were shortwave broadcasts of news and sports events.) AFRS discs included edited versions of commercial U.S. radio broadcasts and programs written and produced by the AFRS. The collections of the Library of Congress include more than 100,000 AFRS and AFRTS program transcription discs. Aside from the NBC collection, the AFRTS collection is the largest collection of radio programming at the Library. By making pressings of radio broadcasts, AFRS became an inadvertent but enormously significant catalyst of audio preservation. There is no larger resource for the study of radio broadcast programming from 1942 to the early twenty-first century than AFRS and AFRTS program transcriptions. Thousands of broadcasts that would otherwise be lost to posterity are preserved on 12- and 16-inch program transcriptions and audiocassettes. Today, however, AFRTS distributes programs by satellite exclusively. The Library of Congress no longer obtains weekly shipments of radio programming from AFRTS.

Because most syndicated radio programs are distributed to radio stations live, via digital feeds from satellite, or by means of digital file transfers via the Internet, rather than in mass-produced physical form, it has become next to impossible for libraries and archives to

---

[29] Testimony of Andy Lanset, archivist, WNYC, New York Public Radio, "Preservation of Radio Collections" session, NRPB public hearings, December 19, 2006, New York.

collect and preserve such programming. Institutions might acquire recorded programming directly from producers or talent associated with programs, but such efforts are labor-intensive and depend upon the generosity of the creators. Subsequently, just as was the case in the era of network radio dominance, most radio programming will not be captured and will be lost to posterity.

Through the American Television and Radio Archive (ATRA) provisions of the Copyright Act of 1976, the Library of Congress has the legal authority to record programming off-air for its collections. The Library is unique in having this authority; however, it is unlikely that the institution has resources or the desire to undertake sole responsibility for preserving contemporary radio. Far fewer programs are produced for syndication today than were 20 years ago, yet many live talk and telephone call-in programs have gained national prominence and political influence.[30] Under the authority of ATRA, the Library of Congress manages an off-air recording project to sample contemporary talk radio.[31] Some 15–20 programs, recorded from broadcasts carried over the Internet, are preserved each month. It is believed to be the only initiative of its kind. The Library's Packard Campus for Audio Visual Conservation in Culpeper, Virginia, includes a room dedicated to the capture of born-digital media with the technical capability of preserving 264 digital streams simultaneously. Thousands of radio stations now simulcast over the World Wide Web, providing a convenient opportunity to record programs aired through the Internet. However, aside from the stations themselves, it is possible that only the Library of Congress has legal authority to make these records for archival purposes. This issue is discussed later in this chapter, in the section on collaboration and coordination.

Noncommercial Radio Station Recordings

Noncommercial radio stations and networks have in many instances served as custodians for their own archives. Below are some examples of public radio preservation programs.

As of the end of January 2007, National Public Radio (NPR) held nearly 64,000 hours of programming that it had produced and another 41,000 hours of "acquired" programming. NPR adds 97 hours of programming to its archive daily, most of which are production elements, not final product. Programming beginning in late April 1999 and thereafter has been recorded digitally and stored on "archival quality" recordable compact discs (CD-Rs). Programming dating from the network's inception in 1971 until mid-1999 was recorded on tape. Programming from 1976 and from the period 1984–1993 has been copied to CD, owing to the extent of hydrolysis, or "sticky-shed syndrome," associated with open-reel recording tape manufactured during that period. NPR has begun to develop a content

---

[30] *Radio and Cable Yearbook 2009* lists 73 producers of radio programming and 53 companies that create syndicated radio programming.

[31] Recorded Sound Reference Center. Library of Congress Web Radio Recording Project. Available at http://www.loc.gov/rr/record/Webradiotoc.html.

management system for the ingestion of recorded programming and metadata.[32]

WNYC, a New York City public radio station affiliated with both National Public Radio and Public Radio International, holds roughly 55,000 audio recordings in many formats. The earliest recording dates to 1927. Roughly 10 percent of the archive is held in storage at a commercial temperature- and humidity-controlled facility operated by Iron Mountain. The WNYC archives have recently been expanded to include the archives of classical music station WQXR.

The Media Library and Archives of WGBH-FM, Boston, holds roughly 30,000 programs dating to 1951 in formats ranging from open-reel tape to digital WAV files. Notable holdings of unique recordings include interviews with performers and composers of a wide range of music, as well as poetry and book readings. Internal policy at WGBH mandates that "defined production materials" from radio and television projects be delivered to the archives upon completion of a project, or on a regular schedule.

Pacifica Radio Archives holds 50,000 reel-to-reel master tapes of programs broadcast on Pacifica from the network's beginnings in 1949, with the bulk of the collection spanning 1960–1990. Contents include interviews, debates, field recordings of demonstrations, documentaries, original radio drama, and live music. Some reels present spliced lengths of both acetate and Mylar tape, hydrolysis or sticky-shed tapes that have "idiosyncratic tracking and tape speeds," and reels that are inaccurately labeled. With grants as well as contributions from individuals, the archive initiated a preservation program in 2002 that has led to preservation of several hundred tapes. According to Brian DeShazor, director of Pacifica Radio Archives, "Continuing the project will require ongoing, secured funding, professional personnel within the archives, additional storage space, and assistance with long-term planning and knowledge sharing."[33] In November 2006, Pacifica held a national on-air campaign to raise funds in support of its preservation activities. The archive also operates an Adopt-a-Tape program where, for donation at a specific level, individuals can select a program for preservation treatment.[34]

---

[32] Statement submitted to the National Recording Preservation Board by David Julian Gray, senior architect, content systems, National Public Radio, as revised April 13, 2007. An e-mail update of March 2010 states that development of the content management system has been temporarily suspended and that NPR archiving remains on CD-R.

[33] Testimony of Brian DeShazor, director, Pacifica Radio Archives, "Radio Recording Collections and Archives" session, NRPB public hearings, Los Angeles, November 29, 2006. Mr. DeShazor noted that the Archive and affiliate KPFK in Los Angeles were conducting an experimental program in which programming content originating since February 2005 is being recorded as MP3s, "identified by date and time code," and stored on hard drives. Upon request by station personnel, listeners, or researchers, programs are burned onto CDs and assigned archive numbers.

[34] In 2007, the Pacifica Radio Archives received supplemental grant funds from the National Endowment for the Arts ($15,000) and the GRAMMY Foundation ($39,000 two-year project beginning October 2007). See http://pacificana.org/public/files/National/BoardReports/20070928-MeetingBook.pdf.

Local Radio Station Recordings

Radio network and transcription service recordings, although of incalculable value, represent only a portion of the broad range of recorded broadcasting. There are more than 14,000 radio stations in the United States.[35] Individual radio stations generate local programming, some of which has been recorded by the stations, sponsors, or talent associated with the broadcasts. Institutional holdings of local radio programming are generally unreported, yet many such collections exist. Noncommercial local stations such as WNYC, New York, and WWOZ, New Orleans, have committed resources to save broadcast recordings of historical significance, but preservation of local commercial radio broadcasts has not fared as well.

Preserving local commercial radio recordings presents unique challenges. Ownership of such stations can change frequently, especially since radio deregulation in the mid-1990s. With changing owners, stations are less likely to invest in the preservation of their history by retaining recorded broadcasts or funding reformatting to save them for posterity. Broadcasting historian Christopher Sterling, in testimony at the hearings conducted for this study, attributed the lack of interest in radio recording preservation by the broadcasting industry to a number of factors: " … a consolidation of the industry, with stations disappearing, with certainly the first and now the second generation of owners who did have a care about history in the field having gone on to radio's happy hunting ground, [and] with the widespread sense in the radio business that there is simply a lack of any revenue potential."[36] Many of the local radio broadcast recordings that have survived have been found in station storage facilities. Some recordings have been transferred to archives and some have been rescued from trash bins by committed senior station staff members and collectors. It is not known how many have been lost, but they most certainly number in the thousands.

Station logging tapes are a potentially rich but neglected source of historical and contemporary radio recordings. Many radio stations regularly made tape recordings of every broadcast hour to create an audio record for use in the case of legal problems, such as profanity issues or Federal Communications Commission license challenges. The tapes were recorded at a very slow speed, so the audio quality is intentionally of very low fidelity. Extant logging tapes may be the only recorded documentation of many broadcast stations. Many of the most respected, as well as most popular, radio programs have not been officially documented. A commemorative compact disc compiled to honor the history of WDIA, the first radio station in the United States programmed by and for African Americans, comprises excerpts of air-checks derived from tapes made by listeners. The station did not maintain a historical archive. Had fans not recorded

---

[35] National Association of Broadcasters. See http://www.nab.org/radio/.

[36] Testimony of Chris Sterling, professor of media and public affairs and of public policy and public administration, George Washington University, and member, NRPB, "Preservation of Radio Collections" session, NRPB public hearings, December 19, 2006, New York.

An Example of Preservation in Practice: The WWOZ Collection

In the early 1990s, when David Freedman and his colleagues at WWOZ Radio New Orleans 90.7 FM began to systematically record live performances of the New Orleans Jazz and Heritage Festivals (Jazzfest), their goals did not extend much beyond capturing as many performances as possible in the best sound quality they could afford within the budget constraints of a community-owned radio station. As New Orleans music aficionados, they recognized the importance of the recordings as unique musical expressions, but as Freeman readily admits, they did not give any thought to the challenges that would arise in preserving these recordings for posterity. Like many broadcasters and audio engineers at the time, they weren't aware of archival best practices that might have been adopted to better position the sustainability of the recordings into the future. Now general manager of WWOZ, Freedman quips, "We were just into saving the music and getting it on the air … if anyone had told us how hard the preservation was going to be, we might not have ever done it in the first place."

People commonly capture sound without regard to its future significance or the care that might be required to ensure that the recordings survive. And there may be times when posterity is served better if people are not thinking about the challenges of preservation. This was one such occasion, because the music recorded by WWOZ is remarkable: live performances of jazz, blues, and zydeco by a unique community of musicians, some of national stature, others local heroes and legends, recorded in musical venues of antediluvian New Orleans. The collection is a unique and vibrant archive revealing a broad musical culture in live performances before an audience deeply in touch with that culture.

Thanks largely to Freeman's efforts, the collection came to the Library of Congress in 2007 under an agreement that will give WWOZ archival-quality preservation files in exchange. Once digitized, the recordings will be available for public listening in the Library of Congress's Recorded Sound Reference Center in Washington, DC.

From its inception as a live-recording production archive to its digital preservation now under way at the Library's Packard Campus for Audio Visual Conservation in Culpeper, Virginia, the WWOZ Collection represents the range of technical, resource, equipment, documentation, and cataloging challenges that arise when institutions and individuals want to preserve sound recordings.

Storage

When Hurricane Katrina hit New Orleans in August 2005, many of the recordings in the WWOZ collection were nearly lost in the ensuing flood. Archives commonly store materials that are not frequently used in remote locations where costs are lower. For collections in circulation or production use, they use more-convenient storage areas, where materials may be at increased risk of environmental damage, theft, or catastrophic loss. While the primary remote-storage facility used by WWOZ and the New Orleans Jazz and Heritage Society remained high and dry, staff were using a second facility, which was located more conveniently to the station, as temporary storage. Many of the master recordings, in use for broadcast productions, were in this temporary storage facility when Katrina struck. They avoided being damaged beyond repair only because the floodwaters stopped rising just inches from the door.

The Recordings

The collection that WWOZ shipped to the Library of Congress consists of 2,223 sound carriers in a variety of live-capture formats that reflect, over the period that these recordings were made, the station's growing financial resources and the adoption of new technologies that offered better sound quality. Beginning with standard stereo cassettes, the station transitioned to DAT cartridges, moved on to CD-Rs, and then entered the world of multitrack recording with 8- and 16-track A-DATs. Festival recordings were made as 24-track digital recordings in a proprietary file format on hard drive units. All of these formats present preservation challenges, ranging from poor-quality tape stock, cartridge fragility, and balky playback characteristics that result in signal dropouts to difficult remixing requirements, hard-to-find playback hardware, and, perhaps most problematic, proprietary software and file format issues that plague the reformatting of early-generation digital multitrack technologies.

The WWOZ collection is similar to other production collections of the period in that each technology upgrade, however much it improved sonic quality, introduced new and significantly more challenging preservation problems. While the widespread adoption of the 96Kz/24 bit Broadcast Wave audio file standard promises to alleviate some of the problems presented by early digital formats, other key components of reliable digital preservation, including metadata standards, file-management practices, and overall information technology infrastructure remain to be addressed.

The original master recordings from WWOZ are typical live-event masters: they are often full concerts—more than two hours long and recorded on more than one tape. They can include dead air and audience chatter as well as long music sets with occasional on-stage introductions. One Library of Congress engineer working with the collection noted that some of the earlier master recordings in the collection are more like field recordings than commercial master tapes. These earlier recordings include periods devoid of musical content and less-than-optimal sound quality. From these masters were produced a variety of broadcast edits that might include interludes of commercially recorded music, radio host talk, and interviews with performers. Still other recordings in the collection are of actual broadcasts—air-checks of programs that include segments from the Jazzfest masters. As a result, the same performances can appear in different settings and on multiple formats, in both edited and raw mixes, completed productions, and off-air dubs. Coupled with the format changes and duplicate copies, this lack of homogeneity further augments the cost and complexity of the preservation work and raises the level of engineering attention and metadata accuracy required to adequately preserve and provide access to the collection. It necessitates thorough cataloging to identify redundancies, careful listening to assess the quality of various versions of the same performance, and informed consideration of the relative risk presented by each format.

Documentation

The recorded contents of the tapes are identified only by handwritten labels made by the engineers on site. The labels include the date, venue, and name of the primary performer or band; only occasionally are sidemen identified. Playlists of song titles, so important for access in the future, are lacking, and retrospectively recovering this data, when possible, is difficult and time-consuming. For this project, music experts at WWOZ will listen to the preserved audio and attempt to provide the Library's catalogers with song titles and additional performer names. Given the thousands of hours of audio involved, this will be a long-term endeavor, and for most archival audio collections, such an effort would not be practical or even possible. Because of the popularity of the Jazzfest, other information resources are available. Several books have been published about the performances, there is a fan Web site with historical information on concerts, artists, and venues, and the New Orleans Jazz and Heritage Foundation has even put a searchable database of Jazzfest concerts on its Web site. Such information resources are often not available for unpublished recording collections, so in this sense, the WWOZ collection is atypical.

Digital Preservation

At the Library of Congress's Packard Campus for Audio Visual Conservation, audio engineers have been preserving WWOZ recordings to current archival standards. The goal is to transfer every recording, unedited, to 96Khz/24 bit Broadcast Wave Files, beginning with the more familiar formats—cassettes, DAT cartridges, and CDs. The station's decisions to use 120-minute cassettes and to record DATs at 32Khz to maximize duration and minimize tape use are unfortunate but not unusual, given the widespread need to control costs. Both practices, however, can affect sound quality and often present real problems at playback; from a preservation standpoint, these were not the best choices. Significant work remains to determine best copies among duplicates, identify masters, supply missing metadata on the recordings, and create the final catalog records.

Assuming that working playback machines can be located, preserving and remixing the multitrack tapes is scheduled to begin in 2011. Working with multitrack audio is relatively unfamiliar ground for archival engineers, who have long focused on reformatting at-risk monaural and stereo recording formats. Because more recent recordings require digitization for access and preservation, expertise with multiple tracks, noise-reduction encoding, and a variety of problematic early digital formats will be essential for audio preservationists. In addition to making faithful transfers, there are subjective aesthetic decisions involved in producing a stereo mix-down of multitrack recordings, and this work has long been the domain of engineers who specialize in the production of commercial recordings from multitrack masters. Once the Packard Campus's born-digital technology is operational and online in 2010, work will begin on extracting the 24-track audio files stored on portable hard drives and bringing them into the audio suites for mixing and transcoding to a non-proprietary, uncompressed file format. This will likely be the final stage in the preservation of the WWOZ collection.

"Best-Possible" Preservation

The Library of Congress and other institutions with well-funded audio programs have the staff and resources to pursue the ideal of best practices in their preservation activities. Because these standards are often beyond the reach of most archives and libraries with recorded sound collections, less costly alternatives are very much needed. More modest, or "best-possible," approaches might include informed and judicious selection of specific recordings for preservation, including earmarking only some items for master-quality preservation. Doubtless, there are other collections of sound recordings perched as much on the abyss as was the WWOZ collection. It is important that institutions of every size, no matter the extent of their resources, provide harbor to important collections lest they be lost altogether.

favorite programs and saved them, the early sound of this pioneer station would be lost.

An additional form of local radio station broadcast recording is *telescoped radio*, i.e., edited compilations of off-air recordings of popular music radio stations retaining only small portions of commercial recordings played during the broadcasts. Telescoped radio recordings are compiled by amateur devotees of local radio broadcasting with the objective of documenting a station's unique "sound" and the style of its on-air talent; they include disc jockey patter, station identification and public service announcements, and advertisements. They are often the only readily accessible documentation of the thousands of local radio stations that developed and refined their own aural styles between the early 1950s and the late 1990s. Telescoped radio recordings are created primarily for trading among compilers and collectors. Few of these recordings are included in libraries and archives that specialize in broadcasting history.

Radio Broadcasts Held Privately

Private collectors have made a great contribution to radio recording preservation. At the hearings for the study, Sterling observed, "With a couple of stellar exceptions, there is no decent program of recording in preservation for commercial radio. ... The primary exception is something called the OTR, or old time radio movement." OTR, consisting largely of private collectors and a few commercial firms, "probably starting in the late 50s or even the early 60s, decided to preserve network radio, the glory days of network radio prior to television. It is thanks to those folks that we have a substantial amount of commercial radio recordings in existence and a variety of collections around the country."[37]

Tens of thousands of tape recordings of vintage broadcasts are held by private collectors. Many of these programs are not represented in institutional libraries and archives. A challenge to broadcast-recording archivists is not only to identify these programs and add them to institutional collections for cataloging and preservation but also to identify the best available copy of each program. Having been copied many times during trading with fellow collectors, most OTR recordings exist in multiple forms, nearly all of them copies that are generations removed from the original. The audio quality of most copies in circulation reflects the sound degradation inherent in analog duplication.

An additional challenge to acquiring private off-air radio recordings is the copyright status of OTR recordings. Old-time radio hobbyists perform an important preservation service in uncovering vintage radio recordings and keeping them in circulation, but these efforts occupy grey areas of copyright and intellectual property laws and procedures. Recordings of pre-1972 broadcasts could not be copyrighted, but every recording has a number of possible rights holders, as discussed in chapter 4 of this study. Little collecting or trading is

[37] Ibid.

performed for profit, but some owners of rare radio broadcast recordings understand the complexity of the rights issues inherent in the recordings and how they complicate access. This has discouraged some collectors from donating their recordings to institutional libraries and archives. As performer and historian Michael Feinstein observed at the NRPB hearings, "[There are] situations that I can think of, particularly in Los Angeles, where there are collections that are in need of preservation but in some instances [the collector] does not want to let go of any of them because of the attendant rights issues."[38]

During the early decades of the audiocassette's primacy as a recording medium, radio ownership was not as concentrated as it is today. Local programming occupied hours of the broadcast day. It is highly likely that the quantity and diversity of "home-born" radio recordings of local programming held by individuals is enormous. Once cassette recording became inexpensive, little cost or effort was required to make recordings. Recordings were made both to be collected and for later listening, or "time shifting," as it came to be termed. While people recording local radio content may not have attached particular significance to those recordings in their own day, they are of increasing interest to historians of radio, politics, and news, as well as to those who study the dissemination of music and ideas. Since these recordings are likely to be incompletely labeled, and stored under less than ideal conditions, they are prime candidates for preservation.

Generally, libraries and archives have been relatively late to recognize the importance of preserving radio broadcast recordings. Most institutional efforts to collect and archive American radio began long after the era of radio's primacy as an information and entertainment medium. Many extant radio recordings are held in personal collections exclusively. Without private individuals' commitment to the medium, the number of lost recordings of significant and influential broadcasts would be far greater than it is. However true Sterling's comments about corporate efforts to preserve radio recordings may be, many individuals working at stations have a sincere interest in seeing that station history is preserved. Additional recordings could be identified and preserved through a program by which libraries and archives convey the importance of radio recording preservation; develop relationships with station owners, engineers, managers, and on-air talent; and publicize the need for preserving radio broadcast recordings in the broadcasting trade press or through organizations such as the National Association of Broadcasters.

Record Company Archives

In June 2008, fire engulfed a portion of the back lot at Universal Studios, Los Angeles, including vaults that housed video and audio. Sprinkler systems were overwhelmed, and low water pressure

[38] Testimony of Michael Feinstein, musician and music historian/archivist, and member, NRPB, "Copyright and Academic Research" session, NRPB public hearings, December 19, 2006, New York.

hampered firefighters. Though stories have circulated to the contrary, Universal has maintained that "nothing irreplaceable was lost" and that copies of audio and video materials existed off site.[39] An account in the *New York Daily News* reported that some Decca label master recordings of Connee Boswell, Bing Crosby, Lennie Dee, and Georgie Shaw were destroyed. However, Peter LoFrumento, Universal Music Group's senior vice president of corporate communications, was quoted as stating, "In one sense it was a loss. In another, we were covered. It had already been digitized, so the music will still be around for many years."[40] However, an episode in which first-generation sound recordings were possibly lost, whether or not surviving in digital copies, kindled anxiety about the full extent of the loss and the location and security of archives held by record companies.

The state of commercial record company archives drew widespread attention with the publication of an award-winning article by Bill Holland in *Billboard* in July 1997.[41] Holland summarized stories that had been circulating for years alleging that major labels had directed that metal parts, safety copies, tape masters, and other first-generation materials be thrown out or destroyed to clear storage space or reduce storage costs. In some instances, these directives were ignored. There are stories of record company employees retrieving discarded materials that awaited trash pickup. Some of these materials were also pulled by alerted collectors or were passed along to them. Other master recordings perished in fires (such as the 2008 Universal Studios fire). Later generations of company management have at times shown scant knowledge of the significant artists who had recorded for their company or participated in sessions that have placed some sort of stamp on history and culture. This lack of knowledge became even more significant as the major labels acquired the catalogs of smaller companies and independents.

Holland's article was mainly about the growing recognition of the historic importance of sound recordings of past decades and the state of initiatives to rescue and preserve vault recordings. In the years since Holland's articles appeared, a general reorientation has occurred. Many recording companies now have their assets stored off site by firms that provide security and housing at controlled temperature and humidity levels.

Representatives of EMI Music, North America, and Universal Music Group, in testimony before the NRPB, described current preservation efforts and challenges. Paul West of Universal explained that judgments are no longer made about what vault materials merit

---

[39] Canadian Broadcasting Corporation Web site. June 1, 2008. "Universal Studios Fire Engulfs Sets, Video Vault, King Kong Exhibit." Available at http://www.cbc.ca/arts/film/story/2008/06/01/universal-fire.html.

[40] Nancy Dillon, "Universal Studies Fire Silences Music of Bing Crosby, Connee Boswell," NYDailyNews.com, June 3, 2008. Available at http://www.nydailynews.com/news/national/2008/06/03/2008-06-03_universal_studios_fire_silences_music_of.html#ixzz0hhRBHAGY.

[41] Bill Holland, "Labels Strive to Rectify Past Archival Problems," *Billboard* magazine, July 12 and 19, 1997. Reprinted at http://www.billholland.net/words/Labels%20Strive%20to%20Rectify%20Past%20Archival%20Problems.pdf.

retention and what is dispensable. "The first rule of thumb is 'Collect and save all' … nobody I think can play God, if you will, in terms of knowing what we should actually keep or what actually we should not." West noted that many reels of recorded tape are not of final, published recordings:

> Only 65 to 75 percent of what is in our library has ever been released. We are dealing with elements. … A lot of the finished product we create is actually the result of gathering elements and basically putting these together for ... production [of] our final product. So, in our world, we do not look at it like having a book or manuscript. … We look at the elements that make up the steps along the way. … If you do not start from the multitrack down through the flat master ... you are, quite candidly, missing the boat.[42]

The resources to preserve analog multitrack master tapes are restricted to record company and other commercial studios. It is unlikely that university and other nonprofit archives have analog tape machines capable of playing back more than two tracks or recording engineers with the experience that would be necessary to collaborate with record companies on the preservation of multitrack masters.

Major labels are grappling with the same challenges facing other archives in selecting which materials require first attention. Paul West observed, "It is going to be maybe a little surprising to hear that some of the stuff that we are in the middle of [preserving] is stuff that probably was recorded about 15 years ago, not something that was recorded 30 or 35 years ago."[43] Discs, metal parts, and stampers are essentially inert, while open-reel tape is subject to several paths of deterioration. More challenging still are early digital assets that may present an entirely different problem. EMI archivist Don Andes observed at the hearings, "We are not talking so much about obsolescence and deterioration of the particular media. … It is a matter of a functional playback device that actually can render and basically allow the migration to preservation."[44]

While established labels and their archivists face formidable challenges, far more record labels—some of them small and independent—have passed from the scene over the years. In some instances, master tapes, discs, and other physical assets have been left unattended or have become scattered. In other instances, the catalog, in part or complete, may have been purchased or acquired by another company or label. Such transactions may include rights to the catalog, but might not include all the physical elements.[45] One historian notes that

---

[42] Testimony of Paul West, vice president, studios and vault operations, digital logistics and business services, Universal Music Group, "Record Company Archivists" session, NRPB public hearings, Los Angeles, November 29, 2006.

[43] Ibid.

[44] Testimony of Don Andes, director, U.S. archives, EMI Music, North America, "Record Company Archivists" session, NRPB public hearings, Los Angeles, November 29, 2006.

[45] With successive sales, the nature of the "rights" themselves can become cloudy, in the absence of written and contractual records of artist and label relationships or of recordings leased by the label originally.

> corporate archives were only as good as the corporations' motivations. Beyond a certain point, companies lacked a compelling reason to preserve recordings that did not hold commercial promise, and if a company went out of business, its archive would not necessarily be maintained, and the continued preservation of the recordings housed therein became more a matter of accident than of intention.[46]

The wheels of commerce also threaten the fate of company-held archives. In recent years, mergers and sales of entertainment units, along with diminished receipts from sales of recordings, have brought about contraction of the industry, high turnover in corporate positions, and diminished corporate continuity that has drained many companies of institutional memory and corporate pride in past achievements. Despite new means of digital distribution, it remains difficult for major record companies to sell to niche markets, and it may not be alarmist to question how long a publicly held company will pay to maintain recordings with little potential commercial value. This could bring about the previously mentioned scattering or destruction of these assets, and the potential loss of important components of our cultural heritage.

Recently, as avenues for the distribution of music have proliferated, many artists have gained more control over their own creative assets. But a number of performers who recorded in the analog era may also control some or even all of the elements from studio sessions. While some have the means to see that analog tapes and discs are properly stored and preserved, others may have neither the focus nor the means to do so, leaving a considerable body of original work at risk. This situation may change, as the studio and work sessions that were seen as all in a day's work at the time begin to take on historical significance, especially for the artists themselves. Testifying before the NRPB in Los Angeles, composer, producer, and recording artist T-Bone Burnett commented on a forgotten session tape that came into his possession:

> Somebody will call and say, "I have got some tapes of yours that you did at Sound City in 1965 and some boxes, do you want them?" And I paid no attention to that. That is the time when I was a kid. That stuff was left all over everywhere.
>
> Now, it is beginning to be a lot more meaningful to me and I'm so grateful to get these things back. And the first thing we are doing is transferring them to digital because ... at the moment, it is the safest, best medium to kind of quickly get things stable.
>
> When we were working on those things in the 1960s, the idea was to get it on the radio and make some money and move on. ... Nobody thought rock and roll would last. So there was no sense of permanence. And maybe that was one of the good things

[46] Jonathan Sterne, *The Audible Past: Cultural Origins of Sound Reproduction* (Durham, NC: Duke University Press, 2003), 327.

> about it too; there was no self-consciousness about its place in history or anything like that. But at this point, I'm ... 58 years old. ... You begin to realize that the things you do in your life actually have meaning and are important.
>
> Barnett Newman says time washes over the tip of the pyramid. And by that, he meant that there is plenty of room at the base of the pyramid to put a lot of things. But that time washes them into the sand very quickly [while] if you put something at the tip of the pyramid, it stays there. And as I have grown older, it has become more and more important to me to put something at the tip, and then it becomes more and more crucial that if you put it there, it is going to stay there.[47]

Burnett's remarks describe the meaning that attaches to sound recordings after the passage of time, a meaning that can be bestowed by their creators, by historians, or by society. They also underscore that if the proper care or preservation of sound recordings is postponed until their significance is realized, it may well be too late. This is especially pertinent to the present era when so many recordings are distributed via the Internet. His observations underline another theme of this study: it is impossible to preserve everything, and it may be similarly impossible to anticipate which recordings will assume greatest significance in the future; consequently, the individuals making choices among collections to be preserved must be sufficiently knowledgeable to assess which recordings most merit attention.

Many archivists, collectors, and scholars are concerned about the long-term security of record company archives. It is hoped that if company archives are closed down, careful consideration will be given to transferring them to an archive that will take long-term responsibility for preservation.[48]

Privately Held Collections of Commercial Recordings

Public institutions were not the first to recognize the importance of collecting sound recordings, and, as a study conducted by CLIR reports, "There is no reason to conclude that libraries hold most of the nation's preservation-worthy audio collections."[49] Record collectors—originally hobbyists—recognized the cultural value of commercially issued sound recordings and began to build personal collections many years before public institutions committed resources

[47] Testimony of T-Bone Burnett, composer, songwriter, performer, and producer, "Metadata" session, NRPB public hearings, November 29, 2006, Los Angeles.

[48] It should be pointed out that the most comprehensive U.S. record company archives are those of the Thomas Edison companies, which stopped making records more than 80 years ago. The archives, composed of thousands of cylinders and discs, research laboratory and company manuscripts, and published documents, are maintained by the U.S. Park Service at the Thomas Edison National Historical Park in West Orange, New Jersey.

[49] Smith, Allen, and Allen 2004, 6.

to collecting and preserving them. Today, some of the most significant, as well as rarest, commercially issued sound recordings remain in private hands, and public institutions acquire many of their most important commercial recordings as gifts or purchases from private collectors. In fact, some of the largest and most specialized recorded sound collections held by institutions and archives could be described as "collections of collections"; that is, large collections had their origins as small collections accumulated by private individuals. Such individuals deserve credit for preserving important commercial recordings dating to the beginnings of the industry, and their efforts have significantly contributed to the preservation of musical and spoken-word recordings.

Cylinder recordings are one example of what private collectors have helped save. Production and sales of cylinder recordings—once the dominant commercial recording medium—were in steep decline before any U.S. institution began collecting them. An informative overview of commercial cylinder production was submitted to the NRPB in support of this study by board member, collector, and independent researcher Bill Klinger.[50] Klinger estimates that U.S. companies published more than 47,000 individual titles before Edison ceased manufacturing commercial cylinder recordings in 1929, that no copies exist of 52 percent of these titles, and that only 17 percent of titles published on wax cylinders before 1902 survive today. It is only because of the diligence of private collectors devoted to the medium that 48 percent of pre-1929 titles are extant. Aside from the Thomas Edison National Historical Park, the three institutions that hold the largest cylinder collections in the United States are the Library of Congress, Syracuse University, and the University of California, Santa Barbara (UCSB). All were acquired from private collectors.

Over the years, private collectors have also provided rare or unissued recordings to record companies seeking to produce reissues. In some instances, the major labels no longer hold the original masters (called *mothers* or *stampers*) that were used in the manufacture of the commercial releases and they may not have vault copies of issued recordings from their catalog. For issues from many smaller but historically significant record labels, studio and manufacturing elements do not exist at all. Private collectors are often the first line of inquiry for a reissue producer seeking pristine copies of issued records, many of which were sold in limited numbers.

Many collectors are in effect private curators, approaching collection development and custodianship with highly focused interests. Some of these independent scholars have published articles and books and have edited reissue recordings that represent their collections or fields of expertise. Many have built their collections within a narrowly defined universe, often achieving completeness within a genre or an artist's oeuvre, and continually replacing copies to

[50] Bill Klinger, Association for Recorded Sound Collections, "Cylinder Records: Significance, Production, and Survival," written statement submitted to the NRPB. Available at http://www.loc.gov/rr/record/nrpb/pdf/klinger.pdf.

upgrade the condition of recordings they hold. These collections may reflect decades of discerning acquisition, significant investments of money, and time-consuming research. Through their study of recorded sound history, many of these collectors have developed expertise in their field of interest unparalleled by professional curators or academics. Their distinct subjects and knowledge of their field often include keen awareness of the cultural value of specific recordings that enter the marketplace, which can aid preservation considerably. For example, in 2009, David Giovannoni, a Grammy Award-winning independent scholar, collector, and co-discoverer of the earliest recordings made, learned from a fellow collector that wax cylinder field recordings made in Africa in the late 1920s by ethnomusicologist Laura Boulton were being sold on an online auction site. These original recordings were not held by the institutions in possession of Boulton's other work. Thanks to the cadre of individuals who focus their interest on early recordings, Giovannoni was made aware of the significance of the auction offer and was able to purchase the cylinders, thereby ensuring that they are preserved for future use.

Every major research library that includes commercial sound recording collections can count among its treasures incomparable recording collections sold or donated by private collectors. Hundreds of such special collections, held throughout the United States, are now accessible to the public. They range from the complete collection of recordings by the composer and bandleader Duke Ellington, donated to the Library of Congress by Jerry Valburn, to the tens of thousands of classical vocal recordings made by artists trained in the nineteenth century, donated to Yale University by Laurence and Cora Whitten.[51]

Recordings held by institutions are rarely documented by item-level cataloging or other detailed documentation, yet some information about these collections is publicly available. And even when preservation of these collections has barely been addressed, collection managers have some awareness of general preservation needs. It is a much greater challenge to address the risk of losing collections about which is little known, or for public policy in the realm of recorded sound preservation to be driven by what cannot be measured. Sound recordings held by private collectors, musicians, and custodians of collections have historical and cultural value that is believed to be significant yet remains largely unknown. These collections pose several major issues that must be considered, such as the identification of private collections, storage and usage of collections, and the disposition of collections that private collectors can no longer keep.

Identification of Private Collections

Who holds private collections, and where are they? What specialties are represented?

"Record collectors" might be characterized as individuals whose

[51] Valburn also sold to the Library of Congress a valuable collection of unpublished recordings by Ellington.

holdings consist of commercially released recordings that may be rare, but probably are not unique. Other individuals might be more accurately described as "recorded sound collectors" in specialty fields, whose holdings generally include released recordings but also may include a host of unique recordings, including interviews and oral histories; off-air recordings of radio broadcasts and actualities; privately made recordings of performances captured on instantaneous discs, tape, or digital media; or recordings of studio sessions, including rehearsal, alternate, and breakdown takes and recording elements that may have been edited into published composite performances. The unique items may have been discovered, won at auction, purchased outright, or received from other collectors or family heirs.

Collectors have also been known to claim (or "save," in their estimation) recordings that major labels periodically disposed of for lack of space or indifference to their possible historical value.[52] There are also tales of serious collectors of specialized material acquiring material surreptitiously. Some of these stories have no doubt been inflated; at the same time many more accounts may lie behind sealed lips or are now beyond the telling. Privately held collections may also include recordings made in violation of policy or law, as in the case of a patron who smuggles a recording device into a concert and walks out with an unauthorized recording. Some of these recordings, though made illegally, were not exploited illegally and may now add incalculably to the performance history of an artist, including the evolution of his or her repertoire or a particular composition with which the artist is closely identified. Unsanctioned provenance does not preclude the possibility that such recordings may be licensed for access or distribution in the future, but the challenges one must overcome to publish the recordings are formidable.

Storage Conditions and Usage

Another issue is the conditions under which private collections are kept and used. Many private collections are stored for periods of time in suboptimal conditions, and collectors' in-use practices for recordings in their collections are a major concern. Some private collectors are dogged in their pursuit of recordings desired for the universe of their interests, but they may give less thought to the caliber of the equipment on which they play items from their collections, using older equipment that has not been maintained (e.g., without periodic replacement of phonograph styli or maintenance of tape transports). Handling practices for analog recordings will affect their condition, and physical damage from improper handling or exposure can be difficult or impossible to remedy. The paper submitted by Klinger in support of this study notes, "Collectors can be very good custodians of their treasured objects. However, many collectors are not well informed about the preferred archival practices that would help to conserve their records; others don't have the resources

[52] These collectors are sometimes identified as "Dumpster divers," although without their plunges into the discards, much would have been lost.

to apply the best practices, even if they wish to." Development of any means of communicating information about safeguards for collections remaining in private hands would be especially beneficial.

Collections held by private individuals are sometimes much more vulnerable to damage than are uncataloged collections housed within an institution's secure walls. Hurricane Katrina, for example, demonstrated how many sound recordings could be at risk or lost entirely. Testimony submitted by a representative of New Orleans radio station WWOZ noted that beyond its own collection

> there are hundreds of smaller, important collections in New Orleans, made by the musicians themselves. Traditional jazz clarinetist Dr. Michael White and virtuoso pianist Henry Butler, to cite two examples, lost their entire collection of master recordings of their life's work. Many other musicians still have recordings in various states of deterioration and obsolescent formats which are at risk of being lost without proper archival intervention.[53]

When considering storage conditions for private collections, the context is usually for analog recordings, but many private individuals hold digital recordings. These present a new set of challenges, some of which may not be adequately addressed by private collectors. Archivists responsible for digital media—CD-Rs, hard drives, and other carriers of digital sound files—understand that all are impermanent and require periodic migration of the data to new media to assure long-term accessibility. Experience has shown that the reliable lifetime of a CD-R created in 2009 is very short in contrast to that of a shellac 78-rpm pressing of a recording made in 1909. Hard drives also have a comparatively brief lifetime and are prone to failure. In sum, institutions and private collectors alike need to preserve their holdings by backing up sound files on multiple drives and periodically migrating those files to new drives to protect against mechanical failure.

The scope of "private collections" is by no means limited to recordings held by collectors. Whereas major record labels once held control of master discs and tapes, artists today increasingly control their original recording materials. Most musicians or groups are now capable of producing a CD or distributing their work in the form of sound files, and responsibility for preserving the primary sound files increasingly rests with the creator. Archives today need to make sure that artists and producers who are distributing their recordings digitally recognize the importance of preservation planning at the time their works are created and sold. Otherwise, their legacy may be lost.

Long-term Planning for Private Collections

Many private collectors fail to make provisions for the placement of their collections, either during their lifetime or after their death.

[53] Testimony of David Freedman, General Manager, WWOZ-FM, New Orleans, Louisiana, "Preservation of Radio Collections," session, NRPB public hearings, December 19, 2006, New York.

A survey of collectors by one major historical record auctioneer revealed that of 644 respondents, only 226, or 35 percent, had arranged for the disposition of their collections after their death.[54] One reason may be the pervasive feeling within the collector community that once in the custody of institutions, collections become less accessible. Some have even likened donating a collection to an institution to sending it into a "black hole."[55] Regardless of why a collector might fail to arrange for the disposition of his or her holdings, the result can be unfortunate. As the Klinger submission points out, "Too often, collectors do not make plans for the ultimate disposition of their holdings. Important collections that took decades to gather, organize, and catalog are frequently broken up and widely dispersed, losing the integrity and accessibility the collection once had, as a localized whole. Worse, entire collections can disappear into the trash heap."[56]

Owners of private collections, or their heirs, have every right to break up collections for individual sales, but in these instances, the subsequent losses extend far beyond the material value of the individual recordings. In some cases, a body of knowledge and history also risks being lost. This may include information about what the collection holds and important details about the recordings themselves—when, where, and under what conditions unique recordings were made; subject content for the purpose of cataloging and basic identification to differentiate one recording from another; and deep background on what is heard on the recordings. Owners of historically and culturally valuable collections are encouraged to identify a proper place where their collections might be placed eventually, even if the collections are not to be passed to the institution until the collector dies or is ready to relinquish them.

Even if transfer of the collection is postponed, transfer of knowledge can begin. Interaction with an institution or archive prior to placement would permit helpful discussion about the collection, including rights and access issues that could be addressed in advance, as well as preservation of the owner's knowledge of the collection content. The benefit to the institution and the private collector alike can be significant, including peace of mind for an owner who would like to see the fruits of his or her effort and ingenuity have a life beyond the collector's span of years.

There are good reasons for collectors who wish their collections to remain intact to make provisions for this prior to their demise. Families often have little or no interest in a collector's holdings, and no sense of whether the collection is of any significance, selectively or as a body. In their haste to ready a deceased family member's residence for sale, relatives and executors may dispose of a collection

---

[54] Survey conducted by Kurt Nauck. The survey results appear in *Nauck's Vintage Records*, no. 41, 118.

[55] Testimony of Tim Brooks, music historian, writer, discographer, and bibliographer, and chair of Copyright Committee, ARSC, "Copyright and Academic Research" session, NRPB, December 19, 2006, New York.

[56] Klinger, 9.

without ascertaining its contents or even compiling a short list of titles or labels chosen at random.[57]

Although many institutions have acquisitions budgets that enable them to purchase published and unpublished sound recordings from private collectors, such institutions often cannot meet the monetary expectations of private sellers. This may be because the buyer and seller fail to agree upon a fair cost; in some cases, for example, the seller may have unrealistic expectations. In addition, estimated values of collections obtained from appraisers may exceed the price a collection can command on the open market. In acquiring a collection, an institution should budget for anticipated costs to rehouse, preserve, and catalog it.

While some collectors would prefer not to see their collections broken up, others would prefer dispersal rather than placement in an institution. By selling the collection in blocks or individual pieces, they feel assured that each item will be more likely to go to a collector who truly wants it. In this perspective, the interests of access are better served by keeping collections *from* archives and institutions, even if it means breaking up a collection that, for scholarly or historical reasons, might be better left intact. This concern of private collectors—this aversion to perceived black holes of inaccessibility—is an important reason why resolving impediments to preservation and access is critically important.

Collections of commercial recordings held by private individuals are a crucial component of audio preservation in the United States. While many of these privately owned collections are likely to remain so, and some are stored under less-than-ideal conditions, the preservation of historical recordings is assured only if the three major parties that can make this goal a reality—collectors, archives, and the recording industry—are jointly committed to ongoing cooperation and communication.

The Views of Scholars and Other Users

Those whose work revolves around historical sound recording archives and libraries—historians, musicologists, collectors, performers—view challenges to audio preservation in much the same light as librarians and curators of audio archives do. This was shown both in testimony presented at a hearing in support of this study and by responses to a series of extended interviews conducted for this study by Nancy Davenport, who was then president of the Council on Library and Information Resources. Davenport's survey was based on discussions with 20 scholars, as well as curators, librarians, and rights holders, held in 2006. Her full report is included in this study as Appendix C.

Davenport's interviews showed that scholars' primary concerns fell into two categories: (1) a desire for better, more detailed tools to

[57] The International Association of Jazz Record Collectors has published a monograph on collection disposal: *Assessing, Insuring, and Disposing of Jazz Record Collections.* IAJRC monograph #1 (Bel Air, MD: International Association of Jazz Record Collectors, 1990). IAJRC is seeking to update it.

aid discovery (i.e., research of collection holdings); and (2) the need to remove impediments to access to recordings in the pursuit of scholarship.

Just as representatives of archives and libraries described the paucity of detailed cataloging and descriptions of their holdings, many scholars interviewed by Davenport expressed dissatisfaction about the difficulty of locating recordings relevant to their research. Davenport summarized:

> The sources of this frustration range from finding no reference to the location of a particular recording to finding insufficient specific information. Many of these recordings are part of library collections (usually kept in the special or non-book collection), but because of work backlogs they have not yet been described in the library's catalog. Moreover, when a library or an archives catalogs large collections, choices may not meet the needs of the researcher in search of a particular recording. For example, a collection might be named for its donor, its label, or the artist. There may be a brief note indicating the number of discs in the collection but no item-level description of each recording. Some catalogs carry detailed information on the better-known materials in the collection but pay little attention to the rest. This situation fails to meet the needs of researchers, who may require details such as the place and date of performance, the names of the musicians, the recording studio and engineer, or even the matrix number. Whether the researcher is comparing multiple interpretations or searching for one exemplar, specific attributes are needed.[58]

The lack of sufficient cataloging or description of collections may result in underuse of institutional audio collections and a consequent adverse impact on allocations of funding for the libraries and archives. Potential users cannot find collections if descriptions are inadequate or not easily accessible. At the same time, institutions may be understandably reluctant to commit resources to provide better access to collections that are rarely used. The same issue arises in regard to access. Librarians and archivists regularly report that users expect free and open access to historic sound recordings held by their institutions. These expectations so greatly exceed legally permitted program actions that users are often dissuaded from using institutional sound collections altogether, further eroding the user support necessary to garner additional resources from the larger institution.

Scholars interviewed by Davenport also noted how the "ease and convenience" of the Internet "contrasted with the difficulty of searching hundreds of library or archive catalogs that may have differing search protocols." The bibliographic utility OCLC is designed to serve as a union catalog that details which libraries hold the specific recordings described in it. The OCLC catalog lists holdings of

[58] Nancy Davenport, "Obstacles to Access and Preservation of Recorded Sound," (see p. 157 of this volume).

thousands of libraries throughout the world. Unfortunately, OCLC catalog records are often inadequate for research on historical recordings. One reason is that institutions lack the resources to create rich catalog records with all of the information about an item desired by many researchers; a second reason is that the OCLC Web search tool WorldCat.org provides nonlibrary users with a scaled-down catalog record that does not display elements some users need.

Davenport's work also revealed scholars' frustrations over access to the recordings themselves. Musicologists who work with recordings often need to transcribe musical passages. They related to Davenport that to do so requires listening to recordings repeatedly, stopping and starting playback frequently, and slowing and speeding recordings. It is now possible to provide such playback services without damaging recordings, since archives and libraries are able to make digital copies of requested recordings for patrons' in-house use. Few institutions provide this service, however. At the hearings for this study, ethnomusicologist Clifford Murphy reiterated this need: "Traveling to these archives is a once-in-a-lifetime experience. Traveling is expensive, and in order to get these musics in one's ears, one needs to hear them more than once in a lifetime."[59]

Another difficulty scholars face is identifying rights holders and securing permission to share recordings with students and peers. For example, a rights holder may be unsure of what permissions he or she may convey, or may fail to respond to a scholar's request. "Interviewees described in detail the time, level of effort, and cost of securing rights. In the absence of a master registry that is updated as rights change hands, scholars must assume responsibility for tracking down the owners. … Multiple interviewees described having to conduct many rounds of rights searches to secure needed permissions."[60]

Davenport prepared a set of seven solutions recommended by some or all of the individuals she interviewed. She interviewed representatives of owners of recording-related intellectual property as well as scholars who make use of historical recordings. Interviewees did not unanimously agree on every solution proposed. For example, the copyright process-related recommendations (4 and 5 below) are unlikely to be endorsed by all content owners. However, implementation of all of the recommendations would undoubtedly increase access to historical recordings.

Davenport's seven solutions are as follows:

1. Create a unified database of sound recordings held by libraries and archives, as well as by individual collectors, to address problems of discovery. Many interviewees suggested that a national recorded sound database be developed and that libraries and archives be strongly encouraged to deposit records of their holdings in it. While the goal is an identification system rich in detail about the performance and artist, with information about the

[59] Testimony of Clifford Murphy, PhD candidate in ethnomusicology, Brown University, "Copyright and Academic Research" session, NRPB public hearings, December 19, 2006, New York.

[60] Davenport (p. 159).

recording's manufacture, institutions should begin to participate with the records currently available about their holdings. Serious individual collectors should be encouraged to deposit information about their collections into this database.

2. Create a unified database of property rights associated with sound recordings to facilitate the location of rights holders. Scholars, performers, curators, and publishers related in detail their efforts to locate names and addresses of rights owners. The interviewees called for a new system to replace the current patchwork approach. This recommendation seeks to develop a voluntary cooperative that would be available to all segments of the recorded sound community.
3. Rewrite the copyright laws to mandate online registration of works owned, sold, or renewed. While the goal of this recommendation is identical to that of the unified database outlined in recommendation 2, the mechanism for its creation and participation would be legally mandated, rather than voluntary. To strengthen this recommendation, some interviewees suggested that it specify that works not registered would automatically fall into the public domain.
4. Rewrite the copyright law to compel rights owners to permit use of their work. Researchers who made this recommendation believe that it is in keeping with the spirit of copyright as it appears in the U.S. Constitution, permitting exclusive use for a short period of time followed by wide availability for the diffusion of knowledge.
5. Affiliate the Library of Congress with at least one library in each state so that the Library's sound recording holdings could be more broadly available. With the ability of digital technology to transfer sound recordings to geographically disparate locations, the Library's collections could be made available for use in every state, minimizing the need for long-distance travel. Each state would have to create facilities for deep, repetitive, and manipulative listening.
6. Create a massive, distributed jukebox of sound. iTunes and other commercial entities have tested and proved a business model that enables users to download a wide assortment of sound recordings at a reasonable price. Interviewees recommended development of a noncommercial variant that would provide better tools for discovery, access, incorporation, and use for casual users as well as scholars. Structured fees would be tied to the level of use—casual use at one fee and performance at a different, presumably higher, fee. The purchase of the material would include the purchase of the rights, and no additional rights clearance would be required. In this model, no institution would relinquish its ownership or physical possession of the underlying recording. As digital copies were made, information about them would be posted to the jukebox. The only centralized organization and enterprise created would be the jukebox Web site and the business and financial operations. Two analogous representations of this

model are eBay, a site through which the transactions take place but where the "content" is distributed throughout the selling community, and AbeBooks, which operates as a centralized point of discovery, access, and business transactions for many out-of-print book dealers.

7. Train librarians and archivists in copyright law. Many of the interviewees described situations in which they had tried to use materials in a library or an archive and been told that the rights to those materials were unclear. In most such cases, the librarian or archivist refused to serve the material, even for listening purposes. The individuals who refused to grant permission generally noted that they were afraid that they or their institutions might be the target of an infringement lawsuit. Scholars think that some curators have become so wary about possible infringement that they are ignoring fair use of the material for scholarly purposes.

Contemporary Recording Formats

Sound recordings made recently may be at as great a risk of loss as those made 100 years ago. The Klinger analysis of cylinder production and preservation submitted in support of this study estimates that only 17 percent of titles published on wax cylinders before 1902 survive in the twenty-first century. There is reason to believe that by 2110, the survival rate of recordings made in the past 20 years could be equally low. Recordings today are published as analog and digital discs, downloadable digital files, and files streamed over the Web. There are few assurances that any of these formats are being systematically archived for preservation. Inherent to each format and its primary means of distribution are challenges to long-term preservation.

Compact Discs

CDs remain the best-selling format for recorded sound in the early twenty-first century. The long-term preservation of CDs is more assured than that of other digital recording formats because they are published in a tangible, physical format and are distributed broadly. Holding copies in widely dispersed places is believed by many to be a form of preservation. Such informal means of preservation may have to suffice for compact discs, as it has for other published sound media, but there are many shortcomings of this ad hoc solution.

First, CDs are not a permanent medium. They are subject to damage from manufacturing defects, misuse, and poor storage conditions. As with every digital format, long-term preservation requires that the digital information on compact discs periodically be migrated to new media. (Bit stream migration is even more essential for CD-Rs, a far less stable medium than mass-produced compact discs.) Only large institutions have the digital infrastructure and staff resources to preserve compact discs for the long term.

Moreover, to be truly accessible, a compact disc in a collection must be individually cataloged in a database available to the public and be available for listening by the community the institution is designated to serve, if not by the general public. Many institutions catalog their holdings to some extent, and provide listening services for their compact disc collections. However, there is no single portal to search holdings of all institutions, and no union catalogs include collections owned by individuals.

Because one of the greatest challenges to comprehensive preservation of compact discs may be the difficulty of identifying all releases, cataloging is especially important as an aid to recording-acquisition specialists. There is no public effort to comprehensively document all releases and ensure that each is held by one or more institutions to guarantee their accessibility in the future. Given the hundreds of companies in the United States that issue compact discs, it is very unlikely that a comprehensive list of published recordings will ever exist.[61] This presents an enormous challenge to institutions attempting to identify and collect comprehensively a specific genre or recorded musical form. While many publishers of compact discs are very small, Internet sales sites have provided a new means of national distribution.

The Library of Congress may be the logical institution to assume responsibility for archiving contemporary published recordings. Section 407(a) of U.S. Copyright Law requires that "the owner of copyright or of the exclusive right of publication in a work published in the United States shall deposit, within three months after the date of such publication—(1) two complete copies of the best edition; or (2) if the work is a sound recording, two complete phonorecords of the best edition, together with any printed or other visually perceptible material published with such phonorecords."[62] Unfortunately, compliance with deposit requirements of the law by record companies is inconsistent, as a small survey has demonstrated. Ten relatively small U.S. record labels, each known for issuing discs of critically acclaimed "indie rock" groups, took part in the survey.[63] Copyright registration records for the year 2007 were surveyed. Of the 10 labels, only 2 registered all or nearly all recordings issued in 2007; the remaining 8 registered no sound recordings in that year.

The compact discs of these small, independent labels may be the contemporary equivalents of the independent record labels that issued country, blues, jazz, gospel, and rhythm and blues recordings in the 1950s. Recordings on those labels are now highly sought after by libraries and archives, record collectors, and music historians; they are difficult to locate and bring high prices in the used-record marketplace. Because the 1950s recordings were issued by small labels, many now out of business, with small numbers of copies released, they often cannot be found in libraries or archives. Consequently, their long-term preservation prospects are in jeopardy.

---

[61] The Archive of Contemporary Music in New York City is purportedly compiling a database of its holdings in an "international discography." See http://www.arcmusic.org/begin.html.

[62] Title 17. Section 407(a). See http://www.copyright.gov/title17/92chap4.html#407.

[63] The data were provided from research conducted by Gail Sonnemann in February 2010. The record labels were Drag City, Ipecac, Jagjaguwar, Kill Rock Stars, Kranky, Matador, Merge, Southern Lord, Sub Pop, and Thrill Jockey.

The goal of the independent ARChive of Contemporary Music (ACM) in New York City is to acquire everything related to international popular music beginning from the mid-twentieth century. ACM Director B. George expanded on the broad acquisitions at this study's hearings in a statement submitted to the NRPB: "So, while ARC applauds any and all archiving and preservation initiatives ... lists of 'important' works, notions of 'best' or 'quality' are laughable. ARC collects what people do. Every generation, every culture must have the opportunity to sift through the full range of what happened as a basis for historical study, entertainment and the creation of new works."[64] The ACM Web site adds, "Taste, quality, marketing, halls of fame, sales, stars and value are as alien to us as they are, well, to aliens."[65]

The ACM may be closer than any other institution to approaching a comprehensive archive of popular compact discs. Its accomplishment, with a minimal staff, is remarkable. The self-described "not-for-profit archive, music library and research" holds more than 2 million recordings. However, it neither migrates CD content nor maintains a listening service for its members or the public. It provides record companies with copies of recordings for reissue when they have no master tapes in their own archives.

While the focus here is CDs, the issues outlined apply to contemporary LP discs as well. LP production and sales never entirely ceased after the advent of compact discs in the mid-1980s, and sales have increased recently. Of interest to many are LP singles, remixes, and expansions of individual musical selections also issued on CD, and recordings released on vinyl LP exclusively. This format is especially important in documenting the development of rap and hip-hop music. It is not known whether any libraries or archives have undertaken efforts to develop comprehensive collections of this format.

The universe of recorded sound is too vast for one institution or group of institutions to assume independent responsibility for its preservation. The range of types of recordings produced is enormous. In addition to rock, hip-hop, country, folk, classical, and jazz music genres, compact discs offer ethnic music (Asian and Latin predominantly, but many others as well), spoken word, children's recordings, and religious music of many denominations. It appears that CD preservation is ad hoc at present, and there is little reason to believe that current preservation efforts are any less scattershot than those of past decades. The number of recordings created daily may be too large to track and preserve comprehensively unless, as private collectors do, institutions with preservation goals focus their interests narrowly or make conscious selection decisions based on quality, or other factors. Clearly, the Library of Congress and the U.S. Copyright Office could exercise more systematically and forcefully the Library's legal entitlement to deposit copies of new works. Institutions should

[64] E-mail from B. George, director, The ARChive of Contemporary Music, to Rob Bamberger, December 2006.

[65] "Why the ARChive?" See http://www.arcmusic.org/begin.html.

consider working together to coordinate collection development and focus acquisitions on specific genres and existing collection strengths.

Born-Digital Recordings

Born-digital media are those created and distributed in a digital form. Sound recordings on compact discs were the first digital medium created for widespread consumer use; most recordings have been created digitally since the mid- to late 1980s. Increasingly, however, more and more audio is not only born digital but also disseminated as a digital streaming or file form. Born-digital sound recordings that are never disseminated in physical forms present even greater challenges for preservation than those posed by compact discs.

The Web has made more audio recordings available for listening than was ever possible before in history. Recordings are both created and distributed in digital form, either as files for download or as streaming media. MP3 audio files can be purchased from Web sites such as iTunes, eMusic, and Amazon. Leading streaming services such as Rhapsody and Lala allow users to listen to audio streams or "leased" (temporarily owned) files for set fees. Social Web sites such as MySpace and Second Life provide a place for performers and fans to post selections for streaming and download. Radio stations simulcast on the net. Music-related blogs often incorporate embedded audio (not always legally) for streaming or downloading. Thousands of informative and entertaining podcasts, many of potential value to scholars, are available through iTunes.com and from their creators' Web sites.

Digital recording and production tools for home computers enable vocalists, instrumentalists, and musical groups to create professional-sounding recordings inexpensively. These tools and the ability to distribute recordings online enable amateur and semiprofessional performers to reach customers directly. The plethora of audio created and disseminated as digital files exclusively led one engineer to remark at the hearings conducted in support of this study, "Archives are dealing with new, born-digital materials while at the same time [they] are responsible for preserving legacy media which may be deteriorating. ... So I am trying to bring the past up to date. I'm trying to keep the present under control. I'm slowly losing my mind."[66]

Sound recordings disseminated in digital form exclusively (download or stream) present institutions with special challenges, beyond the purely technical and beyond those associated with audio preservation generally. They include the ephemeral nature of online digital audio; discovery and selection; digital rights management and legal issues related to capture and file maintenance; prevention of exposure to file-embedded viruses; normalizing (manipulating for standardized handling) a wide variety of file formats; and providing access legally. Discovery and selection, and the inherent legal issues surrounding online sound, may present the most difficult obstacles.

[66] Testimony of Adrian Cosentini, audio/preservation manager for the New York Philharmonic, "Writing About Historic Artists and Ensembles and Performing their Music," session, NRPB public hearings, December 19, 2006, New York.

In a statement prepared for the hearings conducted in support of this study, audio preservation specialist Chris Lacinek quoted an observation made by Howard Besser, professor of cinema studies and director of New York University's Moving Image Archiving and Preservation Program: "In the analog world, previous formats persisted over time. Cuneiform tablets, papyrus, and books all exist until someone or something (fire, earthquake) takes action to destroy them. But the default for digital information is not to survive unless someone takes conscious action to make them persist." Lacinek continued, "Our traditional flawed physical model did not bring total loss, regardless of our inability to perform preservation activities, because it persisted by default. Our digital collections, in contrast, will languish by default. The prospect of total loss is easily foreseeable."[67]

In considering preservation of born-digital sound, archivists must ask the following questions:

- Are we capable, even as a group, of preserving everything?
- Is all of it worth the expense and effort to preserve?
- If not, and selections must be made on what to preserve, who will make them?
- By what criteria will selections be made?
- Can consortia of libraries and archives undertake these tasks cooperatively?

The answers to these questions are not at hand. Until they are, and appropriate actions are taken, audio recordings are being lost. The Web is inherently ephemeral. There are no assurances that any podcasts and other recordings accessible today will be available for listening in a year. The individuals and organizations that post audio on the Web might at any time remove recordings. Any number of circumstances might cause this, including closure of the Web site, a terminated license, or the inability or refusal to pay royalties. If this content is to be preserved, a concerted effort by several institutions will be necessary.

Online audio includes music of all types—studio-recorded and live events as well as literary, political, and educational spoken-word recordings. A concerted selection-and-capture program would be complex to administer. Challenges would include discovering what has been made available and identifying it properly. Record label names and numbers will not be available for identifying online publications. The file names and text used to describe audio may not include sufficient information to discern exactly what has been recorded in the digital file and by whom, or how to differentiate it from identical or other similar recordings. A title alone is clearly insufficient. Names of the performer, composer, and writer, the date and time the version located was posted, and when it was captured

[67] Testimony of Chris Lacinak, Association of Moving Image Archivists and Audio Engineering Society Technical Committee on Archiving, Restoration and Digital Libraries, "Preservation Challenges and Practices in Archives and Libraries" session, December 19, 2006, New York. See also http://www.loc.gov/rr/record/nrpb/pdf/Lacinak.pdf.

all are necessary. Institutions that preserve online audio for the long term will require a standard and persistent set of identifiers interpretable across systems, if they are to identify who has preserved what, prevent redundant capture, and enable cooperation across institutions.

Selection and systematic capture and preservation of online recordings will require measured decisions by a coordinated group of subject-area specialists representing expertise in dozens of fields of music history, literature, politics, cultural history, broadcasting, and more. The task would be formidable, but if the failures of radio and recording company preservation initiatives are any indication, online audio will be lost unless specialists, archivists, and librarians take the initiative. One cannot assume that creators of online audio will preserve their own content and maintain the digital files over time.

Consideration might be given to crawling the Web and capturing all online audio. Technology exists to perform this function. In fact, some argue that this is the only efficient and effective way to preserve born-digital audio recordings distributed over the Web exclusively. However, the primary formats used by record labels and radio stations to distribute sound are low fidelity (MP3, streamed sound). It is not possible to preserve high-fidelity sound if the recording was created, or is distributed exclusively, as a low-fidelity recording. In addition, capture alone, without means to discover what has been preserved, is ultimately pointless. Archivists, librarians, and preservationists might collaborate with music information retrieval specialists to develop new tools and metrics to aid discovery of preserved audio recordings from the Web. Information about music information retrieval developments can be obtained from Web sites created by members of the International Society for Music Information Retrieval and at the society's annual conferences.[68]

Under present laws and many existing licensing agreements, it is not legal to copy much born-digital content to public access servers and provide access to it in an institutional setting. Rights holders have implicitly tolerated using software to capture a streamed radio broadcast and save it to disc for playback later when the action is undertaken by individuals for personal use. It is doubtful whether they would be similarly tolerant of institutional archiving of the same content, which would entail making multiple copies for backup and providing access from servers. The vast number of rights holders of online audio may preclude negotiating blanket licenses to download, archive, and make accessible all born-digital audio. Trade unions, publishers' representatives, and performing rights organizations might agree to permit born-digital audio to be downloaded to a *dark archive*, i.e., one to which access is restricted until the content falls into the public domain. Such organizations represent only a portion of potential rights holders in online content, and funding for dark archives, to which access is by their very nature restricted, may be difficult to obtain. An alternative approach might be to seek authorization to create the equivalent of Library of Congress affiliates that would have

[68] See http://www.ismir.net/.

legal authority to capture and preserve born-digital content and share with the Library the responsibility to preserve these recordings.

Library Streaming Services

Library users expect online access to sound recordings. Many libraries are meeting users' listening needs through subscription services. Companies first aggregate a wide range of contemporary and historical audio recordings into online service packages. Then, for monthly subscription fees based on the number of potential users, a library can stream thousands of audio tracks to patrons throughout a campus—in dormitory rooms as well as within the library itself. These services fulfill a demand for legal, convenient access to a great deal of audio content. However, audio subscriptions are expensive, and a subscriber cannot choose which tracks the subscription comprises, since only whole packages are offered. These services can have a major impact on library audio acquisitions budgets; that is, funds used to subscribe to streaming services deplete resources that might otherwise be used to acquire physical musical formats such as compact discs and preserve their content.

In most instances, libraries cannot save or preserve content from subscription services; when subscriptions expire, access to content is lost. An exception to these restrictions on retention is the licensing agreement developed by OhioLINK (The Ohio Library and Information Network) and two record companies that offer streaming services. OhioLINK is a consortium of 90 public and private university libraries in Ohio. The consortium has entered into an agreement with two record labels, Naxos of America and New World Records; the agreement provides the consortium with rights to copy and then stream in perpetuity the entire catalogs of both companies to "authorized users" (faculty, students, staff, and contractors associated with the member institutions in OhioLINK). The licenses with the record companies also authorize OhioLINK to create digital preservation copies and derivative files of all LPs, cassettes, and CDs controlled by the two companies. These agreements may serve as examples of streaming licenses that augment the markets of the two record companies significantly and ensure the long-term preservation of their publications. The OhioLINK initiative is also an example of the potential benefits of consortial approaches to preservation and access where the costs, real and administrative, are shared by many institutions.[69]

Downloadable-Only Commercial Recordings

A growing number of recordings are being published and sold as *download only*, that is, they are not available on CD and are obtained only as digital downloads from online sellers. Pertinent to present day-to-day library activities are the contractual obstacles to archiving recordings sold as digital files. Download-only recordings, like all digital music files, are controlled by licensing agreements between

[69] The authors are grateful to music librarian Daniel Boomhower for his insights on this issue.

the seller and the buyer stipulating that the music files can be purchased only by individuals and that they cannot be redistributed. Limits on redistribution restrict a wide range of common library functions, including lending holdings, copying them to servers, and making them accessible in classrooms.[70]

Because libraries cannot purchase download-only recordings under a licensing agreement, there is a growing body of recorded music that libraries are not able to add to their collections and circulate to their users. The sale of physical CDs to individuals or libraries gives these buyers limited rights through the "fair use" and "first sale" doctrines—i.e., the rights to copy a recording and sell or loan it. However, most license agreements controlling download purchases prohibit sales and limit copying. One librarian observed, "If libraries cannot purchase 'download only' recordings in the first place, they are not able to preserve the recordings—a vital service of libraries as the keepers of cultural heritage."[71]

A plenary session at the 2009 Music Library Association conference was devoted to restrictions on the storage and use by libraries of 'download only' recordings.[72] In addition, the Music Library Association has organized a Digital Audio Collections Task Force to investigate "issues related to the development of library collections of digital audio files." The case in point during that session was Deutsche Grammophon's "DG Concerts" series, but Deutsche Grammophon is but one of many restrictive marketers. The Metropolitan Opera now offers a "Met Player" service providing access to audio of historical as well as recent performances. The service offers a subscription option of the complete catalog of more than 200 recorded performances or of "rental" (online access for 30 days) to individual performances. Metropolitan Opera's terms of use state, "Except as set forth herein, you may not copy, publish, reproduce, transmit, frame, hyperlink, upload, post or distribute in any way, or create derivative works from the Contents, in any form or in any medium," which precludes distribution within a university campus, retaining a copy for later use, or preserving a copy.[73]

Overcoming Barriers to Audio Preservation

The testimony presented at the hearings conducted for this study, the written statements submitted, and the interviews and research conducted have provided an enormous amount of information about

---

[70] One such licensing agreement, that of the Grammy Award-winning Los Angeles Philharmonic recording of Berlioz's *Symphonie Fantastique*, states, "You represent, warrant and agree that you are using the SHOP hereunder for your own personal entertainment use and not for redistribution of any kind. You agree not to redistribute or otherwise transfer any copies of Content obtained through the SHOP." See http://www2.deutschegrammophon.com/webseries/index.htms?ID=dg-concerts.

[71] Daniel Boomhower e-mail to Sam Brylawski, May 8, 2009.

[72] "What's Next? The Compact Disc as a Viable Format in the Future of Music Libraries." Final plenary session, Music Library Association 78th Annual Meeting, Chicago, February 21, 2009.

[73] See http://www.metoperafamily.org/metopera/utility/terms_conditions.aspx.

barriers to audio preservation and many suggestions to help overcome obstacles that place audio collections at risk.

Storage

While all audio formats have to be reformatted eventually, archival-quality storage, both housings for individual items and the storage environment, can help minimize degradation of sound recordings until they can be copied for preservation. A study conducted by the Image Permanence Institute states, "Today, proper storage may still be an efficient option to improve the preservation of magnetic media until the point at which reformatting becomes necessary to cope with technology changes. Until that time, which will come sooner or later, and until resources are available, maintaining the physical integrity of tape collections is extremely important."[74]

Individual housings for recordings, such as sleeves, reels, and boxes, can protect recordings from contaminants and, in some cases, deter degradation during storage. Archives make significant investments in archival packaging. While individual sleeves and boxes may not be expensive, rehousing a large collection can easily require thousands of dollars. Setting priorities for buying housings can be especially difficult because a variety of products, sold at a wide range of prices, are available for each medium. In some cases, it is not known whether the most expensive products—some costing more than replacement value of the recording they protect—are worth the cost. Archives, libraries, and private collectors need scientifically based information to guide these choices, and that is not available for all media. It is generally agreed, for example, that inner record sleeves made from polyvinyl chloride are not recommended for storage of vinyl discs, such as LPs. Many sleeves are made from other materials, and archives would benefit from guidance on the cost benefits of individual products.

Cylinder recordings are especially vulnerable to poor storage conditions and improper containers. Wax cylinders are susceptible to mold and are very fragile. Celluloid cylinders are subject to malformation from improper storage. To address this problem, the NRPB commissioned the Technical Committee Cylinder Sub-Committee of the Association for Recorded Sound Collections to design an archival cylinder box. After creation of two prototypes and feedback from specialists, design of the box is complete. The Library of Congress has funded the production of the cylinder box molds and manufacture of the first set of boxes, to be delivered in 2010. It is expected that the new box will provide better protection of cylinder recordings and be less expensive than any existing archival cylinder box.

Few storage facilities in the United States provide optimal environmental conditions for audio recordings. The International

[74] *The Preservation of Magnetic Tape Collections: A Perspective.* Final report to National Endowment for the Humanities Division of Preservation and Access. NEH GRANT # PA-50123-03. Rochester, New York: Image Permanence Institute, Rochester Institute of Technology, 2006, 8. Available at http://www.imagepermanenceinstitute.org/shtml_sub/NEHTapeFinalReport.pdf.

Standards Organization (ISO) recommendation for long-term storage of polyester audiotape is a maximum temperature of 11°C (51.8° F) and 15–50 percent relative humidity.[75] It is likely that until the Library of Congress Packard Campus for Audio Visual Conservation opened in 2007, no institutional collection in the United States benefited from a storage facility that meets ISO standards. Increasingly, however, academic collections are being stored in custom-built remote facilities that provide a stable environment that is cooler and less humid than normal room environments, with temperatures that may not be 11°C, but are held constant.

The Davenport report notes, "The lack of space and, more important, of environmentally controlled space, is a common problem for archives and libraries. Storing collections for optimal preservation requires a vastly larger footprint than storing them efficiently does. Weight considerations frequently dictate that recording discs be stored on the lower levels of buildings, where they are more often subject to water leaks and flooding. If a collection arrives with a donor restriction that the contents must be permanently housed together as they were when in the donor's possession, the collection will take more space than it would if sorted by format."[76] Not surprisingly, deficiencies in storage spaces are major threats to collections held privately. Such collections are often stored in attics, basements, and garages with little or no environmental control and on poor shelving that places the collections at risk.

One collection that remains at great risk is that of the Pacific Pioneers Broadcasters (PPB). The organization's Web site notes, "PPB has accumulated one of the largest private collections of memorabilia pertaining to the history of radio broadcasting. Included in this collection are original recording transcriptions, scripts, photographs, publications, equipment, sound effects, and other radio memorabilia." The report continues, "In the past, this material was available to members and bona fide researchers in our PPB Clubroom, located in the basement of the Washington Mutual Building at Sunset and Vine. Unfortunately, this has not been possible since the December 2004 underground power transformer failure, which released contaminants into our Clubroom. Our collection has been sealed there, awaiting resolution of a lawsuit filed by PPB after Los Angeles Department of Water and Power rejected our claim for clean-up costs."[77] PPB has entered into a collaboration with the Thousand Oaks Library Foundation American Radio Archives. If the foundation can raise the needed funds and the collection is salvageable, it will be moved to a new facility at the Grant R. Brimhall Library in Thousand Oaks, California.

---

[75] AES-11id-2006. Audio Engineering Society Information Document for Preservation of Audio Recordings–Extended Term Storage Environment for Multiple Media Archives (New York: AES, 2006). Available at http://www.aes.org/standards/.

[76] Davenport, (p. 163).

[77] See http://www.pacificpioneerbroadcasters.org/archive.html.

Collaboration and Coordination

Many contributors to this study called for greater coordination of preservation activities and collaboration between archives. Without partnerships, institutions cannot make the most judicious use of funding. These partnerships should be extended to the community of private collectors.

The CLIR survey of ARL/Oberlin libraries stated, "There is no authoritative dataset describing the content, location, and preservation status of recorded sound held in special and private collections in the United States. Furthermore, there appears to be no single approach to gathering such data."[78] Both the Davenport and *Folk Heritage Collections in Crisis* reports also cite the need for a single portal or database to search sound recordings. Descriptions of collections and cataloging called for in this statement would serve institutions as well as the research needs of patrons of archives and libraries. New York Philharmonic Orchestra archivist Barbara Haws observed at the study hearings, "Would it not be great if we could easily find a way to share that information because maybe there are reasons to have certain redundancies? ... The Philharmonic and New York Public are in discussions about trying to share digitization in preservation so that if we are preserving one of our concerts and the New York Public Library currently has it in their holdings, we will give them the preserved copy so that they do not have to spend the resources on it. Why should all of us be preserving the exact same thing?"[79]

Preservation of all valuable sound recordings can be assured only by increased collaboration among all types of collections, private as well as public. Currently, institutions allocate reformatting resources to redundant efforts, consuming resources that might otherwise be devoted to other important recordings. However, deficiencies in cataloging and lack of organizational infrastructures are not the only contributors to redundant reformatting. Under present laws, archives are prohibited from sharing digital preservation files. The Library of Congress has proposed establishing a preservation file-sharing "network" to a major U.S. recording company. It is hoped that gratis licenses can be acquired to enable participating archives to share digital files of preserved commercial recordings for access on university and other institutional intranet sites.

It is likely that many institutions have invested valuable resources in saving sound recordings that have already been rescued, possibly years earlier. Institutions should seek all available expertise to evaluate the contents of collections to determine what is truly unique and whether copies in better condition might be located elsewhere. For example, it could appear that a deteriorating reel of recording tape in a scuffed box houses a unique sound recording, but that is not necessarily the case. One institution, presenting at the annual

[78] Smith, Allen, and Allen, 55.

[79] Testimony of Barbara Haws, archivist and historian, New York Philharmonic, "Preservation Challenges and Practices in Archives and Libraries" session, NRPB public hearings, December 19, 2006, New York.

conference of the Association for Recorded Sound Collections in 2009, discussed and played excerpts from a collection of open-reel tapes it had received that were devoted to a major jazz figure. Conference attendees included several people who were familiar with the artist and institutional holdings of the artist's work. These audience members provided titles of works the archive had been unable to identify, and also noted that some of the transfers the archive was excerpting were recordings that had already been transferred, restored, and released—some of them years ago, and with better sound.

Syracuse University's E. S. Byrd Library has recently begun digitizing its cylinder collection for access over the Web.[80] In undertaking this project, Syracuse library managers are intentionally not digitizing any cylinders already digitized and presented on the Web by UCSB's popular Cylinder Preservation and Digitization Project.[81] The two projects are designed to be complementary, and their users would benefit from a cooperative Web portal to enable users to discover and audition both collections through a single search.

It has been noted previously that, through the deposit and American Television and Radio provisions of U.S. copyright law, the Library of Congress has exclusive rights and responsibilities to preserve audio content, including streamed radio broadcasts disseminated on the World Wide Web if that content, by legal definition, is considered to be unpublished. Consideration should be given to whether one institution alone will be able to capture and preserve the enormous number of audio recordings distributed on the Web exclusively, or whether a consortium of libraries and archives might assume this responsibility under the leadership of the Library of Congress. Such a project would require legislative authority or development with rights holders of an array of licenses to permit a partnership to undertake these preservation responsibilities.

A description of a successful audio digitization project where many institutions collaborated in outsourcing preservation may be found in the Collaboration section of chapter 2 of this report.

Access

A 2003 CLIR report titled *Survey of the State of Audio Collections in Academic Libraries* noted that respondents "tended to identify lack of funding as the greatest barrier to access."[82] In the hearings conducted in support of this study and in written statements submitted, many argued the inverse: lack of access might be the greater barrier to preservation funding. In a submission in support of this study, Marcos Sueiro Bal of Columbia University wrote:

> For many libraries [sound preservation] is a very expensive proposal, and the only way to justify it (and/or get funding for it) is thanks to what I like to call the trump card of digital: greatly

[80] See http://libwww.syr.edu/information/belfer/index.html.

[81] See http://cylinders.library.ucsb.edu/.

[82] Smith, Allen, and Allen, 10.

> increased access. Severe copyright restrictions are the wrench that can derail the whole system, so materials are not digitized.[83]

As the Web has made access to recordings technologically easier, user demands and expectations for ready access have increased. Funders of audio preservation reformatting require that writers of grant proposals include a plan for providing access. One hearings participant observed, "In today's funding climate there is no funding for dark archiving," that is, preservation in which access to the audio is withheld or restricted until the works enter the public domain. He emphasized that requests for funding for audio materials, of which nearly none are in the public domain, have enormous difficulty when competing against proposals for preserving materials that can be disseminated on the Web.[84]

Frustration over obstacles to accessing historical sound recordings were repeatedly expressed at both hearings conducted for the study, in the written submissions received for the study, and in the interviews conducted by Davenport.[85] More directly, a seventh-grade student testified in Los Angeles that "the preservation of music is meaningless if this music is not accessible."[86]

One could argue that many recent developments related to access to sound recordings—e.g., increased expectations of free access to recordings and evidence of lessening respect for rights of creators by consumers—have placed rights holders to recordings at a disadvantage. Total receipts from sales of sound recordings have fallen significantly in the past 10 years (though some argue that the music industry is financially healthy overall).[87] Thanks to the Internet, millions of desktops and mobile computers now have access to tens of thousands of recordings, but not always by means within laws, and not necessarily providing appropriate compensation to producers, artists, and songwriters. At the same time, collecting and preservation institutions (libraries and archives) are publicly debating some rights holders over the exact scope of fair use of copyrighted materials. In the twenty-first century, the public and scholarly communities have come to expect ready access to sound recordings. It is extremely unlikely that society can or will return to a time when consumption of music and recordings is dominated by sales of multitrack albums or individual songs on discs. Whether through wholly legal means or not, the public has come to take convenient access to deep ranges of recordings for granted. The clock cannot be turned back.

Hearings testimony and written submissions to this study, as well as interviews with librarians, archivists, and scholars who use

---

[83] Statement submitted to the NRPB by Marcos Sueiro Bal. Available at http://www.loc.gov/rr/record/nrpb/pdf/bal.pdf.

[84] Testimony of David Seubert, audiovisual archivist, University of California, Santa Barbara, "Copyright and Intellectual Property Issues" session, NRPB public hearings, November 29, 2006, Los Angeles.

[85] See, for example, Clifford Murphy's testimony.

[86] Testimony of Jasper DeAntonio, student, Polytechnic School, NRPB public hearings, November 29, 2006, Los Angeles.

[87] See http://www.scribd.com/doc/7697646/Popular-Music-Rethinking-The-Music-Industry.

historical recordings, show that the historical recorded sound community respects the rights of creators of recordings and recognizes that creators must be compensated for their work. Receipts from sales to libraries and the scholarly community contribute significantly to businesses related to historical sound recordings. Archives and libraries, as well as users, have long shown willingness to pay to listen to recordings; few expect access to recordings free of charge. But they are acutely aware of thousands of recordings to which access is denied. As doctoral candidate Clifford Murphy observed at the New York City hearings, "unreissued recordings are part of the historical and traditional fabric of our nation's regional cultures. Indeed, by choosing not to reissue regional recordings or vernacular musics, copyright holders are doing damage to regional culture and are essentially denying America's working class ... and ethnic communities access to their own expressive culture."

Several archives and libraries have undertaken ambitious projects to make portions of their holdings accessible over the Web. Some significant examples of audio collections accessible to the general public are the American Memory, Performing Arts Encyclopedia, and American Folklife Center Web sites of the Library of Congress; the Cylinder Preservation and Digitization Project and the Center for the Study of Democratic Institutions Audio Archive at UCSB; the Black Gospel Music Restoration Project at Baylor University; and the Frontera Archive of Mexican-American Music at the University of California, Los Angeles. The latter two projects provide access to complete recordings through the campus intranet sites, and 30- to 50-second samples to the general public through public Web sites. In the fall of 2010, the Library of Congress will launch a "National Jukebox" Web site, which will present more than 10,000 recordings from discs of the acoustical era of sound recording (1900–1925). A license to stream these recordings was granted to the Library by Sony Music Entertainment.

The Andrew W. Mellon Foundation has supported several initiatives related to audio archiving and sound preservation. The foundation has also provided support to the Database of Recorded American Music (DRAM) Project, an online audio-streaming service that offers content from more than 2,000 recordings on 15 labels, including New World Records.[88] Even though the project was created by record labels that own the rights to the recordings the project distributes, DRAM found it difficult to acquire licenses to provide online access to those musical works. Its efforts are documented in an informative case study included in a report by the Berkman Center for Internet and Society at Harvard University and commissioned by the Mellon Foundation.[89] At the New York City hearings in support of this study, Donald Waters discussed several issues related to access and preservation. Concerning the DRAM Project

[88] See http://www.dramonline.org/page/about.

[89] The Digital Learning Challenge: Obstacles to Educational Uses of Copyrighted Material in the Digital Age. A Foundational White Paper. Available at http://cyber.law.harvard.edu/media/files/copyrightandeducation.html.

and licensing recordings for educational use, he observed:

> I am not so enthusiastic about digital media that I would suggest that policies and legal regimes need to be changed to favor use without respect for the prerogatives of owners and other rights holders. However, I would certainly join those who would point out that the interest of preserving the cultural record and making it widely available should take precedence over efforts to protect rights holders that cannot be found and whose works are thereby orphaned. Instead, I would focus … attention on some of the more subtle policy issues that affect use, and especially educational use, of sound recordings.
>
> … one of the more remarkable findings of their project [DRAM] was the difficulty it had reconciling the federally mandated royalty regimes with a subscription model targeted to educational use. Put simply, the royalty regime is aimed at pay-per-use and educational use is deeply inhibited by such a regime. Often, study requires repeated use of a work by many students or by a single scholar who is carefully analyzing the piece. If they are required to account for each and every use and pay for them even at discounted rates, study and education simply will not happen. … Pay-by-the-drink requirements conflict with educational use at a deep level and distributors like New World Records are in a precarious position as they try to offer and price subscription models to colleges and universities that appear to encourage unlimited use and then, on the other side, are required to pay rights holders for each and every use.[90]

Looking at audio preservation as a business, it can be further argued that access and preservation are inextricably linked. Richard Wright, a senior engineer at the British Broadcasting Company and a leading participant in the European PRESTO preservation initiatives, has called attention to the concept of calculating preservation costs on the basis of use:

> The true cost of an asset is total life-cycle cost. The true benefit is related to the number of times that asset is used over the life cycle. Although not every use has equal benefit, overall more media issued from the archive means more benefit to the broadcaster and to the wider public service. Therefore a simple way to combine transfer cost, life-cycle cost, and the significance of new service opportunities is to translate those new opportunities into a predicted rate of item usage. Options for preservation can then be compared, in monetary terms, on a "cost per use" basis. A significant conclusion of the PRESTO survey is that archive preservation strategy should aim at the "lowest cost per use" over the life cycle of the new media, NOT at the lowest transfer cost.[91]

---

[90] Testimony of Donald J. Waters, December 19, 2006.

[91] Richard Wright, "Preserving Europe's Memory: PRESTO Shows How to Preserve Multimedia in the Most Cost-effective Fashion," *Cultivate Interactive* 7 (July 2002). Available at http://www.cultivate-int.org/issue7/presto/.

If audio preservation programs are to develop, access issues must be resolved. Processes to efficiently license unpublished and out-of-print recordings for dissemination must be devised. Innovation in license agreements is necessary to enable legal archiving and controlled access to preserved audio recordings. With such tools, libraries, archives, and the preservation community as a whole can work collectively to ensure preservation of audio heritage and, at the same time, to benefit creators and producers of recordings.

Advocacy

Many contributors to this study addressed the need to provide further support for the preservation of sound recordings, and to educate the public and policy makers of the importance of audio preservation and the necessity for additional resources to ensure this heritage is available to posterity. Effective advocacy often focuses on a crisis that, if not addressed, will have catastrophic consequences. Although recordings do not face the dramatic risks that confront nitrate motion picture film, millions of sound recordings, including early cylinders, unpublished recordings on instantaneous media, and contemporary born-digital recordings, are at danger of loss or have already vanished. Contributors to the study suggest that a number of approaches to preservation, with the objectives of drawing in different constituencies, might be most effective.

The Public

Two NRPB members, Michael Feinstein and Christopher Sterling, agreed at hearings that the general public understands the need for preservation when it has personal relevance. Sterling recommended identifying and publicizing important missing recordings and recounted public involvement in trying to locate a copy of the first Super Bowl, a television broadcast recording that may still remain at large. Feinstein spoke of "creating an interesting story."

> It is like reality television. You create a whole drama around the preservation of a recording or recordings. One of the examples that I have spoken of before is the missing Bruce Springsteen demos, something that will really ignite the public—"Oh my God, that does not exist any more."… I think that it is those kinds of examples that make most people pay attention because the assumption with the commercial recording is that it is untouchable, that it exists in an archive, and it is safe. And educating people that a certain percentage of those masters are gone is important. I think it is by the way most things are disseminated today which is reality programming, if you will.[92]

Announcements of the National Recording Registry afford an annual opportunity to emphasize the importance of audio preservation. The Librarian of Congress is directed by Congress to name a

[92] Testimony of Michael Feinstein, December 19, 2006.

group of "culturally, historically, or aesthetically significant" recordings to the Registry each year, to be added to the collection of the Library of Congress.[93] In recent years, the NRPB has commissioned a radio series about recent Registry recordings for airing on public radio stations.

The radio series *Lost and Found Sound*, produced by the Kitchen Sisters and Jay Allison, was a regular segment on *All Things Considered*, the NPR evening news program, between 1999 and 2002. The series featured historical recordings from archives and private collections, and provided historical contexts through interviews with their owners, archivists and librarians, and subject-matter experts. This popular feature raised consciousness about the value of historical recordings and the importance of their preservation.

In its written submission to the study, WGBH in Boston suggested that public consciousness about audio preservation could be raised by adapting a model of "Home Movie Day," an annual event featuring screening of home movies and other amateur films.[94] WGBH also proposed that "recognition within the nation's schools of the annual additions to the [National Recording Registry] might plant the seed about the importance of preservation. On-line access to these recordings and a short curriculum outline for selected age groups would be an added benefit." The station also recommended that "Support for non-profit institutions to develop and implement protected on-line access to historical recordings should be encouraged. This is not only for the public's benefit as a direct link to their historical past, but a great tie-in with schools for students to access primary source materials."[95]

Educators and Scholars

At the New York City hearings, Donald Waters noted that scholarship related to sound recordings now extends beyond the three fields of specialists that traditionally made the most use of recordings—musicologists, ethnomusicologists, and folklorists:

> Preservation of musical sound recordings depends on a growing knowledge base of the cultural importance of such recordings. Recordings are themselves a way of preserving an otherwise ephemeral performance and making them broadly available through audiences that may never have heard them or may never have been intended to hear. … And specialists … are turning to sound recordings as one of many kinds of evidence for analyzing a broad variety of historical, sociological, economic and psychological dimensions of social and cultural life.[96]

---

[93] National Recording Preservation Act of 2000. Public Law 106-474.

[94] See http://www.homemovieday.com/.

[95] Written submission by Mary Ide, director, WGBH Archives; Jon Solins, program director, WGBH Radio; and Jeffrey Nelson, FM archivist, WGBH Radio, January 26, 2007.

[96] Testimony of Donald J. Waters, December 19, 2006.

Waters recommended that administrators of sound recording collections enlist the assistance of their users to promote audio preservation.

> Scholars in a growing number of disciplines who are building and spreading knowledge and understanding of sound recordings as cultural evidence can provide a rich, deep and articulate source of motivation and justification for building, preserving and providing access to collections of musical sound recordings.[97]

Advocacy for audio collections and preservation must include promoting collection subject matter, expanding use of the collections, and collaborating with patrons and scholars on interpretation of the collections. In addition, creators of recordings must recognize the importance of preserving sound recordings, what can be done at their inception to promote preservation, and how recordings might be used in the future. At the New York hearings, Smithsonian Folkways Director Dan Sheehy suggested that if those who make recordings "frontload the whole documentation process with the notion of preservation and the utilization of that preservation for education purposes, I think we will be a lot further along."[98]

Resources for Preservation

Not surprisingly, adequate funding for audio preservation is of great concern to all parties involved with sound archives and libraries, as the submission to the NRPB from ARL points out:

> Sound recordings have been available since the late 19th century and audio archives thus represent a large amount of materials in a wide range of physical formats that may require an investment in time and funding that may be more than the Nation's libraries individually can accomplish. For ARL member libraries and other large institutions with expansive holdings, piecemeal action regarding preservation is sure to result in significant losses of valuable cultural and historical information. Preservation of large quantities of unique content presents significant challenges for individual libraries. No institution currently has sufficient resources to ensure preservation of even all the unique materials they hold.[99]

All known evidence reinforces ARL's observation that funding, when available, is piecemeal. In 2009, Safe Sound Archive, a Philadelphia business that provides audio and video preservation services, surveyed 84 of its clients to ascertain common sources of funding for audio preservation projects. Safe Sound received 56 responses. The survey found that

- Twenty-one (38 percent) of the 56 respondents were funding their audio preservation work from the regular budgets of their

---

[97] Ibid.

[98] Testimony of Dan Sheehy, director and curator, Smithsonian-Folkways Recordings, NRPB public hearings, December 19, 2006, New York.

[99] Adler and Hahn, January 26, 2007.

institutions. Nine projects were supported by donations to the archives. Of the 30 internally funded audio preservation projects, 4 could not be completed for lack of adequate funding.

- Eighteen of the 56 respondents attempted to fund their projects with grants from national organizations such as the Grammy Foundation, the National Endowment for the Humanities, or the Association for Recorded Sound Collections. Twelve of the 18 (66 percent) were successful in obtaining funding from these organizations.
- Eight projects (14 percent) were funded through local grants (e.g., state programs, community foundations) or program-specific organizations. All eight projects were completed.
- Of the 56 respondents, 46 (82 percent) were able to secure full funding for their projects; 10 (18 percent) were not. At least eight of the respondents reported seeking funds from multiple sources and being turned down by one or more of those sources.

Given the limited nature of the survey, one must be careful about drawing broad conclusions on the basis of its findings. Many major archives maintain in-house audio preservation facilities and would not be required to outsource to a service such as Safe Sound. Yet institutions with in-house facilities also compete for preservation grants.[100]

Collectively, participants in the survey obtained grants from all six major national sources of funding for audio preservation (i.e., the Grammy Foundation, The Andrew W. Mellon Foundation, the National Endowment for the Humanities, the Institute of Museum and Library Services, the Association for Recorded Sound Collections, and the Save America's Treasures program). It is not known whether the cited 66 percent success rate in awarding of grants from national programs is representative of all audio preservation applications received by these programs, or how the figure of 18 percent that were unsuccessful in obtaining preservation funding correlates to broad circumstances nationally.

The fact that local programs funded 14 percent of the projects shows that collections with regional interest conceivably have broad options for support when institutions have the resources to explore local funders and solicit their support. Identifying potential funders of audio preservation can be challenging. A useful guide recently published by the Library of Congress and the Foundation Center lists hundreds of national and regional foundations that have supported preservation projects of libraries, archives, and museums. The guide includes a regional index and a detailed index of the subjects of collections supported, but it does not indicate which foundations have a record of providing funds for audio preservation.[101]

---

[100] The National Archives, Library of Congress, and Smithsonian Institution, which hold large and significant audio collections, are excluded, as U.S. federal agencies, from consideration for preservation grants from NEH and IMLS.

[101] Library of Congress and the Foundation Center, *Foundation Grants for Preservation in Libraries, Archives, and Museums* (Washington, DC: Library of Congress, Preservation Directorate, Conservation Division, 2009). Available at http://www.loc.gov/preserv/foundtn-grants.pdf.

The Indiana University collections survey case study notes that all three of that institution's audiovisual digital preservation projects are supported exclusively by grants.

The ARL submission stresses the need for development and support of a national funding strategy:

> Funding concerns present enormous challenges to research libraries engaged in preservation of audio recordings. Institutions need sufficient funding to help pay for preservation conversion and long-term access to these resources. For example, in institutions where resources may already be limited, the additional costs of even surveying the condition of collections of recorded sound may prove prohibitive. But this is an important step that we must take.
>
> The costs to our institutions of maintaining audio recordings are not insignificant. The combination of obsolete formats and the equipment used to play them means that preservation conversion to digital formats is both necessary and expensive. Furthermore, designing, establishing and maintaining conversion and storage facilities will require initial funding and ongoing support. A national funding strategy is needed to address these pressing preservation and access concerns before we lose these valuable and unique resources.[102]

Developing a national plan that ensures adequate funding to meet the audio preservation needs of archives, libraries, and users would be an enormous challenge. Congressional appropriations to preservation funding agencies are generous, but do not begin to meet national needs. The U.S. Congress has directed the Library of Congress to establish the nonprofit National Recording Preservation Foundation (NRPF) to support audio preservation. The law creating the foundation includes provisions for Congress to match funds raised by the foundation. The Library of Congress has created the foundation, but the initial work has been stymied by the challenges of raising required seed money and developing a sustainable business plan.

It has been suggested that those who purchase audio recordings online should be provided with an opportunity to make a voluntary contribution to audio preservation, but that approach would require agreement and cooperation from providers of digital audio products. To date, aside from the Grammy Foundation, no company or organization associated with sound-recording businesses has provided financial support to audio preservation initiatives.

Many broadcasting stations overseas are state supported. Resources to preserve recordings of their broadcasts are often included in station and network budgets or supplemented by government funds. Noncommercial radio stations in the United States appear to have recognized the importance of preserving their recorded history to a greater degree than have commercial stations. Their efforts will

[102] Adler and Hahn, January 26, 2007.

benefit from support by the federally funded Corporation for Public Broadcasting "American Archive" initiative.[103] However, thousands of recordings held by noncommercial radio stations remain at risk of loss. At the hearing conducted in support of this study, Sterling remarked that the profit-making requirement of commercial broadcasting in the United States "totally blinds [the broadcasting] business to any sense of its own history."[104]

The challenges ahead are enormous, and current prospects for continual funding to sustain national audio preservation needs are poor. Regarding the dire need for sustained funds for preservation, NRPF Chair Bill Ivey has stated, "It is just too big; it cannot be justified at an appropriate level in marketplace terms. There has to be some way in galvanizing enough enthusiasm so that the public interest gets served through public dollars that get allocated."[105]

If it is true that the marketplace cannot supply all resources necessary to ensure sustained preservation, advocacy and enhanced access may be able to generate new resources. Adequate funding for audio preservation will come about only as a result of dedicated commitments from all parties, including creators, rights holders, institutions, consumers, and the government.

---

[103] Descriptions of the American Archive project and its accomplishments to date may be found at http://www.cpb.org/aboutcpb/financials/appropriation/justification_11-13.pdf (page 18) and http://pressroom.opb.org/press-releases/opb-completes-american-archive-project.

[104] Testimony of Chris Sterling, December 19, 2006.

[105] Remarks by Bill Ivey, director, Curb Center for Art, Enterprise, and Public Policy at Vanderbilt University, at NRPB public hearing, December 19, 2006, New York.

CHAPTER 2

Technical Issues in Digital Audio Preservation

Introduction

The transition from preservation on analog media (i.e., open-reel tapes as the target preservation medium) to digital media has brought enormous challenges to archives, along with the opportunities and promises of the digital domain. The greatest technical challenges faced by audio archives today are those associated with the transition to digital preservation: new procedures and tools, a new and complicated lexicon, formidable and time-consuming documentation requirements, daunting storage and information technology (IT) responsibilities, and an incomplete set of standards and best practices—and all of this only after significant up-front investment of money to create technical infrastructures necessary for digital preservation.

For decades, archivists have harbored hopes of discovering a permanent preservation medium—preservation's own Holy Grail. They have now acknowledged the futility of the quest. There will never be a permanent preservation medium, at least one practical enough for widespread use. Any medium used for sound recording will eventually deteriorate. When preservation copies took the form of analog audiotape, archives produced a succession of fresh copies over time as the old tapes deteriorated—a process that some call *migration*. Each fresh copy suffered *generation loss*, losing a little quality when compared with its predecessor. In contrast, the production of high-quality digital audio files means that subsequent copies produced in digital migrations will be bit-for-bit identical with their predecessors; no quality will be lost. But the digital environment is not risk-free: bits can be lost during storage or when files are migrated. These risks can be mitigated by good data-management practices.

Preserving digital audio recordings means that the recordings must be actively maintained. Such maintenance requires an institutional commitment to periodically duplicate or refresh files and to verify their integrity. In the digital domain, preservation is not a single action; it is a process that requires systematic and continuous attention. The returns to an archive making the investment in digital preservation are substantial. Whether working with analog tape or a digital file, the objective of audio preservation reformatting is a transfer of the source audio modulation, which captures and maintains the full integrity of the audio from the original disc or tape to the highest degree possible. A core of best practices seems to have evolved over the past 40 years of preservation reformatting, but it is neither comprehensively documented nor, in all cases, backed by science.

Consensus on Recommended Practices and Issues to be Resolved

In support of this study, the National Recording Preservation Board (NRPB) convened a group of experienced audio engineers and archivists in 2004 to discuss best practices in the capture of audio from analog discs and tapes. The roundtable discussion was conceived additionally as a *gap analysis* of preservation engineering, that is, a means of determining what knowledge, techniques, and tools preservation engineers still need in order to create high-quality transfers. A publication summarizing the discussions, *Capturing Analog Sound for Digital Preservation: Report of a Roundtable Discussion of Best Practices for Transferring Analog Discs and Tapes*, outlines the processes and documents general agreement among the participating engineers.[106] The publication also includes a set of "broad recommendations for improving the practice of analog transfer for preservation," a set of "core competencies" for preservation engineers, recommendations for relevant coursework for audio engineers undertaking preservation, and 15 recommendations for future work. A second roundtable discussion, devoted to digital preservation issues, was convened by the NRPB in March 2006.

The Technical Committee of the International Association of Sound and Audiovisual Archives (IASA) has published two highly respected and frequently cited guides to audio preservation, *The Safeguarding of the Audio Heritage: Ethics, Principles and Preservation Strategy*[107] and *Guidelines on the Production and Preservation of Digital Audio Objects*.[108] The guidelines, commonly referenced as "TC-04," have

[106] Council on Library and Information Resources, National Recording Preservation Board (U.S.), and Library of Congress, *Capturing Analog Sound for Digital Preservation: Report of a Roundtable Discussion of Best Practices for Transferring Analog Discs and Tapes* (Washington, DC: Council on Library and Information Resources and Library of Congress, 2006). Also available online: http://www.clir.org/PUBS/reports/pub137/pub137.pdf.

[107] International Association of Sound and Audiovisual Archives. *Standards, Recommended Practices and Strategies. The Safeguarding of the Audio Heritage: Ethics, Principles and Preservation Strategy* (Aarhus, Denmark: International Association of Sound and Audiovisual Archives, Technical Committee, 2005).

[108] International Association of Sound and Audiovisual Archives, and K. Bradley, *IASA-TC04 Guidelines on the Production and Preservation of Digital Audio Objects: Standards, Recommended Practices, and Strategies* (Aarhus, Denmark: International Association of Sound and Audiovisual Archives, Technical Committee, 2009).

become the benchmark of digital audio preservation best practices; they are generally seen as the best guide to professional preservation practice.

More recently, engineers at Indiana University and Harvard University published *Sound Directions: Best Practices for Audio Preservation*, a report on work conducted under a grant from the National Endowment for the Humanities. *Sound Directions* outlines the audio preservation workflows of the Archives of Traditional Music at Indiana University and Archive of World Music at Harvard University. The project and resulting publication, edited by Mike Casey and Bruce Gordon, acknowledges the work and recommendations included in *Capturing Analog Sound* and TC-04 and concentrates on workflow and best practices related to creation of digital files, metadata describing the files and processes undertaken to create the file, and long-term file maintenance. The report includes a useful and well-defined series of 47 best practices.[109]

Cumulatively, TC-04, *Capturing Analog Sound*, and *Sound Directions* provide a valuable and authoritative road map to the best practices for audio preservation, as well as clear outlines and rationales for the means and processes chosen to achieve professionally produced and sustained audio preservation. To some degree, however, these road maps may be too abstract to guide all but archives with the highest level of resources and expertise for implementing a professional digital preservation program. The terrain that most archives navigate is largely uncharted and usually marked by considerable technological, financial, and human obstacles. Best-practices guidelines reflecting the consensus of experienced professionals are invaluable for archives with enough resources to implement them. For many archives, however, such guidelines may fail to meet on-the-ground needs and may set the bar too high. Some organizations respond by ignoring the guidelines entirely, failing to realize that short of best practices, they still have responsible and creditable options. The preservation operations of many archives will benefit from an established set of minimum standards that must be met, as well as best practices to which to aspire.

While most practitioners yearn for the establishment of standards for audio preservation, some differences of outlook and opinion exist within the technical community. At hearings conducted by the NRPB in New York City, a representative of Columbia University noted that "specifications and best practices for conversion are still under debate nationally. The recommendations of the Audio Engineering Society, the International Standards Organization, and the International Association of Sound and Audiovisual Archives do not always agree."[110] Agreement on standards and best practices would provide archives and institutions with a sense of direction

[109] Mike Casey and Bruce Gordon, *Sound Directions: Best Practices for Audio Preservation* (Bloomington, IN: Indiana University; Cambridge, MA: Harvard University, 2007).

[110] Testimony of Emily Holmes, assistant director of preservation reformatting, Columbia University, "Preservation Challenges and Practices in Archives and Libraries" session, NRPB public hearings, December 19, 2006, New York.

for investing resources and developing educational curricula. Most important, agreement on standards would enable the exchange of ideas across the entire community on such critical topics as developing more efficient means to store files for the long term and, to the extent allowed by copyright law and licensing agreements, sharing preserved files.

Specific targets have yet to be set in some instances: issues remain to be resolved and gaps to be bridged within the audio preservation community. Nonetheless, there is agreement in principle on the following seven points:

1. Digital technology is a given: the analog era has ended.
2. Linear pulse code modulation is a given; digital audio files should be *transparent*, i.e., audibly indistinguishable from the original.
3. Preservation transfers must be *flat*, that is, without any imposed equalization of the frequency range or use of restoration techniques to mitigate defects or limitations in the recording.
4. Digital audio preservation files must be produced at high sampling and bit rates, and be uncompressed.
5. Storage must be planned for the long term.
6. Rich metadata must accompany preservation files.
7. Professionalism is an essential component of audio preservation.

1. Digital technology is a given. Although digital formats present challenges, they must at this time be the format of choice to achieve the objectives of recorded sound preservation. Older formats, especially analog recording tape, deteriorate with time—both physically and sonically—whether or not they are stored under ideal conditions of temperature and humidity. They cannot be copied without audible signal loss and introduction of *noise*. In addition, raw tape stock is difficult to obtain, as are professional-grade recording machines.

At the same time, all digital media, including recordable CDs, DVDs, and professional DAT formats, fail over time. Experience has shown that these are not long-term preservation formats; moreover, the incidence of failure in even a relatively short time span has been both a surprise and a disappointment. To most digital preservation professionals, a permanent medium is not only unobtainable but is also no longer considered necessary to assure long-term preservation.

Well-designed and properly managed digital preservation programs accept media impermanence as a given. Because digital audio files can be copied with relative ease, and with no loss of audio quality, preservation systems are designed and built to manage encoded content over the long term. These so-called digital repositories, discussed in detail later in this chapter, monitor file integrity and assure that digital files are migrated to new media as necessary.

Still, at hearings conducted in support of this study, some participants expressed lingering doubts about digital audio preservation. These doubts were based on apprehension about inadequate institutional commitments to support digital infrastructure and on the enduring desire for an audio storage format that would not deteriorate over time. Nearly all audio is now created digitally, and while we cannot afford to dismiss it as untrustworthy, neither can we trust it without question. To most professionals, the advantages of digital preservation outweigh the disadvantages, but digital preservation is a resource-intensive, long-term series of processes, not a one-time action.

2. File formats and wrappers. The adoption of linear pulse code modulation (PCM) for digitally encoding audio is nearly universal. However, while there is consensus about linear PCM, archives are not in full agreement about file formats and packaging. Linear PCM bit streams may be contained within a number of types of file "wrappers." Many preservation engineers recommend the BWF (broadcast wave format) file wrapper, a European adaptation of Microsoft's WAVE format, which allows more metadata to be stored in its file header than can be entered and stored with a file in the basic WAVE format. The selection of WAVE or BWF as the preferred format for preservation is based in part on its widespread adoption as a digital audio file format for production purposes. However, concerns about BWF have been expressed by some who find even its expanded structure inadequate for full metadata requirements, and who have encountered problems with the metadata embedded in BWFs being read properly by digital audio workstations and editing software.

The WAVE file format cannot exceed 2 gigabytes in size, a concern to some engineers. Some preservation engineers recommend the RF64 file format, which can exceed the size limit of regular WAVE files. Multitrack sound files can be stored as multiple monophonic files (a separate file for each channel of a recording) or interleaved (all channels multiplexed into a single file), and many engineers have expressed a preference for one approach over the other. However, digital audio workstations do not support interleaved file types in the same manner; for this reason, many engineers desire a standard method to support differing file formats across all workstations.

The audio interchange file format (AIFF) is another viable, noncompressed audio file format that is sometimes used for audio preservation. The IASA TC-04 document recommends WAVE or BWF files, perhaps because of their popular edge over AIFF in the commercial recording field. It is broadly agreed that file, and component, interoperability has become a critical factor in audio preservation. Will the audio file made today be playable 25 years from now? Will hardware and software made 25 years from now know how to read the audio and embedded metadata in playback files made today? Linear PCM bit streams and WAVE and BWF wrappers are transparent: self-evident in content with a relatively simple structure. The formatting of audio recorded on commercial compact discs (the compact disc format is not a file format) is more complex, but the ubiquity of audio CDs and public documentation of the technical specifications for the format provide reasonable assurances that such discs will be interpretable for many decades. Proprietary digital formats, with no public documentation, are at the greatest risk of being unplayable in the near future.

3. Flat transfers. Those outside the community of archivists and sound engineers often confuse preservation and restoration, or assume they are two words for the same thing. They are not. *Preservation* is the creation of a faithful copy of a recording from its original. *Restoration* is a separate operation that applies filtering or other signal-processing technologies to a copy of a file, but never to the original. The objective of preservation is to make transfers of analog and born-digital files that are flat—as faithful to the original as possible. No signal processing should be applied. Flat digital files contain the most information or content that may facilitate restoration or post-preservation reprocessing in the future, especially as new restoration technologies are developed.

The issue of flat playback for preservation is made more complex by instances where the original recording signal was intentionally altered during the recording process. Millions of discs and tape recordings have been made with the application of playback equalization curves (e.g., NAB, RIAA, CCIR) or Dolby noise-reduction systems, which boost or attenuate ranges of audio frequencies to compensate for equipment or recording medium limitations. Sound recordings recorded with playback curves or Dolby reprocessing can be heard as intended only if they are played back through circuits or software that decode the altered signal. There are two key challenges in preserving such recordings: (1) identifying which recordings have had signal processing applied and determining which type of process was used (e.g., Dolby A, B, or C; the RIAA curve; or an older equalization curve); and (2) applying the appropriate curve or de-emphasis to properly decode the signal. Most preservation specialists argue that the altered signal should be compensated for (removed) in an initial transfer for digital preservation. Proprietary processing systems such as Dolby noise-reduction processes are held closely by their creators and will be especially challenging to compensate for in playback decades from now.

4. Sampling rates and compression. There is consensus that preservation files should have high sampling and bit rates, and be uncompressed. When sound files are compressed, inaudible or redundant elements of the original sound recording are discarded. Compression creates a significantly smaller digital file that, in turn, requires less storage space. There are "lossy" and "lossless" compression codecs (programs for encoding). In lossy compression, information that has been lost because of compression cannot be restored, except by returning to the original recording to make a fresh transfer. Several popular consumer formats for digital sound recordings—including MP3 and MPEG4 AAC—are lossy and severely compressed; they are unacceptable for preservation files because the audio is not as richly reproduced as possible. Whether lossy or not, any digital file compressed in accordance with codecs is at risk of not being interpretable decades from now. A thorough and useful survey of digital formats has been conducted by Caroline Arms and Carl Fleischhauer and is available on the Library of Congress Web pages.[111]

5. Storage and content management. Long-term storage of digital files is one of the major issues for which standards, resources, and assistance are eagerly sought. It is more than just a hardware issue because long-term preservation requires the migration of digital files over time. At different levels of file management, the physical devices holding digital information will vary. Digital files may be captured on specialized, nonconsumer tape formats, or on hard drives that may provide interim storage. More sophisticated systems—dubbed by specialists as "digital repositories"—might include small managed environments with tape backup, or larger-scale systems that provide for periodic migration of files. Some consider CD-Rs and DVD+/-Rs appropriate only for listening copies. Most archives do not have the resources to create their own repositories or to contract with independently managed, off-site repositories. Nonetheless, repositories will likely be the most suitable and reliable means and process for protecting recorded sound.

6. Metadata. A wide array of metadata is required for digital preservation. Without systematic collection of structured information related to content, format, and other attributes of the audio files, digital preservation is ineffective. At the same time, the creation of metadata is one of the most challenging and expensive aspects of a digital audio preservation program. The creation of metadata for preservation projects requires trained staff and automated tools.

7. Professionalization. Digital preservation requires trained professional staff. Much audio preservation to date has been undertaken on an ad hoc basis by part-time staff or student workers, without adequate oversight by engineers. As summarized in a written submission to the NRPB by ARL, "Staff with appropriate technical expertise is a key resource for effective preservation programs."[112]

Professional capture of audio and conversion to digital files is only an initial step of digital audio preservation. This chapter discusses several other components of a digital audio preservation program and outlines some of the challenges archives are facing, as discovered in research, roundtables and hearings conducted for this study, and discussions with professionals.

---

[111] Sustainability of Digital Formats Planning for Library of Congress Collections. Available at http://www.digitalpreservation.gov/formats/.

[112] The Library of Congress National Recording Preservation Board (NRPB) invited written comments and submissions by the public on the subject of recording preservation in late 2006 and early 2007, at the time hearings on audio preservation were conducted in New York City and Los Angeles. Written submissions to the NRPB are published by the Library at http://www.loc.gov/rr/record/nrpb/nrpb-comments.html#responses.

Metadata

Preservation and use of digital audio files is critically dependent upon *metadata*, or documentation about the files. Analog media, such as discs and tapes, are themselves physical, and their content is documented on the equally physical containers and labels that hold them.[113] Digital audio files, by contrast, exist discretely. Understanding the identity of digital files depends upon information that may be stored within the file itself or be entirely separate from the recording file. Either way, compatible software for interpretation is required. Metadata identifies content so that it may exist free of individual physical containers with labels, on media such as hard drives or data tapes. With such separation comes a greater necessity for information about the recording and its form as a digital file. Comprehensive preservation metadata documents content, technical processes, administrative rights and permissions, file formats, and the relationship of project files to one another. Metadata "provides the framework for digital audio preservation and ... forms an essential component of the virtual object."[114]

Although the word *metadata* is new to many people, the concept is as old as libraries themselves. Cataloging data that describe books or other items in a library is a form of *descriptive* metadata. One purpose of structured metadata is to enable exchange of information about digital files, as well as the files themselves. MARC (machine-readable cataloging) formats are some of the oldest metadata standards. When libraries began to create MARC standards in the 1960s, their primary objective was to permit the ready exchange of cataloging information among institutions and automated systems. Because preservation metadata must be communicated between systems and must persist over time, standards are crucial.

Generating and maintaining metadata is one of the most expensive and technically sophisticated components of the preservation process. Metadata requires complex applications to compile and store. Testimony provided for this study showed that archives undertaking preservation desire a clear and realistic universal metadata schema to enable sharing and migration among systems, and tools to create metadata efficiently. At this time, most preserved files are accompanied by little metadata, even at institutions that promote the use of administrative and technical metadata on their Web sites and in other publications.

Several types of metadata are needed for preservation of content in digital form.

Descriptive metadata. Descriptive metadata for digital objects is comparable in some ways to traditional cataloging; it describes the content of a sound recording, including performers, participants, and titles of works represented on it. Several formats have been

[113] It must be noted that unpublished recordings, including commercial studio master tapes, are often inadequately identified and insufficiently detailed. They may also not be in their original containers, which can cause them to be misidentified.

[114] Casey and Gordon, *Sound Directions*, 60 (pdf p. 68).

developed for communicating descriptive metadata. In addition to MARC formats, library and archive communities have developed a simpler Dublin Core set of data elements and the more complex XML-based MODS (Metadata Object Description Schema) schema.

Administrative (technical) metadata. This metadata describes physical and technical properties of the source recording and corresponding digital file(s). It also includes *digital provenance* data—that is, data identifying the equipment on which the source recording was played during digital capture, the hardware and software making up the workstation, machine settings, when and where the transfers were made, and the identity of the recording technician. Also included is information provided by the recording technician that is specific to the original recording and the transfer process that will account for any anomalies noted in the preservation copy.

Administrative metadata (rights). This category includes information about ownership of, and rights to, the recording. It includes data pertaining to copyright of the original recording—date, owner, status, and contact information, among other elements. Rights data are based upon information provided with the recording itself and may be incomplete. However, the "lack of such descriptive [i.e., rights-related] data elements," one writer notes, "places an even larger burden on those who would like to make use of the works," to fully identify the rights holders, and the absence of such information has contributed to the large population of orphaned works. "The provision of descriptive data elements that can be transmitted with the work itself should facilitate subsequent uses of the valuable intellectual content that the work represents."[115] A challenge inherent in recording rights data is maintaining such information over time. Several parties may own rights to different aspects of one recording and, over time, each of these rights might be sold, licensed, transferred, or expire.

Structural metadata. Structural metadata might document the exact location of a selection within an audio file or the relationship of one file to another among a set of files. Many audio digital preservation projects produce images of containers and labels. Structural metadata record the relationships between files in a digital object and make possible the presentation of those files as a composite virtual object.

Metadata Models and Standards

Archivists and institutions would welcome agreement about the basic metadata that must be created and how it should be collected and managed. At roundtables convened in support of this study, participants expressed a need for a "universal core audio metadata schemata," and proposed that it be created by the Library of Congress, in collaboration with groups such as the Audio Engineering Society (AES) or the National Academy of Recording Arts and Sciences (NARAS).

Data models and tools have been developed for creating and

[115] Karen Coyle, "Descriptive Metadata for Copyright Status," *First Monday* 10, no. 10 (3 October 2005). Available at http://www.firstmonday.org/issues/issue10_10/coyle/index.html. The California Digital Library has developed and maintains *On-line Guidelines for Digital Objects* at http://www.cdlib.org/inside/diglib/guidelines/.

managing preservation metadata and managing preservation files. Most of these designs are complex models, systems, or schema that are best suited for preservation programs in larger institutions with highly developed IT infrastructures. None has been widely adopted. Concern has been expressed over the number of fields of metadata included in some schema. If the number of fields were to be scaled down to accommodate smaller archives with limited resources, the issue then becomes what data are most essential.

Integration and standardization among the range of metadata formats in use is an additional challenge. There are no schema or practices so widely adopted and commonly used that they are read and interpreted by all professional audio editing and preservation software. For example, while BWF files are in broad use and can be read by nearly all audio software, much of this software ignores the segments ("chunks") in BWF files containing metadata that supports preservation—the information that differentiates BWF files from common WAVE files.

One purpose of metadata is to support the life cycle of digital files. The information held by metadata is essential to the long-term maintenance of preservation files by repositories. A widely accepted framework for a digital repository is the Open Archival Information System (OAIS). The National Aeronautics and Space Administration developed OAIS for the long-term storage, management, and retrieval of digital files or information packages. OAIS models packages for submission, or ingestion, of digital files to a repository; the archival functions performed by the repository; and dissemination of the files held by the repository. In other words, the OAIS framework provides a common language and structure for defining the functions, data, and actors in a repository.

The object framework of OAIS is accommodated by the METS (Metadata Encoding and Transmission Standard). Developed by the Digital Library Federation and maintained by the Library of Congress, METS is a standard for "encoding descriptive, administrative, and structural metadata regarding objects within a digital library."[116] METS is a communications format that defines data elements and a modular XML structure for communicating metadata and content in the same digital package. The system provides "wrappers" around metadata elements that apply to a set of digital files, comprising a digital "object." A METS object might include a range of administrative, descriptive, and technical metadata of various schema.

The AES has developed several audio metadata standards. Although these standards were created to meet the needs of professional engineers in the commercial recording sector, they are of potential value in audio preservation work. One standard, referred to as "AES31," has been of particular interest to audio preservation engineers. As noted by the *Sound Directions* project:

> AES31 is an international standard designed to enable simple interchange of audio files and projects between workstations.

[116] See http://www.loc.gov/standards/mets/mets-schemadocs.html.

> Part 3 [AES-31-3-1999] includes a format for the communication of edit decision lists, called Audio Decision Lists (ADLs) in the standard, using ASCII text that is human-readable but also may be parsed by software. AES31-3 is used in archival work to model the relationship between the source recording and resulting digital files. It provides a standard way to link the various files that are created, sometimes through multiple stops and starts during transfer of a deteriorating source, thereby reconstructing the source recording. Without it, future researchers are left with one engineer's interpretation of the edit points.[117]

AES has developed a number of metadata standards and is in the process of developing more. AES-X098B will define administrative and technical metadata fields for documenting content in digital audio objects. AES-X098C is a schema in development to describe the process history of a digital audio file, namely, what was done to the file, when, by whom, and with what equipment.

Metadata Tools

The need for tools to create and manage metadata is widely acknowledged. Several projects are under way to build such tools and to make them available to the commercial recording sector and to preservation archives. The *Preserving Creative America* initiative of the Library of Congress's National Digital Information Infrastructure and Preservation Program (NDIIPP) has supported a project being carried out by the firm BMS/Chace, which provides audio reformatting and information technology support to the entertainment industry, and with the active cooperation of the Recording Academy, to create a "standardized approach for gathering and managing metadata for recorded music and developing software models to assist creators and owners in collecting the data." The Library of Congress press release announcing this work notes, "A standardized metadata environment will allow content creators, record labels, individuals and cultural heritage institutions to document, archive and manage 'born digital' recordings effectively."[118]

Creating metadata is a particular challenge for small and medium-size archives. Some of the most sophisticated tools work well for the institutions for which they were created but are difficult to integrate into the workflows of other studios. Harvard and Indiana Universities, for example, have created impressive tools for collecting metadata as part of the *Sound Directions* project. These applications are being offered to other archives free of charge.[119] However, given the variety of tools for metadata gathering and archiving—and the absence of a comprehensive turnkey application—in-house programming resources are needed for professional-quality audio

---

[117] Casey and Gordon, *Sound Directions*, 7 (pdf p. 15).

[118] "Digital Preservation Program Makes Awards to Preserve American Creative Works." Library of Congress press release, August 3, 2007. Available at http://www.loc.gov/today/pr/2007/07-156.html.

[119] The *Harvard Sound Directions Toolkit* is available for download without charge at http://hcl.harvard.edu/libraries/loebmusic/aps/sound_directions.html.

preservation. In the second phase of *Sound Directions*, launched in 2007 and continuing into 2010, the Indiana University team is focusing on automating many of the manual practices developed for collecting metadata. Scripts are being written to gather technical metadata, create audio decision lists and derivative files, generate checksums, and move files. These scripts may not be applicable to systems other than those at Indiana, but the project report will provide a model for creating such programs that would have more general applicability. Concurrently, the project is developing an audio technical metadata collector, an open-source Java application to collect and generate metadata.

Many institutions outsource their audio preservation and require that associated metadata be delivered along with the digital files produced. Again, the absence of common documentation practices or standards can be an impediment to this work. Preliminary metadata is often created before reformatting and accompanies tapes and discs sent out for preservation. This metadata can take many forms, e.g., a database or spreadsheet, and might include a variety of elements. Consistency in what the metadata represents can be an issue. In the case of a tape, metadata might describe the physical source medium, individual sets of data for each intellectual work found on the tape, or both. Contractors reformatting the work might be required to write software to migrate the data into the form used in the preservation studio, and migrate the information back into the form in which it was sent. This undertaking diverts resources that, were there standard metadata schema, might be devoted to reformatting additional collections.

Columbia University, with funding from The Andrew W. Mellon Foundation, is investigating challenges inherent in the exchange of digital audio files and their associated metadata created for preservation. The originators of the project emphasize that its goal is not to break new ground but to build on existing work (e.g., *Sound Directions*, METS, the standards being created by AES, and other initiatives) to establish a comprehensive workflow for processing audio recordings. Working with Safe Sound Archive in Philadelphia, the Columbia University project is investigating preservation practices and metadata issues in particular. At its conclusion, the project intends to report specifications for software to collect, amend, and return preservation metadata that can be ingested into preservation repositories with minimal effort. The specifications will not be a standard or application for metadata creation, but rather something that can be provided to programmers, and that will be available to others at no charge. Given the challenges and costs inherent in creating and exchanging metadata, this is a project of potentially great importance that merits close watch.[120]

The Mellon/Columbia project also addresses a number of major challenges in the use of preservation metadata that are of concern to audio archivists: creation of standards and recommended practices;

[120] See https://www1.columbia.edu/sec/cu/libraries/bts/mellon_audio/index.html.

widespread adoption of standard practices to ensure viability of the data over time; resources required to create, or write, metadata; and the integrity of metadata over time, as files are exchanged and read by systems other than the ones in which they were created.

In 2008, the Library of Congress's NDIIPP established the Federal Agencies Audio-Visual Digitization Working Group.[121] This informal body reviews best practices and examines emerging standards. It is working to codify a set of best practices for audio preservation projects within the federal government, and to develop tools that will benefit audio and video preservation activities of federal and nonfederal archives alike. Initial plans include an investigation of options for embedding metadata in WAVE files, including the BWF subtype.

Two related issues are determining how much metadata to embed within audio files and when to embed it. As has been noted, while the BWF file format is commonly used for audio preservation, the broadcast extension (*bext*) segment offers a limited number of fields for metadata. These are free-text in format, i.e., they do not use the XML markup preferred by many archivists and information scientists. In addition, the permitted numbers of characters in each field is limited. There are few standard practices for formatting BWF-embedded metadata, least of all among archives. Many audio applications may be unable to read this data accurately, if at all. For preservation workflow and for internal archiving, there may be a need to embed only minimal metadata. In contrast, when content is disseminated, a great deal of metadata may be called for. Thus, an archive may place a handful of data elements in a file at production time (e.g., an identifier, the name of the archive, the date the file was produced). Later, when the file is provided to an end user, the archive may embed a richer set (e.g., descriptive, rights, structural, and technical metadata). To use the terminology of the OAIS reference model, such an archive will require that its repository system embed metadata in the dissemination information package that is created in a response to an end user's request. The Federal Agencies Audio-Visual Digitization Working Group is exploring several of the issues pertaining to embedded metadata. Its findings and recommendations will be made available on the group's Web site.[122]

For the adoption by sound archives of METS, AES31, and other complex schema, software must be developed to collect and structure this metadata—and of crucial importance—to read and interpret it. Widespread adoption of professional digital preservation practices for audio is undercut by circular dependencies. Metadata schema and file formats will not be widely used until archivists are assured that present and future software can read and interpret them easily. At the same time, developers will not write software unless they are assured of a wide user base. A preservationist recently commented,

[121] The group is led by Carl Fleischhauer, program officer, Library of Congress National Digital Information Infrastructure and Preservation Program. Its Web site is at http://www.digitizationguidelines.gov/audio-visual/.

[122] See http://www.digitizationguidelines.gov/.

"One can define chunks and schema, but if they are not supported they will die on the vine."

Metadata Documenting Authenticity: Checksums

Checksums, more accurately referred to as "hash algorithms," are a form of data that can be used to confirm that the content of a digital file has not changed over time, and that copies created during the course of long-term preservation are identical to the original. Checksums are integer values computed from the content of a file, maintained separately as a reference, and recomputed later to verify the file and determine whether it has been corrupted during storage or migration. When a file is transmitted or copied to a new medium, an archive can generate a new checksum or hash value for a given file and then compare it with the previous checksum or hash value, in an effort to authenticate that the file has not been corrupted during transmission or duplication. Several software tools are available to create checksums and hashes; at least one popular digital audio workstation model creates a proprietary checksum that cannot be read by other systems.

Although recorded sound preservationists regard checksums as critical to long-term preservation, few archives create them routinely in audio preservation projects. This may be because checksums should be stored in separate files, and not embedded into the digital audio files. This practice requires forming and maintaining related databases, or the creation of METS wrappers. Either solution calls for automation tools and human resources that are not available to most audio preservation projects. Specialists often express the desire for easy-to-use, open-source tools for purposes like this.

Identification Metadata

An additional form of metadata discussed at both the hearings and roundtables conducted by the NRPB is the *persistent identifier*, a unique identification code created for every recording preserved and associated with that file permanently, no matter where it resides. It was suggested at the second engineers' roundtable that persistent identifiers (embedded in a digital file) might prove useful if a digital file is separated from its descriptive or other metadata. Persistent identities could also prove useful when sharing files. Persistent identifiers that tie to descriptive metadata about a work represented in a digital file (e.g., cataloging data about a book) or reference URLs are common. There are no widely adopted practices for assigning persistent identifiers for preservation files. The Federal Agencies Audio-Visual Digitization Working Group has recommended that identifiers not only be assigned but also be embedded in files.[123] Acknowledging the wide variation in practice, however, their guideline does not specify *which* identifiers. The guideline accommodates the fact that several federal agencies employ multiple identifiers (e.g., references to cataloging of the source recording, identification of the

[123] See http://www.digitizationguidelines.gov/audio-visual/documents/wave_metadata.html.

shelf number of an original tape, and file-level identifiers), any or all of which might be embedded in their preservation files.

Whatever metadata schema is ultimately used to store or communicate preservation information about a sound recording, digital preservationists and engineers broadly agree that metadata should be created at the inception of every recording event, preferably when the sound is first recorded, and during later events, such as making copies to support preservation or access. Elizabeth Cohen, an NRPB member and past president of the AES, noted at one of the engineers' roundtables, "Our job is to teach people how to record things for an archive; how, from the moment they start recording, that material has information with it that allows them to archive it intelligently, and that is our long-term goal here." At the same session, recognizing the importance of having metadata arrive at the preservation archive along with newly acquired items, another participant asked, "How do we get this down to the individuals who are recording broadband in their basement with a podcast and things like that? How do we get them to be creating the kind of metadata that we [archivists] want?"[124]

Exactly what kind of metadata do archivists want? Settling upon a set of core metadata is difficult. Participants in several of the forums convened in support of this study expressed the desire for a "core preservation metadata element set"—an essential minimum need for small as well as large archives. Some hoped that the Library of Congress and the NRPB, in collaboration with such organizations as the National Academy of Recording Arts and Sciences, IASA, and AES, might lead an effort to create the element set for technical and administrative metadata, accompanied by an explanatory data dictionary.

Repositories and Long-Term Storage

Curation of digital audio files is an ongoing process. Digital files are commonly stored on hard disc drives, data tapes, and CD-Rs or DVDs. None of these media was designed or intended for long-term storage. Custodians of digital preservation media cannot "shelve it and forget it" but must establish and follow systematic processes to monitor files for their integrity. Periodically, digital sound files will need to be refreshed by migrating them to new formats.

While reformatting on digital media has become common, archives still need professional tools and resources to assure the long-term viability of their digital audio recordings. As a participant at the second engineers' roundtable noted, "A lot of what we've been talking about in digital preservation essentially is the cycle of migration and ... [removing] ourselves from the shelf life debate of optical media, hard disk, etc."[125] The establishment of, and reliance upon, a trusted digital repository (TDR), a storage system designed to

[124] Uncredited statement at NRPB Engineers' II conference, March 11, 2006, Washington, DC. Tape 1B. Unpublished.

[125] Uncredited statement at NRPB Engineers' II conference, March 11, 2006, Washington, DC. Tape 3A. Unpublished.

"provide reliable, long-term access to managed digital resources to its designated community, now and in the future," may obviate need for such a debate. A TDR performs "a range of interrelated tasks and functions." More than passively storing digital content, it is designed "to ensure the ongoing management, access, and security of materials deposited within it." It includes routines to verify the integrity of its files; it complies with the OAIS model; it is protected by firewalls; within it are backup and redundancy systems; and it is financially structured for long-term sustainability. [126]

Indiana University's written submission to the hearings conducted for this study summarizes the need to define, document, and disseminate models of preservation repositories with various functionalities, including the following:

- creating detailed and specific best practices for operating these repositories[127]
- modeling service-level agreements between content providers and preservation repositories
- assuring long-term data integrity and authenticity issues
- modeling how potential threats to content will be addressed, including such issues as obsolescence, failure of hardware and software, malicious behavior, human error, disaster, and others, including the development of proposed solutions
- developing migration strategies and tests[128]

Though regarded as an ideal solution to long-term preservation, few TDRs are in place. Several universities are building or testing their own TDRs but few, if any, are fully functional. A repository capable of meeting all its desired objectives is immensely expensive to develop and test. Most professionals, including leaders in audio preservation, are using local, small-scale storage systems or are interacting manually with university storage facilities. Often, the best a university preservation program can accomplish is to load its digital preservation files onto the university's servers and depend on those files being backed up during regular cycles of the systems.

As of 2008, a small number of third-party digital storage services were available to archives. Although not promoted as a TDR, OCLC's Digital Archive, which provides file integrity monitoring and maintenance of multiple backups at off-site facilities, may be the most sophisticated service available at this time.[129] One hundred gigabytes of storage (approximately 100 hours of preservation-quality

[126] *Trusted Digital Repositories: Attributes and Responsibilities.* An RLG-OCLC Report. (Mountain View, CA, RLG, May 2002). Available at www.oclc.org/programs/ourwork/past/trustedrep/repositories.pdf.

[127] Konrad Strauss has noted that such recommendations should also include suggestions for file aggregation techniques (creating "tar" or "rar" archive files) and files for mass data storage systems and the creation of non-proprietary utilities to create these archive files.

[128] "Sound Directions: Digital Preservation and Access for Global Audio Heritage." Statement submitted to the NRPB by Mike Casey, associate director for recording services, Archives of Traditional Music, Indiana University, January 31, 2007. Available at http://www.loc.gov/rr/record/nrpb/pdf/Indiana.pdf.

[129] See http://www.oclc.org/digitalarchive/overview/default.htm.

stereo audio) is estimated to cost $750 per year.[130] With competition and continuing declines in digital storage costs, it is likely that prices charged by TDRs will decrease, but the service of a TDR is likely to continue to represent a formidable investment for a midscale archive. Assuming, however unlikely, that there is no decline in the price or discount for a large-scale customer, storing 1,000 hours of audio (1 terabyte [TB]) for 25 years could cost $187,500 over that term. Barebones Web-based storage offered by Amazon Web Services presently costs $180 per 100 gigabytes ($45,000 for 1 TB of data over 25 years; file transfers and requests are available at additional charge). Amazon's overview of the service does not describe features that would be expected of a digital preservation storage system, such as disaster preparedness and security processes verification of the integrity of the files.[131]

Several preservationists have expressed hope for the development of regional, nonprofit, consortial repositories.[132] Archives not affiliated with an institution large enough to design, build, and support its own exclusive TDR might fill their long-term digital storage needs by leasing space on a communal TDR, presumably at a cost significantly lower than that of existing services. One project in development that might meet these criteria is the Audiovisual Archive Network (AVAN). The Mellon Foundation is funding development of a business plan for AVAN, intended to provide public and educational access to moving-image (and possibly audio) content as well as to TDR services. Little has been published about the exact specifications of AVAN and its costs to users. Until the network is developed further, it remains unclear whether AVAN can meet the needs of archives seeking affordable TDR services. A prototype of the network is being built in 2010.[133]

Immediate Solutions for Preservation

As audio archives look to the future for reliable and affordable systems to maintain digital recordings, their most immediate needs are for guidance in creating digital files that can be sustained for the long term. An element of this is recommendations on best practices for selection and care of interim storage media. All too often, preservation projects are not continuing beyond the media and systems judged by large institutions and professionals as "interim." Additional provision needs to be made for a migration strategy to assure that audio captured on CD-Rs or data tapes will be protected in the long term.

Sound engineers commonly believe that the CD-R is a poor and unreliable long-term preservation format; nonetheless, it has become

[130] Barbara Quint, "OCLC Introduces High-priced Digital Archive Service," Information Today Inc., May 2, 2008. Available at http://newsbreaks.infotoday.com/nbReader.asp?ArticleId=49018.

[131] See http://aws.amazon.com/.

[132] The concept has been proposed by Carl Fleischhauer in several discussions, and is suggested in the Indiana University submission to NRPB preservation hearings.

[133] See http://www.archivenetwork.org/index.html.

the storage workhorse of audio preservation. Although there are no statistics to prove it, it is feared and believed that most audio is preserved as digital files on CD-Rs. Considering the complexity of the stages of recommended practices for digital preservation and the many supporting digital files created in the process of preservation—which at Indiana University include master files, production master files, delivery files, metadata, images and text, and digital wrappers, all of which are intended to be supported by an IT infrastructure—the predominance of CD-Rs is not surprising. By comparison with the poorer shelf life of magnetic recording tape, CD-Rs initially seem to be a considerable step forward, and for many archives they are the only feasible choice. Small archives do not have the resources to build repositories, and most of these archives may have had little introduction to solutions other than CD-R storage. At the second engineers' roundtable, a participant remarked that the choices shouldn't be, "We either go with archival optical media such as gold CD-Rs [or], if you can't do that, then you simply have got to step into a large, managed IT repository."

In some archives, portable hard disc drives substitute for CD-R storage. CD-R backups are often generated from the drives. The configuration is conceived as a low-cost solution for digital storage. Such a system could be an improvement over storage on CD-Rs exclusively, and adequate for an archive with limited resources, but there is no assurance of systematic migration of the data on the drives to new media. Unless the data's integrity is monitored, and periodic migration guaranteed, a hard disc drive sitting on a shelf may be no safer a medium than a CD-R.

Two preservation programs surveyed for this report built storage configurations that, while well short of being TDRs, use sophisticated IT. Yet the host institutions of these programs do not have the resources (hardware, staff, or both) to create the recommended checksums for their preservation files. They lack automated ingestion systems. Files are moved to the server manually, and there are no means to generate anything approaching the metadata required to build a METS object. For example, in one institution, some descriptive metadata is included in the BWF made in the preservation program, but little technical metadata is recorded. Another academic institution reported designing a MySQL database in-house (coded by students) for storage and presentation of technical metadata. In that operation, the storage of files was local, on RAID arrays in the archive. The files are backed up daily, on an incremental basis, and weekly, in full. But data have been lost because of faulty validation processes. Both archives create and retain CD-Rs of their content, for backups, or for patron access.

These two arrangements are examples of professional efforts to maintain digital audio preservation files despite restricted financial and technical resources. Reports from several institutions indicate that these file maintenance strategies are significantly more sophisticated than those undertaken in most digital preservation scenarios. It is also important to note that the two systems described above could be developed only because the audio archivists who commissioned them had some computing and audio studio expertise. These archivists designed their preservation studios as well as the storage systems. Individuals in the audio archivist field rarely possess the skills needed to design and implement a preservation program at that level of detail. Professional audio preservation programs require sound engineers, programmers, catalogers, resources, and individuals capable of designing and building IT infrastructures for long-term storage. Digital preservation "cannot be sustained by generalists," as one archivist noted.[134]

The Columbia University metadata project funded by the Mellon Foundation will provide valuable guidance on metadata content for archives preparing digital audio files for long-term storage. Recognizing that many archives would benefit from additional assistance in preparing preservation files for long-term storage while full digital storage facilities and services are not yet at hand, recording engineer John Spencer and the Technical Committee of the Association for Recorded Sound Collections (ARSC) are working to develop the concept of a *transitional repository*, i.e., a set of procedures to be followed to ensure that digital audio content is suitable for ingestion when a fully functioning preservation repository is available. The ARSC transitional repository project will comprise Web publication of a set of best practices for interim storage formats, data management and tracking, metadata collection, minimum sets of metadata, and other topics.

Best Practices and Best-Possible Practices

At the public hearings conducted for this study and in written submissions, concerns were raised about how to help small archives and institutions with limited resources. A submission to the hearings by Virginia Danielson of Harvard University proposes a "national program that can lead collectors and curators to engineering guidance from professionals accustomed to the issues of preservation and storage for the treatment of their collections." One suggested model is the Fund for Folk Culture's "Preserving America's Culture Traditions" (PACT), which supports small folklife archives by sending "'circuit-rider' experts to a number of collections across the country with the goal of making practical and well-informed plans for audio preservation in the separate archives."[135] PACT is a limited project at this time, but it may be a model that could be scaled to assist curators of all types of sound collections. Groups such as the Conservation Center for Art and Historic Artifacts, the Education and Training Committee of ARSC, and the Northeast Document Conservation

[134] Research into archive practices described in this section was conducted by phone interviews and e-mail exchanges between members of the Association for Recorded Sound Collections and Sam Brylawski in the spring and summer of 2008.

[135] "Toward a National Audio Preservation Program." Written statement submitted to the NRPB by Virginia Danielson, Richard F. French Librarian and Curator of the Archive of World Music, Eda Kuhn Loeb Music Library, Harvard University, January 31, 2007. Available at http://www.loc.gov/rr/record/nrpb/pdf/harvard.pdf.

Center regularly conduct workshops that address digital audio preservation. The sessions are well attended, indicating a demand for instruction and information about digital audio preservation.

The hearings and engineers' roundtable discussions conducted by the NRPB brought forth a desire for additional formalization of standards and for a Web site that compiles composite best practices and recommended preservation workflows. Currently, there is no central source to consult for recommended practices. One hearing participant expressed that there are many "emerging" and "de facto" standards that could be formalized, adding, "I also think that doing such a thing, creating a regional repository or regional centers, would help progress standardization."[136]

Some perceive the criteria for audio preservation set forth in the IASA, Harvard-IU, and NRPB publications as complex and costly to implement. It has already been suggested that criteria that raise the bar too high might only foster hopelessness and a broad disregard of any recommendations. Two engineers testifying at the hearings proposed that best practices might vary according to the capabilities of the organization: digital conversion at the best-*possible* sampling rate, and adoption of the best-*possible* means to monitor, maintain, and migrate files. "What we find is that within the range of standards and [best practices], what is singularly most important is that the project be designed around what the institutional infrastructures [are] capable of. If you have somebody in the paper archive that has a small collection of audio, the collection is going to be different than if you are dealing with a major university digital libraries program."[137] The Collaborative Digitization Program's *Digital Audio Best Practices* was recommended as a useful and readable guide to digitization that is tailored for a lay audience.[138]

The call from the audio preservation community and many institutions for direction on best practices fosters a conundrum with potentially serious implications for saving sound. Many participants in the hearings for this study were troubled about the large amount of preservation work undertaken by amateurs, such as college work-study students. A second concern was potential misallocation of limited resources. Given the enormous amount of audio that will have to be copied for preservation if it is to survive, operational efficiencies were frequently discussed at the hearings and roundtables conducted for this study. Participants generally agreed that a number of efficiencies in duplication practices could be achieved, but not without losses in quality. Furthermore, those compromises, the attendees

---

[136] Testimony of Chris Lacinak, Association of Moving Image Archivists and Audio Engineering Society Technical Committee on Archiving, Restoration and Digital Libraries, "Preservation Challenges and Practices in Archives and Libraries," session, NRPB public hearings, December 19, 2006, New York.

[137] Testimony of George Blood, Safe Sound Archive; and Adrian Cosentini, Audio/Preservation Manager for the New York Philharmonic, at the closing panel, NRPB public hearings, December 19, 2006, New York.

[138] Digital Audio Working Group. Collaborative Digitization Program. 2006. *Digital Audio Best Practices* (Version 2.1) Aurora, Colorado. Available at http://www.bcr.org/dps/cdp/best/digital-audio-bp.pdf.

emphasized, must be known in advance. Preservation sound engineer George Blood paraphrased Pareto's principle by speculating that 80 percent of audio recordings require very little intervention during transfer, but the remaining 20 percent might require 80 percent of the time invested. Blood proposed what he termed "process engineering":

> We need to find ways to reliably, accurately, and safely process the vast majority of recordings. The resources—time, money, management, assessment, et cetera—are not and will not be available to process even a fraction of the audio and moving image assets that are out there. … The solution lies not in making more money available to those without but in finding a way to make it more affordable for all.

In considering the 80 percent of his work that requires "little intervention," Blood speculated that "you might be able to use work-study students to transfer a mountain of cassettes; you are not going to give them delaminating acetates, at least, not a second time."[139]

A recent study of magnetic tape collections conducted by the Image Permanence Institute at the Rochester Institute of Technology recommends developing "automated tape transfer" technologies.[140] In the second phase of the *Sound Directions* project, Indiana University plans to study efficiencies such as simultaneous transfers and automation. While many desire efficiencies and are aware of the need to study their costs and benefits, experts at the second engineers' roundtable warned that introducing efficiencies exacts an inevitable trade-off in quality, and that archivists need to be fully aware of the measure of that trade-off. The dilemma, as set forth at the second engineers' roundtable, is "how to be efficient without spoiling everything."[141]

European radio and television broadcasting archives appear to be at the forefront of research and implementation of preservation duplication efficiencies. The PRESTO and PrestoSpace projects, funded by the European Commission, were conceived to ensure the preservation of the hundreds of thousands of audio and video recordings held by European broadcasting archives through collaborations with researchers and commercial venders to solve specific engineering challenges and create high-throughput "preservation factories" for reformatting.[142] The recently opened Library of Congress Packard Campus for Audio Visual Conservation includes facilities for simultaneous, multistream reformatting of magnetic tapes. Planners of the center note that the keys to the success of the work are selection of recordings most appropriate for this preservation approach, use of

---

[139] Testimony of George Blood, NRPB public hearings, December 19, 2006, New York.

[140] Jean-Louis Bigourdan et al., Image Permanence Institute. *The Preservation of Magnetic Tape Collections: A Perspective*. Final Report to the National Endowment for the Humanities Division of Preservation and Access, December 22, 2006. Available at http://www.imagepermanenceinstitute.org/shtml_sub/NEHTapeFinalReport.pdf.

[141] Uncredited statement at NRPB Engineers' II conference, March 10, 2006, Washington, DC. Tape 2B. Unpublished.

[142] See http://prestospace.org/project/index.en.html.

professional equipment, diligence in maintaining the equipment, and attentiveness to quality assurance.

Standard archival practice is to retain originals even if they have been preserved. If the digitization process incorporates efficiencies, such as multiple, simultaneous streams that prevent full aural monitoring or sampling for quality assurance, retention of originals is even more critical. Future opportunity and technology may enable a second pass to achieve a superior transfer.

In March 2009, PrestoPRIME, a successor program to PrestoSpace, was launched. The European Union committed 12 million euros to PrestoPRIME. The ambitious objectives for the program include creating a digital preservation network; developing tools to create and manage metadata; creating a rights management system, as well as an "audiovisual fingerprint registry"; and establishing a networked "European-networked Competence Centre" to provide training, deliver advanced digital preservation advice and services, and publish economic guidance and business models.[143]

Collaboration

Achieving some efficiencies doesn't require compromises. For example, several participants at the hearings and roundtables proposed collaborations among archives that might support audio preservation. At the hearings conducted in Los Angeles, Russ Hamm described his work to preserve a collection of audiotapes of San Diego folk festivals and concerts of the 1960s recorded by Lou Curtis. Although he did not have the resources to digitize the recordings for preservation, Hamm has established a partnership with University of California, Los Angeles, to preserve the tapes.[144]

The written submission by Mike Casey of Indiana University suggests that for audio recordings held by smaller institutions to survive, there must be "mutually-beneficial partnerships between larger and smaller institutions" and "mutually-beneficial partnerships between smaller institutions and the private sector."[145] A common form of collaboration between small archives or collectors and large institutions has been loan of at-risk recordings to the larger institutions for preservation duplication. Under these arrangements, the original collection, usually of unpublished tapes, instantaneous discs, or cylinders, is duplicated. One preservation copy is retained by the institution performing the preservation and another copy is provided to the original owner. (The originals might remain with the larger institution or be returned with the preservation copies.) Such arrangements are beneficial to both parties. Disbursing two copies makes the material more accessible for research and begins to fulfill

---

[143] See http://wiki.prestospace.org/pmwiki.php?n=Main.PrestoPRIME.

[144] Testimony of Russ Hamm, representing the San Diego Folk Society, "Copyright and Intellectual Property Issues" session, NRPB public hearings, November 29, 2006, Los Angeles.

[145] Written statement of Mike Casey, submitted to the NRPB January 31, 2007. Available at http://www.loc.gov/rr/record/nrpb/pdf/Indiana.pdf.

the widely endorsed preservation philosophy that has been dubbed LOCKSS ("lots of copies keep stuff safe"). However, unless authorizations are obtained from all rights holders of the content of the recordings (performers, authors, composers, etc.), such collaborations, resulting in multiple preservation and/or access copies, are usually illegal under U.S. copyright law.

As challenging as planning and implementing digital preservation may be, archivists and engineers are also concerned about proper storage of original media—CD-Rs, discs, tapes, cylinders, and wires. Many archives do not have temperature- and humidity-controlled storage environments for their collections. Participants in the hearings and roundtables also proposed establishing regional centers where original media could be safely stored.

Many collections are in need of sleeves, boxes, reels, and other conservation supplies. At the hearings and roundtables it was suggested that archives pool resources to purchase supplies in bulk quantities to lower per-unit costs. The practice might be extended to include supplies and tools for reformatting, such as record styli. To meet a long-articulated need, the NRPB commissioned the Cylinder Subcommittee of ARSC's Technical Committee to design an archival cylinder box. The design is now complete. Experts believe the container will cost less than any existing archival cylinder box, and that it may be superior for long-term storage. Hardware, including related parts and documentation, might be acquired and maintained by consortia, which could loan specialized playback machines to institutions as needed from hardware banks located at regional centers.

Until recently, most audio preservation focused on unique, at-risk recordings. Digitization of mass-produced commercial recordings was a low priority.[146] This situation has been slowly changing; libraries and archives are more commonly digitizing commercial recordings to provide access. Providing access to a digitized recording enables students and scholars to study a recording in depth and allows repeated audition without harming the recording through multiple playback or requiring that trained staff be on hand to provide listening service.

The creation of listening copies may be relatively common, especially for library audio reserves and academic course-management systems (e.g., Blackboard). But the practice may be illegal technically because the number of copies of a recording that can be made by libraries and archives is sharply limited under U.S. copyright law. If limited copying for access could be accomplished within the law, archives and libraries might be able to share these files and reduce redundant digitization of recordings. In his testimony before the

[146] Two software programs have been developed to help collection managers set priorities for audio preservation. Both are available as free downloads. The Field Audio Collection Evaluation Tool (FACET) developed at Indiana University is available at http://www.dlib.indiana.edu/projects/sounddirections/facet/index.shtml; Columbia University's Survey Instrument for Audio and Moving Image Collections may be found at http://www.columbia.edu/cu/lweb/services/preservation/audiosurvey.html.

NRPB, ethnomusicologist Clifford Murphy outlined how limited access to rare New England country music recordings has impeded his research. Murphy expressed a corollary concern that lack of access to sound recordings may affect academic research because the theme and scope of the research may have to be modified to suit the universe of recordings that can be studied. If recordings needed for study were held by a group of libraries and available through a local library, the needs of scholars might be met.[147] Such a program would depend significantly upon descriptive metadata, formatted to a common standard to allow digital content to be shared among many libraries and archives and queried by researchers.

Closer cooperation among copyright holders, intellectual property owners, and libraries could be advantageous to all parties. Libraries and intellectual property owners would benefit from increased collaboration in the creation of metadata. Participants at the second engineers' roundtable suggested that libraries and recording creators should collaborate on tools to create descriptive and technical metadata at the time of creation of a file, further suggesting the assignment and embedding of a persistent identifier by the U.S. Copyright Office when a recording is registered. A participant at that roundtable noted, "We all have different agendas, but somehow there is this pool of data or this resource in the middle that [we] wish we could share."[148] Discussions indicated that some redundancies, as well as inadequacies, in metadata creation might be overcome if descriptive metadata creation tools were developed and made available to all creators of digital audio recordings.

Most institutions that hold audio collections do not maintain in-house preservation reformatting facilities and must rely on contracted services. Whether these services are contracted collaboratively or not, smaller institutions need guidance when outsourcing preservation. In testimony for these hearings, Emily Holmes, assistant director for preservation reformatting and reprography at Columbia University Libraries, observed that "institutions that cannot establish in-house conversion labs will need reputable service bureaus that can meet preservation standards and they will need agreed-upon mechanisms to evaluate these service bureaus, and model contracts and other tools."[149]

An audio-digitization project undertaken by the Collaborative Digitization Program in Colorado (now BCR) has been cited as a model for shared outsourcing for digitization. The project, funded by a grant from the Institute of Library and Museum Services, encompassed a wide range of activities, including cataloging, creation of preservation metadata, exhibitions, and digitization, related to 2,000 audio recordings held by 40 libraries, museums, and archives in

[147] Testimony of Clifford Murphy, Ph.D. candidate in Ethnomusicology at Brown University, "Copyright and Academic Research" session, NRPB public hearings, December 19, 2006, New York.

[148] Uncredited statement at NRPB Engineers' II Conference, March 11, 2006, Washington, DC. Tape 3B. Unpublished.

[149] Testimony of Emily Holmes, NRPB public hearings, December 19, 2006, New York.

Colorado. The process by which the recordings were digitized is of particular interest.[150]

Digitization of all 2,000 recordings was outsourced to one company. BCR established specifications for the digitization services, selected the vendor through a competitive-bidding process, described each recording in a consistent manner, created a model for metadata to be collected by the vendor, and operated as the sole liaison with the vendor on behalf of the many institutions that owned the recordings. The vendor that performed the work, Safe Sound Archive, in Philadelphia, saw the job as "a single project with 2,000 items," with one invoice, common specifications, and a volume of similar work that resulted in a significantly reduced per-item cost to the vendor. In testimony for this study, George Blood, president of Safe Sound Archive, noted that by consolidating digitization needs, the larger participating institutions saved 20 percent of what they would have paid for digitization had they contracted for the service separately and that the smallest organizations, with as few as 15 items digitized, realized savings of 80 percent.[151]

The Application of Science

Historically, the foundation of recorded sound preservation practice, education, and training has rested upon the empirical knowledge of its senior engineer practitioners. First- and second-generation leaders in recording preservation and restoration (audio cleanup and remastering for reissue) were usually sound engineers whose careers did not begin in audio preservation. They learned specialized preservation techniques on the job, through trial and error, or from informal instruction from senior colleagues.

More recently, the field has begun attracting recording engineers with solid backgrounds in science, advanced degrees in relevant disciplines, and early career commitments to the field of preservation. This development is recognized as of benefit to the field and been encouraged by many. Donald J. Waters, program officer for scholarly communications at the Mellon Foundation and strong supporter of developing preservation standards and tools, observed at the New York City hearings:

> One of the biggest impediments for the Foundation in providing funding for the preservation of sound recording is not just the lack of widely disseminated best practices but the relative absence of a scientific approach to and basis for these practices. Sound engineering typically as taught and practiced in the U.S. is

[150] Leigh A. Grinstead and Nancy Allen. Sound Model: An Infrastructure for Digital Audio. March 2007. IMLS Final Report LG-30-04-0214-04. In 2007, Collaborative Digitization Program merged with the Bibliographical Center for Research (BCR). The full report is no longer available online. However, many appendices from the report may be found on the BCR Web site, as well as an excellent guide to audio digitization practices, *Digital Audio Best Practices*, Version 2.1. http://dignevada.bcr.org/dps/cdp/best/digital-audio-bp.pdf.

[151] Testimony of George Blood, NRPB public hearings, December 19, 2006. New York.

> a handicraft transmitted by apprenticeship and aimed primarily at producing recordings for commercial distribution. We need to attract more of these engineers into an academic setting as practitioners.[152]

A variant of this view was expressed in a submission to the NRPB by Marcos Sueiro Bal, an engineer at Columbia University: "We must phase out the era of 'it has personally worked for me so far' in favor of a more scientific, peer-reviewed basis. Especially with the tools available today to analyze audio, it seems destructive not to use objective measurements (although I am always the first to admit that the ear is our best measurement instrument)."[153]

In recent years, greater awareness of the importance of audio preservation and the transition to digital preservation has resulted in increased research and development relevant to audio preservation and engineering. A number of institutions in the United States and in Europe are developing noncontact means for the playback of grooved audio media, a technology that would be ideal because it would reduce the frequency of contact playback with a stylus. Among these efforts is the work of a team at Lawrence Berkeley Laboratories on the Berkeley campus of the University of California. Physicists, engineers, and programmers at the laboratories are developing two systems for reading and interpreting lateral and vertical grooves of discs and cylinders.[154] The IRENE (image, reconstruct, erase noise, etc.) system, now being tested at the Library of Congress, optically scans the groove floor of laterally recorded discs. The more complex and data-intensive task of mapping cylinder grooves, which are vertically recorded ("hill and dale"), is being tackled by a second system, which utilizes a confocal microscope to capture three-dimensional images that can be processed and interpreted to reproduce the sound.

These sophisticated, noninvasive systems hold promise for audio preservation. With these tools, pieces of broken records can be "played" and their original content reconstructed digitally. IRENE may make possible high-throughput digitization of 78-rpm discs to create digital files for access. Proper play of 78s depends upon many factors, including the caliber of turntables equipped to play early shellac recordings, the matching of styli to groove size, and the ability to determine and set proper pitch by adjusting the speed of playback. Quality transfer of a single selection can be time-consuming. Owing to the relatively stable composition of 78-rpm shellac discs,

---

[152] Testimony of Donald J. Waters, program officer for scholarly communications, The Andrew W. Mellon Foundation, NRPB public hearings, December 19, 2006, New York.

[153] Written submission to the NRBP by Marcos Sueiro Bal. Available at http://www.loc.gov/rr/record/nrpb/pdf/bal.pdf.

[154] The work at the Lawrence Berkeley Laboratories is described at http://irene.lbl.gov. Three other projects conducting research in noncontact playback are the Visual Audio project at Swiss National Sound Archives (http://project.eia-fr.ch/visualaudio/), the Sound Archive Project of the University of Southampton School of Engineering Sciences (http://www.sesnet.soton.ac.uk/archivesound/home/), and the French "Clareety" project (described at http://prestospace.org/training/images/Proto-Clareety.pdf).

they have been a low priority for preservation reformatting. The three-dimensional mapping process now under development at the Lawrence Berkeley Laboratories could make possible the preservation of tens of thousands of wax and celluloid cylinders that are now totally inaccessible. This would be an enormous benefit because all cylinders are at risk of deterioration; early wax cylinders are highly susceptible to mold as well as breakage. The digital representations created by both IRENE and the three-dimensional systems can be interpreted and processed by virtually smoothing over physical imperfections that mar the sound recorded. Software can also achieve any necessary pitch correction. The laboratories' achievements are the product of research, experimentation (with off-the-shelf hardware), skilled professionals, and close collaborations between preservation engineers, audio specialists, and scientists. The work has been supported by nine organizations, including the NRPB.[155] It is a model of scientific collaboration, energetic fund-raising, and creativity. From its inception, it has also added to our understanding of analog groove media. In early 2008, IRENE was enlisted to play, for the first time, an experimental recording made in 1860 by Édouard-Léon Scott de Martinville that had not previously been heard.[156]

The work of the Lawrence Berkeley Laboratories notwithstanding, audio preservation research in the United States is limited. Several facilities in the United States have addressed audio-related conservation issues, such as research related to physical preservation of legacy media, but quantitative analyses of transfer or reformatting processes are lacking. In contrast, many audiovisual preservation-related research projects have been undertaken as part of the European broadcasters' PrestoSpace project.[157] As with every technology-based activity, increasingly sophisticated and effective tools are being produced that are available to the professional audio community. Many of these have benefited audio preservation as well as production work. With ample funding, preservation studios are able to exploit technological advances developed for commercial production. With careful planning and adequate funding, clean, interference-free signal chains may be assembled, and outstanding hardware enlisted for preservation transfers.

Professionally designed studios are among the components needed to accomplish the best-possible audio preservation work. Audio preservation studios at the Library of Congress Packard Campus were custom-designed by acousticians to provide the best-possible environment for critical listening while monitoring preservation transfers.

[155] Funders of the Lawrence Berkeley Laboratories' work include the U.S. Department of Energy, the John Simon Guggenheim Foundation, the Institute of Library and Museum Services, The Andrew W. Mellon Foundation, the National Academy of Recording Arts and Sciences, the National Endowment for the Humanities, the Library of Congress, the National Recording Preservation Board, and the University of California. See http://irene.lbl.gov.

[156] See First Sounds Web site, http://www.firstsounds.org/.

[157] PrestoSpace Public results are available at http://prestospace.org/project/public.en.html.

Listening skills and knowledge of recording content can be as important to audio preservation engineering as a background in physics and other sciences. More so than preservation digitization of books, video, and images, audio preservation is an art as well as a science. The art of audio preservation is in the requirements of acute listening skills and experience. Playback of analog media often entails the selection of styli and adjustments to playback speed. The skills needed to perform these activities are informed by careful listening, experience with the media, and familiarity with the recording content. Videotape transfers exploit tools such as vectorscopes and video-level devices and strict engineering rules and standards that informed the creation of the item to be preserved. Audio preservation benefits less from objective tools and standards.

This study's hearings and roundtables showed that professionals desire quantitative tools to supplement what they learn from their trained ears. In preparation for the second engineers' roundtable, Ken Pohlmann drafted a paper defining criteria to evaluate analog-to-digital converters for preservation.[158] The Federal Agencies Audio-Visual Digitization Working Group is exploring the measurement of system performance and developing specifications and tools that will determine whether digitization systems meet those specifications. The intention is to permit archives to evaluate their preservation transfer systems (or those of their contractors) to ensure that they are as transparent as possible. The need for a performance assessment tool was a topic of discussion at the second engineers' roundtable.

Audio preservation, especially restoration (the enhancement or aural repair of a recording), has benefited from several tools employing applied technology. Prominent among these is the Plangent Process. A common problem with analog tape is wow and flutter. Another is pitch fluctuations caused by slight variations in the speed of the recording master during the recording process. The Plangent Process, developed by engineers, adjusts the pitch of audio played from a magnetic tape by identifying and analyzing ultra-high frequency signals on a tape—bias signal—and then adjusting playback speed by regulating the frequency of the ultrasonic information. The process is a powerful restoration tool. Like most other signal processes, it should be applied after a flat transfer from the original source has been completed. The Plangent Process system is not sold or leased; it can be used only by outsourcing. It is possible that this may put its cost out of reach for all but the most well-funded preservation programs. The company's Web site notes that a related system designed to correct audio captured from off-center disc pressings

[158] Ken C. Pohlmann, "Measurement and Evaluation of Analog-to-Digital Converters Used in the Long-term Preservation of Audio Recordings." Paper written for roundtable discussion, "Issues in Digital Audio Preservation Planning and Management," March 10–11, 2006, Washington, DC. Available at http://www.clir.org/activities/details/ad-converters-pohlmann.pdf.

or misshapen cylinders is under development as well.[159] Engineers Nadja Wallaszkovits and Heinrich Pichler in Vienna are also conducting research on the use of the high-frequency bias signal for audio restoration.[160]

Many engineers and archivists who contributed to this study in the hearings and roundtable discussions agreed that the audio preservation community has neither articulated its research needs adequately nor formed and exploited scientific and technical alliances. Several participants in the second engineers' roundtable expressed interest in establishing national committees to advise on agendas and priorities for audio preservation research. Lawrence Berkeley Laboratories physicist Carl Haber, one of the developers of the IRENE system, suggested at the second roundtable:

> The thing is to communicate on preservation problems to the scientific community. … To a certain extent, the scientific research organizations can also be proactive if they recognize that reaching out to new communities will be a good thing for society or in their self-interest. ... A broader way to do that is basically to try to just bring out the message of what your problems are through scientific journals, magazines, presentations … or whatever the modes might be. A more top-down method would be to really deal with the scientific leadership. … I think the archival community should prepare, if it wants to go and engage more deeply with the scientific community, some sort of a report that would be written in a way that the scientific community would find easily accessible, outlining [broadly] the challenges and the technologies and the methods that you think that you need, almost like a shopping list.

Perpetuating the Craft of Preservation

Most contributors to this report expressed support for the incorporation of more science into sound preservation. Without intending to minimize that need, many participants at the hearings and roundtables convened by the NRPB also urged that a means be developed to capture the immense knowledge and experience of today's senior practitioners so that it might inform transfer and preservation now and in the future. At the New York hearings, Emily Holmes observed that "it is concerning that the older generation of sound engineers who understand analog formats and equipment is being replaced by younger generation too often familiar only with digital formats."[161] At the same hearing, George Blood expressed similar thoughts: "We

[159] Information about Plangent is available at http://www.plangentprocesses.com/. Many other tools for audio restoration are available. Sonic Solutions' NoNOISE software restoration tools are available as a plug-in to ProTools digital audio workstations (http://www.digidesign.com/index.cfm?navid=115&itemid=3180). Tools developed by CEDAR Audio are sold as both hardware and plug-in software (http://www.cedar-audio.com/).

[160] Paper presented at JTS2007, described at http://www.jts2007.org/program.htm.

[161] Testimony of Emily Holmes, NRPB public hearings, December 19, 2006, New York.

are fast approaching the time when many key people, long retired, will no longer be available to share their firsthand experience. Very little of the knowledge available within the trade has been developed systematically, much less collated and distributed systematically, such as in textbooks or imbedded in peer-review journals."[162] In 2008, the British Library published a 340-page manual on transferring historical sound recordings by Peter Copeland, conservation manager at the British Library Sound Archive.[163] The publication, representing career-gained knowledge of a respected preservation engineer, begins to address concerns such as those expressed by Holmes and Blood.

Several participants in the NRPB hearings suggested that a broad, structured apparatus be established to capture, vet, and share the skills and practices of experienced preservationists. One suggestion was the creation of a public Web site in which best practices and recommended workflows would be compiled and updated, after peer review, by a group of preservation engineers. At the Los Angeles hearings, Russ Hamm, recounting his efforts to seek preservation for the Lou Curtis folk music collection, noted a need for an "organized knowledge base for how to go about this business." Hamm recounted his attempt to acquire preservation information from the listserv sponsored by ARSC and administered at the Library of Congress. Over time, the listserv has served many as a valuable source of information about hardware, media shelf life, disaster management, and other important topics. He hoped that the answers he needed might be found on the mailing list, but was frustrated by its lack of organization and superfluous posts. Konrad Strauss, director of recording arts at the Indiana University Jacobs School of Music, has noted that the restoration techniques and processes of many engineers have been developed over years of experimentation and are proprietary. In an e-mail he stated that, "I think that this knowledge could be considered intellectual property. For example the Plangent Process is very effective, but it is not a free service. So while harvesting audio preservation knowledge is a good idea, a system will have to be developed to reimburse engineers for sharing their hard-earned knowledge. Some, I'm sure, will be willing to share it for free, but others may want some kind of remuneration."[164]

At the hearings in Los Angeles, Robert Heiber, of Chace Productions, an audio postproduction facility, recommended

> establishment really of some form of a consortium of resources that archives could approach. It could be not-for-profit, it could be done at a modest cost … where the small archive will go for oversight and peer review and help in development of a project. I'm a huge believer that regardless of the steps that you take, if you architect a project properly and you get the right road

[162] Testimony of George Blood, NRPB public hearings, December 19, 2006, New York.

[163] Peter Copeland, *Manual of Analogue Sound Restoration Techniques* (London: The British Library, 2008). Available at http://www.bl.uk/reshelp/findhelprestype/sound/anaudio/analoguesoundrestoration.pdf.

[164] E-mail from Konrad Strauss to Brenda Nelson Strauss, June 17, 2009.

> map, then it does not matter how far you get down the road in the beginning as long as you know where the end result is going to lead and you know that that is going to be a successful outcome.[165]

Conservation and Material Science

An overwhelming number of audio recordings located throughout the United States are at risk of deterioration. Given the relatively small number of these recordings likely to be reformatted for preservation in the near future, responsible custodianship of original materials, including defensive steps to inhibit deterioration, is essential. As they confront this task, caretakers of audio collections seek assistance from scientists to better understand physical risks to audio materials, to minimize or defer these risks, to deal responsibly with emergencies, and to guide choices when setting priorities for reformatting recordings.

Archivists are aware of many inherent threats to individual media formats but often lack information about the causes and progression of chemical or physical changes, or proven remedies, and knowledge of when a recording will ultimately degrade until it can no longer be played. The hearings and roundtables revealed a wide range of conservation issues of interest to archivists and engineers. Many participants cited the need for scientifically tested and proven cleaning solutions, techniques for cleaning discs and cylinders, and more knowledge about the degradation mechanisms that affect cylinder recordings.

Additional study of magnetic tape properties as they relate to conservation is a priority for many archivists and engineers. A major threat to relatively recent (1970s–1990s) polyester-based magnetic tape is binder degradation, or hydrolysis, the breakdown of the "glue" that adheres the magnetic particles to the base physical carrier that serves as the tape backing. Tapes suffering hydrolysis, also called "sticky-shed syndrome," squeal when played. The most common remedy for hydrolysis is to bake the tape at low heat for several hours. However, many archivists question the effectiveness of baking and are fearful of possible long-term effects on the media baked. They wonder whether a better remedy might be found. Older, acetate-based tapes are at risk for a number of additional threats. Little is documented about acetate tape, which may exhibit symptoms similar to those of hydrolysis. It is known, however, that baking acetate tape will exacerbate the condition. Acetate tapes are subject to many other problems as well, largely undocumented. According to Richard Hess, a leading tape preservation engineer

> The biggest risk, but not yet a huge problem, for older tapes that used cellulose acetate as a base film is vinegar syndrome, which destroys the base film. This has been a huge problem with

[165] Testimony of Robert Heiber, president, Chace Audio, "Metadata" session, NRPB public hearings, November 29, 2006, Los Angeles.

> magnetic motion picture film (for sound—essentially thicker tape in film widths with sprockets). We are not sure if these mag films are an outlier or the "mine canary" for what will happen with the thinner, narrower acetate audiotapes.[166]

In a study conducted by the Image Permanence Institute at the University of Rochester, 17 institutions were surveyed on tape preservation. Survey responses "projected a sense that magnetic tape collections are not under strategic preservation control." The survey further confirmed the lack of quantitative data on the state of preservation of tape collections in the participating institutions and the difficulty of developing nondestructive testing methods for media. The institute did not discern what they termed "a general pattern" of tape deterioration. The study made three recommendations for magnetic tape preservation. The first is that tape collections could benefit from improved storage conditions. ("Proper storage is the single most important factor for preventing media decay throughout large collections. Providing cooler and drier storage conditions would increase the life span of tape collections while they await transfer.") Second, the study recommended that development of automated tape transfer should be supported. Finally, it recommended that priorities be established for transfer of magnetic tape recordings to new media.[167]

Research and publications related to the material science of sound recordings have contributed to the conservation of audio carriers. In 1959, the Library of Congress published *Preservation and Storage of Sound Recordings*, which described the results of research undertaken on the physical composition of discs and tapes, with analysis of the types of degradation that threaten each medium and recommendations for archival housings and storage.[168] The work, funded by the Rockefeller Foundation, was the first of its kind. Many of its conclusions still guide conservation of analog audio media. However, in light of subsequent research, some of its recommendations are no longer valid. The Library of Congress Preservation Research and Testing Division recently expanded its work related to recordings and conservation. The division is researching the use of Fourier Transform Infrared Spectroscopy (FTIR) to nondestructively test audiotapes for hydrolysis. The work is intended to identify sticky-shed tapes and the causes of that problem. Other audio-related work being undertaken in the division includes investigations into possible uses of portable FTIR devices by collection managers when prioritizing collections for preservation; studying magnetic

---

[166] Richard Hess contribution to ARSCLIST, August 27, 2008, "Tape Degradation (was ELP Turntable & earlier RIAA EQ software)." Archived at http://cool.conservation-us.org/byform/mailing-lists/arsclist/2008/08/msg00362.html. Mr. Hess's Web pages, at http://richardhess.com, include much information of potential value to holders of tape collections.

[167] Jean-Louis Bigourdan et al., *The Preservation of Magnetic Tape Collections*, 64. Available at http://www.imagepermanenceinstitute.org/shtml_sub/NEHTapeFinalReport.pdf.

[168] A. G. Pickett and M. M. Lemcoe, *Preservation and Storage of Sound Recordings* (Washington, DC.: Library of Congress, 1959).

media in changing environments, utilizing a scanning electron microscope; tracking error rates on compact discs; and continued collaboration with the developers of the IRENE system.

In discussions about incorporating more science into audio preservation, several participants at the second engineers' roundtable suggested formation of a national preservation advisory committee. The proposed group might guide research and provide support to justify new directions in preservation. An alternative suggestion, significantly more ambitious, was to establish a national media laboratory where preservation research would be centralized and conducted. Such a laboratory would focus on preservation science by developing and maintaining testing methods, assisting in the establishment of standards, and training new specialists.

CHAPTER 3

Development of Curricula in Recorded Sound Preservation and Archives Management

Introduction

A number of universities now offer academic-degree programs in film preservation and archives management. Audio preservation and archives management present a far less encouraging picture. While several universities offer courses that relate to audio preservation, none offers a degree program that trains professionals in audio preservation and archives management.[169] "Current preservation education within traditional library and archival studies programs," concludes one study, "does not provide adequate preparation in the areas of technical and managerial expertise to deal with the preservation of digital collections, audiovisual media, or visual materials."[170] Furthermore, the study notes, there is a need to integrate preservation education and training into graduate-degree programs rather than into workshops or seminars that "cannot adequately convey the theoretical knowledge, technical expertise, or scientific methods needed for certain jobs."[171]

---

[169] The 1994 plan for furthering film preservation prepared by the Library of Congress under the auspices of the National Film Preservation Board recommended a "systematic graduate program" for developing a cadre of film-preservation specialists. Three notable degree programs surfaced between 1996 and 2003—the L. Jeffrey Selznick School of Preservation at the George Eastman House (1996), the Moving Image Archival Studies program at the University of California, Los Angeles (2002), and the Moving Image Archiving and Preservation program at New York University (2003).

[170] Karen F. Gracy and Jean Ann Croft, *Quo Vadis, Preservation Education? A Study of Current Trends and Future Needs*, Pt. 1: Academic Institutions, 5. Available at http://www.sis.pitt.edu/~kgracy/Quo_Vadis_pt1.pdf. This study has greatly informed this chapter.

[171] Ibid., 12–13. Gracy and Croft theorize that the lack of integration of preservation into library information science programs may owe something to the fact that preservation is perceived to be a "collection of practical information and skills rather than a discipline grounded in theoretical knowledge and research."

This chapter focuses primarily on the development of degree programs in the underlying sciences and essential management practices of recorded sound preservation. But education, no matter how important, can serve only as a foundation. There are, and will be, further needs, including (1) dissemination of technical knowledge and practical experience with standards and evolving practices, (2) opportunities for continuing education to keep current with developments and new practices in the field, and (3) opportunities for professional development. As one witness remarked at a National Recording Preservation Board (NRPB) hearing, most archivists and librarians are only "paper trained" in the maintenance, monitoring, and migration of digital files because the digital realm is still new, and digital preservation encompasses a complex range of technical and management issues.[172]

The community of individuals familiar with legacy media is shrinking. A system must be developed to ensure that the generations of engineers and archivists who have had no experience with analog recording formats will gain familiarity with the physical properties of, and best methods for preserving, legacy media.

A group of audio preservation engineers attending a January 2004 meeting sponsored by the NRPB issued a list of recommendations that included research initiatives to investigate potential new methods for cleaning analog tapes and discs and for treating magnetic recording tape that has undergone hydrolysis. Other recommendations called for better methods of disseminating the results of research, such as developing a "Web-based clearinghouse for sharing information on how archives can develop digital preservation transfer programs" and initiating an effort to "collate relevant audio engineering standards from organizations."[173]

A common theme emerging from discussions in the field and from conversations with preservation managers, archivists, and engineers is that the introduction of recorded sound preservation and management programs at educational institutions, however necessary, is but a beginning. It will take time to develop university programs; broader initiatives for sharing knowledge cannot wait.

The NRPB commissioned the Kilgarlin Center for Preservation of the Cultural Record at the University of Texas at Austin's School of Information to compile a bibliography identifying and assessing the current literature for audio preservation. The compilation, which underscores the interdisciplinary nature of the recorded sound preservation field, is posted on the NRPB Web site.[174]

---

[172] Testimony of Adrian Cosentini, audio/preservation manager, New York Philharmonic Orchestra, NRPB public hearings, December 19, 2006, New York.

[173] For a complete list of task force recommendations, see *Capturing Analog Sound for Digital Preservation: Report of a Roundtable Discussion of Best Practices for Transferring Analog Discs and Tapes*. (Washington, DC: Council on Library and Information Resources and Library of Congress, 2006), 14. Available at http://www.clir.org/pubs/abstract/pub137abst.html.

[174] The bibliography is available at http://www.loc.gov/rr/record/nrpb/.

Scope and Objectives of Education in Recorded Sound Preservation

Programs at schools of library and information science (LIS) typically offer one course in preservation; a 2003 survey revealed that only two schools offered more than three courses, and more than 60 percent of the faculty teaching preservation courses were adjunct instructors.[175] These meager offerings reflect, in part, a broad, ongoing restructuring in the traditional LIS curriculum. The scope of the degree program is expanding. In fact, the word *library* is being used less and less in descriptions of degree programs. *Information science* or *information studies* are now the preferred terms, and some critics believe such programs place "undue emphasis on the creation and distribution of digital resources, subverting the original concerns and drives of the preservation agenda."[176]

The ascendance of digital media has dramatically altered the landscape for education in the traditional components of librarianship. These observations can be made:[177]

- In recent years, LIS programs have come to include coursework in information management and information technology (IT). Technologies in these fields are constantly advancing, and special efforts will be required to develop curricula that prepare students for rapidly changing workforce needs.
- The expected changes in the technologies associated with recorded sound preservation will require ongoing adjustments in library practices and in sound-archives management. It will be more important than ever that preservation managers and engineers keep abreast of technological developments associated with digital content creation and preservation. Continuing education, once regarded as potentially career-enhancing but optional, will become essential. Appropriate courses must be designed.
- The increasing number of obsolete analog media makes it even more urgent to develop degree programs in recorded sound preservation. Sound-preservation and sound-archives specialists should be familiar with the physical characteristics of legacy media to ensure that they can properly handle and store these materials as well as identify recordings in the most urgent need

[175] Gracy and Croft, *Quo Vadis*, 22. A survey response from 41 academic institutions found that "thirty-two schools currently [offer] preservation, however, almost sixty percent of them offer only one course (usually an introductory survey course), seven schools offer two courses, four schools offer three courses, and only two schools offer more than three courses."

[176] Ibid., 14–16. Concern that the management of digital resources might increasingly dominate librarianship and diminish the importance of preservation may have some foundation. Materials that have been reformatted from one analog medium to another and are kept in proper storage conditions with playback equipment available may not require attention for many years, if they are left undisturbed. In contrast, digital files will require cycling and continuous migration every five years or so to assure their integrity and accessibility.

[177] These observations are informed by a meeting held in Austin, Texas, July 20–21, 2006, and sponsored by the NRPB at the University of Texas Kilgarlin Center for Preservation of the Cultural Record. The purpose of the meeting was to identify the major elements and core knowledge to be taught in a master's degree or an advanced certificate program.

of attention. Familiarity with the characteristics of each format's sound—and the ceiling of expectations—is essential to good-quality transfers.

- A generation of specialists with experience in legacy media is disappearing, as is equipment on which to play analog recordings such as open-reel tape or wire recordings. Fewer and fewer people are familiar with the care and repair of older equipment. Many of these individuals are collectors or hobbyists, not necessarily academic or industry experts. This fund of knowledge and expertise is not being documented professionally and is not being passed on in any systematic way to individuals studying audio engineering and who will work with legacy formats in libraries and archives.
- Managers in institutions that hold a significant number of recordings will need a grounding in the history of the period of these recordings, the impact of recording technology, and the aesthetic and cultural impact of the recordings. Likewise, they will need to know enough about personages, recording artists, and the significance of the material recorded to make informed decisions about setting priorities for preservation activities.
- Managers will require much more than technical knowledge of recordings and a sense of history and culture. Directors of archives will increasingly require that such individuals have formal training in advanced management skills. These skills include organizational theory and behavior, contracting and project management, facilities planning, cost analysis, and budgeting.
- Meeting all these objectives may founder on one unavoidable truth: audio preservation work is neither an especially remunerative nor secure profession. Institutional funding for audio preservation is commonly very limited, and few professional positions are available. In addition, many positions at universities and other libraries and archives are funded by grants and have an uncertain time horizon.

The interpolation of audio preservation training into other degree programs may be the most promising approach to attracting individuals to audio preservation. At most schools, courses in recorded sound preservation are adjuncts to broader degree programs. Audio is often combined with "audiovisual" because better employment opportunities are thought to lie in the latter direction. The specialization that many students develop in audio is for studio recording and production, not preservation. This should not be surprising. Transfer work does not offer significant career-development potential; additionally, the work can be tedious. It could not be the sole focus of a degree program. Consequently, the field of recorded sound preservation would likely benefit significantly from graduate academic programs that combine technical, scientific, and managerial training, as well as instruction in the history of audio formats.

An additional option might be to establish a certificate program in preservation for audio technicians that could be an appropriate educational track for preservation transfer engineers. However, it is not clear that a graduate-level educational institution would want to offer a certificate program, and indeed, whether graduates of such a program alone would meet the needs of archives. Assurance of the preservation of our audio heritage will increasingly depend on professional engineers and archivists, but it is not apparent how large a workforce the market will be able to absorb in the near and mid term. It is likewise unknown how many institutions have the resources to meet the salary requirements of more than one or two graduate-degreed engineers and archivists. Most beneficial would be the creation of permanent positions with secure funding at libraries and archives with significant holdings of sound recordings.

Career tracks, salaries, and job security, as well as curricula, need to be rethought. Additional professionally trained reformatting engineers are essential to ensure that at-risk audio is reformatted to accepted archival standards. The 14 core competences in media analog capture outlined by audio preservation engineers at a roundtable meeting convened in January 2004 might well be met by a one- or two-year certificate program similar to that conducted for film archiving by Eastman House in Rochester, New York.[178] These core competencies represent the *technical* training required—necessary but possibly not sufficient. At the symposium, "The Great Migration: Audio Preservation in the Digital Age," held in November 2007," the director of a well-respected audio reformatting company was asked what he looked for in applicants for positions as preservation transfer engineer. His first priority was a broad background in the humanities and "Western civilization."

A prototype of a curriculum is described in the pages that follow. As will be seen, developing effective educational programs and courses of study requires not only mastery of the details of course content and syllabi but also an awareness of several broader considerations. Attention is paid elsewhere in this study to the physical media that have been the carriers of sound from the late-nineteenth to the late-twentieth centuries. Those who design degree programs must be mindful of how digitization has altered the landscape in the realm of recorded sound. It has become so simple to capture sound in a digital format that the hours of original sound recordings being generated each day are likely—from the point of view of the preservation community and its resources—to reach epic proportions.

Recording lacquers and quality audiotape were expensive; as a result, decisions were made about the value of making a recording before it was made, thus limiting the number of sound recordings and films created. With digitization, by contrast, the costs of creating moving-image and sound recordings are negligible. Now, recordings may be made with little forethought; decisions about their worth come after the fact. Individuals are now recording the sounds and images of their daily lives with inexpensive, handheld digital equipment. This digital information is then transferred to physical storage and becomes subject to all the vulnerabilities that necessitate

---

[178] *Capturing Analog Sound for Digital Preservation*, 15–16.

preservation attention. Audio archivists will need to be able to select what is of sufficient cultural or aesthetic value to be worth the cost of preservation.

Individuals entering the field of information management will need a background in the humanities. Archivists will need to be culturally and historically literate to make selection decisions, and such literacy cannot be gained strictly in the classroom. Managers will require such literacy to understand how collections are used and to help devise means by which potential users can identify or discover audio of interest. Discrete born-digital sound media (that is, sound not embedded in Web sites or other mixed media) will be easier and less expensive to reformat than analog audio; the process might be better described as transcoding than as reformatting. Once processes are established for specific hardware and source file formats, and quality assurance practices are built into the processes, migration of the bits requires significantly less real-time monitoring, or none at all. However, adequately organizing born-digital sound, whether through catalog records, finding aids, or new means of descriptive access, will require cultural literacy, creativity, and innovation, as well as knowledge of standard archival practices.

The preservation task will be facilitated by archivists who have a keen sense of the audience for their sound collections and who can anticipate emerging interests. Historians are using audio recordings to a greater extent than ever before. "Audio studies" or "sound studies" has emerged as a serious field of cultural study. Audio archivists must keep abreast of fields of study related to their collections and of the developing audiences for such collections. Even publicly funded archives may advance preservation objectives by building constituencies and cultivating current patrons of targeted collections. The tie between preservation and access, as well as the constant evolution and emergence of new distribution models, requires that archive managers continually assess technologies and processes for access in order to meet new demands and to anticipate new markets. Those who design educational programs will need to emphasize that today's archivists can no longer be passive and can no longer regard their tasks as strictly technical.

Designing a Curriculum

As noted earlier in this chapter, the Library of Congress, under the auspices of the NRPB, commissioned the Kilgarlin Center for Preservation of the Cultural Record to convene a task force to identify the extent of current educational opportunities in "audio archiving, engineering and preservation."[179] The task force intended that the identification of core knowledge and skills, as well as the names designated for the three educational and professional tracks described

[179] The full text, *Report of a Task Force Discussion to Define Prerequisites, Core Knowledge, and Graduate Educational Directions for Sound Preservation Professionals, and to Review an Annotated Bibliography of Audio Preservation Resources*, appears as Appendix B to this report.

below, be a hypothetical design that might launch discussion and inspire refinement.

The technology for capturing sound is now 130 years old. A major premise of the task force's deliberations was that preserving that sound requires a cadre of specialists, including archivists, preservation managers, and engineers at all levels. There can "no longer be universal specialists," the report notes. Toward that end, the task force set out to identify the knowledge and skill sets that a curriculum in the field would need to provide.

Parsing those skills among different paths of training is not easy. The task force report notes:

> Those who develop, catalog and reference sound collections and those who manage their preservation have overlapping knowledge requirements. Likewise, audio preservation managers need to have a solid grounding in the work of audio preservation engineers. However, for the nation's vast store of small sound collections held in archives, libraries and museums, one audio professional may need to know a good bit about all aspects of the field.

In sum, professionals will need to have a varying blend of theoretical, managerial, and technical skills. The objectives of effective management and preservation of sound cannot be achieved if management and technical skills are entirely divided.

At present, very few training opportunities are directed toward preservation engineers and preservation managers. Most individuals in the field gained their initial training as recording engineers before migrating to preservation fields, or obtained degrees in LIS or the humanities and learned audio-reformatting techniques on the job. Task force members noted that, given the complexities of digital audio technology, the fast rate of change, and the enormous body of works in need of preservation, the field requires professionals trained specifically to manage and preserve audio archives.

Before setting out a hypothetical curriculum, task force members identified knowledge and experience that might be considered prerequisites to entering a master's degree or certificate program. Among these were a comfort zone in the hard sciences (mathematics, chemistry, and physics); knowledge of acoustics and the associated technology (for preservationists); critical-listening skills; an ability to communicate both orally and in writing; and—ideally—relevant experiences in ethnomusicology, oral history, radio, or music.

While some of these areas could be incorporated into the degree program, the task force expressed hope that students would eventually possess higher-level prerequisite knowledge and skills at the time they enter their education and training programs.

As described in detail below, the task force created three educational tracks, each of which shares some elements with the others. The program for the *audio preservation engineer* focuses on training in audio transfer. The *audio archivist* and *audio preservation manager* will apply additional skills and practices in cataloging, storage of audio materials, prioritizing work, and planning for the periodic migration of digital sound files. These individuals are likely to be vested with management and decision-making responsibilities; they must also have a grounding in cultural literacy and history. Finally, they must have the motivation and curiosity to stay abreast of current affairs and sociocultural developments.

The two managerial positions—audio archivist and audio preservation manager—are not hierarchical with respect to one another. Neither is more likely than the other to launch a candidate into the directorship of a major archives or library. The intention of the task force was to design educational and career tracks that would help spawn a leadership cadre.

1. Audio Archivist: The task force included in this track not just archivists but also librarians and curators of recorded sound collections. The archivist's training would include both "practical and theoretical" education as well as prerequisites to a "broad and versatile background." The latter would include some knowledge of history so that the archivist could assess the relative significance of sound collections for both acquisition and preservation.

Core knowledge and skills of the audio archivist would include the following:

- appreciation of the historical and philosophical underpinnings—the "why" behind preservation;
- a foundation in recorded sound, including the science, technology, and structure of sound carriers and their audio properties;
- understanding of storage and environmental requirements;
- ability to set priorities for and match resources to best protect and preserve specific collections;
- mastery of techniques of reformatting analog recordings for preservation;
- understanding of the requirements of metadata systems to ensure that metadata are comprehensive and accessible to other institutions;
- ability to maintain the integrity of digital files; and
- collection-management skills, including archival processing; knowledge of copyright and intellectual property law, cost analysis and budgeting, and project management; ability to write grant proposals; and a range of human resources skills.

2. Audio Preservation Manager: The task force agreed on the need for a new type of audio preservation specialist, to be called an audio preservation manager. Members concurred that a master's degree curriculum designed to teach preservation management of recorded sound would need to be broad and "well-rounded," including courses in administration, materials science, and technology. Such a curriculum would prepare audio preservation managers to oversee decision making and to address the wide-ranging preservation needs of recorded sound collections. Task force members concurred that larger college and university communities would be best suited to provide the necessary breadth of coursework in the humanities and sciences as well as in LIS. Such institutions are also more likely to have audio collections that could provide a laboratory environment for applying skills learned in the classroom. A certificate of advanced study might accompany the LIS master's degree to signify that the student has satisfactorily completed additional study in audio preservation and collection management.

Core knowledge and skills would include many of those noted earlier for the audio archivist. For example, a basic familiarity with recording transfer is essential to supervise engineers and to maintain quality control.

Additional areas of training for the audio preservation manager would include, among others:

- ability to assess technology and to design a reformatting lab;
- comprehensive knowledge of administrative and technical metadata; and
- thorough grounding in digital archiving, including media refreshment, conversion, format and metadata repositories, and authentication.

3. Audio Preservation Engineer: Education and training for this position would draw largely from the sciences to develop professionals skilled in the science of transferring analog sound to digital formats for preservation. The task force noted that recorded sound transfer, although informed by science, is also an art, requiring acute listening skills and a basic understanding of and sensitivity to the programs to be preserved. Also required are familiarity with electrical engineering, acoustics, and psychoacoustics, along with an ability to apply this knowledge to specific analog formats. Preparing individuals to follow this track would best be accomplished in a large, interdisciplinary academic community that could also provide laboratory opportunities.

Core knowledge and skills for the audio preservation engineer would include training in the foundations of recorded sound and preservation, with targeted courses in techniques for preservation and reformatting of audio, audio engineering, digital archiving, equipment-maintenance needs, and creation of metadata. One of the challenges in curriculum design may be integrating coursework in support of audio preservation with at least some coursework in library science.

Doctoral Studies. The report notes a need for "empirical and theoretical scholarship" to further recorded sound preservation objectives. Task force members underscored a need for the LIS discipline to support doctoral study in the field of preservation. Potential areas for advanced research are included in the task force report.

CHAPTER 4

Preservation, Access, and Copyright: A Tangled Web

Introduction

The basis of copyright law in the United States lies in a constitutional mandate to "promote the progress of Science and useful Arts, by securing for limited Times to Authors and Inventors the exclusive Right to their respective Writings and Discoveries." U.S. copyright law grants broad rights to creators and producers but also includes provisions intended to further preservation and fair use of copyrighted materials. Many contributors to this study, however, believe that recorded sound preservation in the United States is critically affected by restrictions and limitations, as well as by the range of exclusive rights outlined in U.S. copyright law.

To a significant degree, copyright law has been overtaken by developments in digital technologies that have rendered obsolete decades-old conventions relating to the creation and distribution of sound. One consequence of this obsolescence is that the copyright laws now in force in the United States place public policy at odds with furthering and accelerating recorded sound preservation. There are few obstacles, other than resources, to a copyright holder preserving its own recorded sound property. However, current law fosters significant conflict between the institutions with primary responsibility for preserving the nation's recorded sound heritage and the legitimate interests of intellectual property and copyright owners who face the growing challenge of protecting their property from piracy and other forms of illegal use.

The inherent relationship of copyright law to recorded sound preservation is not obvious to the public or to policy makers. The impact of copyright law on the preservation of, and access to, sound recordings was of concern to Congress when it mandated that the National Recording Preservation Board (NRPB) of the Library of Congress explore the issues within this recording preservation study, as specified in Section 124 (b) of the National Recording Preservation Act of 2000. Among the issues addressed in that section, two relate directly to copyright law and its effect on preservation and public access. Quoting the language of the act, these issues are

> 4. Current laws and restrictions regarding the use of archives of sound recordings, including recommendations for changes in such laws and restrictions to enable the Library of Congress and other non-profit institutions in the field of sound recording preservation to make their collections available to researchers in a digital format.
>
> 5. Copyright and other laws applicable to the preservation of sound recordings.[180]

The need to address copyright law while working collaboratively with rights owners is further mandated in the act, which directs the Librarian of Congress to

> implement a comprehensive national sound recording preservation program, in conjunction with other sound recording archivists, educators and historians, copyright owners, recording industry representatives, and others involved in activities related to sound recording preservation, and taking into account studies conducted by the [National Recording Preservation] Board.[181]

Additionally, the act directs that a number of specific activities be carried out under this national preservation program, including the requirements to

> 1. coordinate activities to assure that efforts of archivists and copyright owners, and others in the public and private sector, are effective and complementary [...]
>
> 3. increase accessibility of sound recordings for educational purposes.[182]

Most U.S. Sound Recordings Are Protected through 2067 and Beyond

The uncoordinated development of federal and state copyright law, as it relates to sound recordings and the works interpreted on them, has caused confusion for more than a century. This confusion stems from the unique status of sound recordings within federal copyright law. Published sound recordings did not come under federal copyright protection until February 15, 1972; unpublished sound recordings made after that date received federal protection in 1978; and foreign sound recordings made at any time received federal copyright protection starting in 1996. All U.S. recordings, both commercially released and unpublished, created before February 15, 1972,

---

[180] *National Recording Preservation Act of 2000*, Public Law 106-474, 106th Cong., Sec. 124 (b) (4) and (5).

[181] Public Law 106-474, Sec. 111 (a).

[182] Public Law 106-474, Sec. 111 (b) (1) and (3).

are protected by a complex network of disparate state civil, criminal, and common laws.[183] Accordingly, sound recordings are unique among all creative works in the United States insofar as the effective term of copyright protection for even the oldest U.S. recordings, dating from the late nineteenth century, will not end until the year 2067 at the earliest (i.e., 95 years after the placement of sound recordings under federal protection in 1972). Thus, a published U.S. sound recording created in 1890 will not enter the public domain until 177 years after its creation, constituting a term of rights protection 82 years longer than that of all other forms of audiovisual works made for hire.[184]

Studies to Date

Recognizing the unique nature of recorded sound copyrights, especially for early and historic recordings where preservation and access concerns are the most vital, the NRPB commissioned three studies examining copyright and other rights as they pertain to various categories of pre-1972 recordings. These studies included publications on

1. issues relating to the digital preservation and dissemination of pre-1972 commercial sound recordings,[185]
2. the preservation and dissemination of unpublished pre-1972 recordings,[186] and
3. the impact of laws in 10 states on the use of sound recordings.[187]

These reports analyze complex legal issues in detail and are integral components of this study. They provide a foundation of legal assessment for this chapter's analysis of how copyright issues often conflict with and can discourage library and archival best practices for preservation and access.[188]

---

[183] Peter B. Hirtle, "Copyright Term and the Public Domain in the United States," http://copyright.cornell.edu/resources/publicdomain.cfm.

[184] 17 U.S.C. Section 301(c). If the recording was unpublished, it would still not enter the public domain until 57 years after other unpublished works became freely available.

[185] June M. Besek, *Copyright Issues Relevant to Digital Preservation and Dissemination of Pre-1972 Commercial Sound Recordings by Libraries and Archives* (Washington, DC: Council on Library and Information Resources and Library of Congress, 2005).

[186] June M. Besek, *Copyright and Related Issues Relevant to Digital Preservation and Dissemination of Unpublished Pre-1972 Sound Recordings by Libraries and Archives* (Washington, DC: Council on Library and Information Resources and Library of Congress, 2009).

[187] Program on Information Justice and Intellectual Property, Washington College of Law, American University, under the supervision of Peter Jaszi with the assistance of Nick Lewis, *Protection for Pre-1972 Sound Recordings Under State Law and Its Impact on Use by Nonprofit Institutions: A 10-State Analysis* (Washington, DC: Council on Library and Information Resources and Library of Congress, 2009).

[188] The FY2009 Omnibus Appropriations Act (P.L. 111-8) directs the U.S. Copyright Office to conduct a study on the "desirability of and means for bringing sound recordings fixed before February 15, 1972, under federal jurisdiction." The study, to be delivered to Congress not later than two years from the enactment in March 2009 of the bill, is to cover "the effect of federal coverage on the preservation of such sound recordings, the effect on public access to those recordings, and the economic impact of federal coverage on rights holders. The study is also to examine the means for accomplishing such coverage." Its release is certain to also inform and figure into any debate over amending U.S. copyright law.

Resolving the conflicts between copyright law and recorded sound preservation entails the consideration of issues that are even more sensitive in the digital environment than they were in the analog era.[189] These issues include unauthorized file sharing, performing rights, and Internet transmissions and dissemination. But many of the statutes intended to protect intellectual property owners from violation of their rights have unintentionally created an unnecessarily restrictive environment for preservation. The problems analyzed in this chapter include assessments of how

- elements of current copyright law are incompatible with best practices for digital preservation;
- copyright law and regulation do not provide libraries, archives, and museums with sufficient latitude to preserve and furnish copies of recordings for research and educational use;
- the lack of clarity in the law creates a threat of litigation that imposes a self-limiting atmosphere and prevents legitimate uses of sound recordings by cultural institutions to further their educational and research missions;
- the ability to provide wide access encourages the preservation of historically, culturally, and aesthetically significant audio materials;
- copyright considerations limiting access discourage private collectors from donating major collections to public institutions because of the perception that recordings held by institutions are less accessible than those in private hands; and
- the study of the nation's social and cultural history is adversely affected by the terms of protection provided sound recordings under current copyright law.

Preservation and Access

Because the interests of preservation and access have become joined, it might seem that the objectives of both should be mutually reinforcing. But copyright law may stall or imperil both, with the result that access becomes irrelevant for sound recordings that are lost for want of preservation.

Before the advent of digital technologies, it was assumed that research access to analog recordings would take place only on-site: to hear a rare or unique recording, one had to visit the institution where it was held. Duplication of recordings was cumbersome and inherently limited and time-consuming because it had to be carried out in real time. Additionally, the fidelity of every subsequent analog generation was poorer than that of its predecessor generation, much as the sharpness of a document declines with every successive photocopy.

Today, the ease with which digital audio files can be created and transferred has fed a growing expectation for instant access to sound

[189] In such a climate, it will not be surprising if some criticize this study for being overly acquiescent with the status quo and "soft" on copyright, while others declare that it demonizes copyright holders and is dismissive of their legitimate interests.

recordings held by archives and subsequent personal, on-demand listening. Because institutions frequently do not hold rights to the sound recordings in their collections and cannot make the material accessible, the likelihood increases that they will find it even more difficult to attract the resources needed to preserve important collections in the first place. A 2004 report published by the Council on Library and Information Resources notes that

> although the right to preserve and the right to make accessible are legally distinct, preservation reformatting is so labor-intensive that it makes sense for institutions to do it only if access is foreseen in the near term. ... Some digital distribution rights are therefore necessary to provide incentives for preservation investment. In the academic setting, this means distribution for fair use.[190]

The broad accessibility of digital technologies in the late twentieth and early twenty-first centuries has fostered a widespread and passionate debate among communities with an interest in sound recordings—the sound recording industry, rights holders, scholars, consumers, and legislators. Creation and duplication of digital sound recording files is widespread. Recordings can be acquired through legal, licensed online purchases, but they may also be shared through *ripping*, i.e., using unauthorized, often illegal, methods to capture and then disseminate sound files over the Internet.[191]

Some individuals, groups, and Web site managers knowingly violate copyright law and make in-print, protected recordings available free from Web sites, incurring significant losses of revenue to performers, composers, and recording companies. A majority of those who make historical sound recordings available on the Internet likely have no familiarity with copyright law; they assume that recordings from the late nineteenth and early twentieth centuries, owing to their age, are in the public domain. But the chain of misunderstanding does not end there. Some Internet users mistakenly assume that if they can access a work on the Internet (works generally regarded as older and thought to be unavailable) it is in the public domain. They do not understand that the public domain constitutes the aggregate of works not protected by copyright law; it has nothing to do with the setting in which a work appears.

Rights holders support the interests of preservation in principle, but their concerns over protection of intellectual property have magnified since digital technologies have made possible the

---

[190] Abby Smith, David Randal Allen, and Karen Allen, *Survey of the State of Audio Collections in Academic Libraries* (Washington, DC: Council on Library and Information Resources, 2004), 16.

[191] *Ripping* is the use of computers, digital technology, and software to create MP3 or other relatively small and easily transferable, compressed files from commercial compact discs. Free software to "rip" CDs is included with home computer music playback and file organization applications such as iTunes and Windows Media Player. The software often includes an advisory that the software should be used strictly for capture and copying within the law. In short, the means to capture and make copies of sound recordings may or may not be illegal; it is the purpose for which the software is used that may violate copyright law.

near-instantaneous distribution of sound recordings. When users have an ill-informed sense of entitlement to immediate access, the scene is set for the perfect storm. At the center of this storm are librarians, archivists, and curators, who find themselves faced with responsibilities for preserving culturally important sound recordings for posterity and for serving their constituents (or meeting funding requirements) by making those recordings accessible.

In some cases, institutions and individuals who try to comply with copyright law may find themselves violating it—or at least pushing the envelope—if they attempt to preserve at-risk recordings and make out-of-print works available for what they regard to be defensible purposes. No focused thought has been given to whether these purposes are, in fact, permitted by copyright law. In other instances, copyright law governing sound recordings, especially those made before 1972, is so complex that it seems impenetrable. In still other cases, librarians and archivists simply believe the law is overly prohibitive. Finally, expertise to interpret the law may be unavailable or beyond the means of the institution in need of consultation. When even responsible individuals and institutions cannot find clear guidance in law owing to its complexity, it becomes increasingly likely that the law will be inadvertently broken or, at the other extreme, interpreted in an unnecessarily restrictive manner. In the perception of the public, copyright law has a reputation for being overly restrictive. This perception fosters a dismissive attitude toward the law in communities that can hardly be characterized as rogue elements of society. An individual representing one institution has noted that, unless or until instructed to cease and desist certain practices, his organization was compelled to "fly under the radar" to support its mission.

Launching an audio preservation program staffed with trained individuals and equipped with the proper tools requires a significant up-front investment. Establishing and maintaining repositories to sustain the resultant digital copies requires additional investment. For these reasons, external funding is often essential. It is virtually impossible, however, to attract grants and donors to support preservation of collections that will not be accessible once preservation occurs. Access is often crucial to attracting support for the preservation of specific collections or recordings. As a study conducted for CLIR noted, "In the digital realm, where ready access drives demand for use, putting more audio on-line must be one of the core strategies to drive the demand for preservation."[192]

The competing interests of copyright compliance and recorded sound preservation become apparent if the agenda of archivists is set against the provisions of copyright law. While copyright law does not absolutely prohibit archivists from digitizing analog commercial recordings on legacy media, many view the conditions under which many of these activities are permissible as narrow and antithetical to preservation best practices. The NRPB's public hearings on audio

[192] Smith, Allen, and Allen 2004, 21.

preservation revealed a number of copyright-related concerns of archivists, educators, record industry executives, collectors, and the public. Priority recommendations included the following:

1. to use sound recordings for educational purposes without violating the Digital Millennium Copyright Act (DMCA)[193];
2. to enable archives to share copies of digitized sound recordings among themselves for the purpose of eliminating redundant efforts to preserve commercial recordings held in many institutions or existing in multiple copies, and, in so doing, assure that as many legacy recordings as possible can be saved and be made publicly accessible in digital formats;
3. to harmonize the term of protection for sound recordings with that of other intellectual property formats, and to explore possible benefits of harmonizing U.S. and European terms of protection;
4. to foster better methods of identifying rights holders for proposed uses of sound recordings that require prior authorization from rights holders;
5. to make out-of-print and/or orphan recordings available to the public over the Internet;
6. to permit making copies of recordings before their sound quality has deteriorated;
7. to clarify the legal definition of "obsolete" media to allow application of routine archival best-practice standards to preservation reformatting of legacy analog media; and
8. to extend fair-use provisions to pre-1972 recordings as national policy.

Copyright and Access

In commissioning this study in P.L. 106-474, Congress directed that focus be given to "current laws and restrictions regarding the use of archives of sound recordings, including recommendations for changes in such laws and restrictions to enable the Library of Congress and other nonprofit institutions in the field of sound recording preservation to make their collections available to researchers in a digital format." Many of those submitting written statements or oral testimony to the authors of this study agreed about the importance of access. In hearings held in Los Angeles, one participant stated forcibly, "The preservation of music is meaningless if this music is not accessible."[194]

---

[193] In mid-2009, record companies and Internet distributors announced plans to create "virtual" albums: multisound packages for downloading that might include album notes, art, lyrics, photographs, and videos. If digital rights management is applied to these virtual albums, efforts to preserve them in their entirety could be in violation of DMCA provisions. See, for example, Matthew Garrahan, "Apple Joins Forces with Record Labels," *Financial Times*, July 27, 2009, available at http://www.ft.com/cms/s/0/28129982-7a18-11de-b86f-00144feabdc0.html?nclick_check=1; Casey Johnston, "iTunes store to add enhanced liner notes, extra media to album purchases," July 27, 2009, available at http://www.tuaw.com/2009/07/27/itunes-store-to-add-enhanced-liner-notes-extra-media-to-album-p/; Ryan Nakashima, Will iTunes 'Cocktail' Juice Album Sales? Linux Insider, July 28, 2009.

[194] Testimony of Jasper DeAntonio, November 29, 2006.

Treatment of Sound Recordings under U.S. Copyright Law

The term of legal protection for U.S. sound recordings, in comparison with that for all other copyright-protected works, is unprecedented in length—from the beginnings of recorded sound in the nineteenth century until 2067, when federal law will preempt state and common law protections. Some individuals and groups are concerned that, in keeping with the recent trend to extend the term of U.S. copyright protection for other media, pressure will be sustained to extend the 2067 date of federal preemption even further.[195]

Liability for copyright and common-law infringements may occur regardless of whether money is exchanged for sound recordings. The present system of long-term legal protections for sound recordings does not take into account varying degrees of historic interest in individual recordings or wide-ranging inequities in their economic value. For example, a scholar researching the history of vaudeville might have a strong interest in hearing recordings made by the first vaudevillians—recordings that came before the recording horn. These performers may have been headliners in their time, but today their names are virtually unknown. While scholarly interest in these recordings is high, their economic value to the property holder is negligible. However, legal restrictions governing access to a cylinder produced in 1909 are the same as those governing a compact disc made in 2009, even though it is highly unlikely that the 1909 recording has any revenue potential for the rights holder.

A study commissioned by the NRPB found that "rights holders appear to have few real-world commercial incentives to reissue many of their most significant recordings." In *Survey of Reissues of U.S. Recordings*, survey researcher and historian Tim Brooks reviewed a sample of 1,521 recordings made between 1890 and 1964 and found that rights owners have made available 14 percent of historic recordings that they control.[196] The percentages are small in early periods; they approach 35 percent after 1954. Decisions by labels to allow titles they control to go out of print are often based on the demographic of the potential audience for these recordings: each generation seems to develop a sense of nostalgia for the music of its late youth and early adulthood. This does not bode well for the reissue of recordings that have already passed out of the realm of lived experience. This will progressively discourage the reissue of early sound recordings, irrespective of their historic importance.[197]

The term of copyright for sound recordings in the European Union (EU) creates an interesting twist. Sound recordings in Europe

---

[195] John Bloom, "Right and Wrong: The Copy-right Infringement," National Review Online, November 22, 2002. Available at http://www.nationalreview.com/comment/comment-bloom112202.asp.

[196] In his sample, Brooks chose to include recordings in which scholars, students, and the general public have shown the greatest interest, as documented by their inclusion in widely used discographies in several fields of music and speech. See Tim Brooks, *Survey of Reissues of U.S. Recordings* (Washington, DC: Council on Library and Information Resources and Library of Congress, 2005), 3. Available at http://www.clir.org/pubs/abstract/pub133abst.html.

[197] Ibid., 7-8.

are protected for 50 years. Brooks discovered, among his sample, that while 14 percent of historical U.S. recordings have been made available by rights holders, an additional 22 percent of historical U.S. recordings are available on European or unauthorized domestic releases. The percentage availability is skewed to earlier periods no longer protected by copyright in Europe. In virtually every category or genre of music, more historic recordings are made available by non-rights holders than by rights holders for every period up to 1945.

This suggests that while rights holders may deem that there is insufficient market for them to even meet the expenses of reissuing their historic catalog, interest in their early catalogs is still sufficiently high to encourage non-rights holders to try to make the material available. Current U.S. copyright law drives this activity overseas.[198] The lack of harmonization between the copyright term for sound recordings in the United States and those in Europe has created conflict as well.

The *Gowers Review of Intellectual Property*, a study commissioned by the British government to review a proposal to extend the term of copyright protection from 50 years to 95 years (both retroactively and prospectively), concluded that such an extension was not supported by economic analysis. The study noted, "In a system where all works receive maximum protection for the maximum term, the vast majority of works remain in copyright despite not being economically viable for the rights holder."[199] Proponents of the extension argued that it would reduce the disparity between performers/producers and composers, who have protection for life plus 70 years. Proponents also maintained that extending the term would provide an incentive to invest in new music and encourage right holders to make works available to the public.[200] While the effort to extend the copyright term for sound recordings in the EU is moving forward, proposals under consideration do not provide retroactive protection. Recordings made prior to 1959 would, in the EU, remain in the public domain.

The Gowers study concluded that most sales of sound recordings occur in the first 10 years after their initial release, and that "only a small percentage continue to generate income, both from sales and royalty payments, for the entire duration of copyright. ... Extension would only raise revenue for a small minority of sound recordings, keeping the vast majority locked up." Securing rights and clearances is already extremely difficult in many cases. Under some scenarios, Gowers suggests, protection could even hurt creators because of the difficulty in securing rights from estates and heirs and in

[198] Ibid., 8, 9, 14.

[199] Andrew Gowers, *Gowers Review of Intellectual Property* (November 2006), 52 (pdf p. 57). Available at www.hm-treasury.gov.uk/d/pbr06_gowers_report_755.pdf. The proposal to extend the copyright term, initially defeated, was revived in late 2008.

[200] Ibid., 49 (pdf p. 54). The author cites a study by PricewaterhouseCoopers, *The Impact of Copyright Extension for Sound Recordings in the UK* (2006), which found that, owing to the contractual relationships struck between performers and labels that require performers to compensate the record company for its investment, few performers collect royalties. "Eighty percent of albums never recoup costs so no royalties are paid to the creator," the study reported.

identifying the rights holders.[201] No comparable economic study has been conducted in the United States.

Rights and Access to Recorded Sound Collections

Access to sound recordings is also affected by whether the holding institution controls the rights to make a recording available in the first place. The existence of digital technology can make it unnecessary for someone wishing to hear a unique or hard-to-find sound recording to travel to the library or archive holding that recording. But sharing preserved audio files is illegal under the current law.

The rights to share files may sometimes not be conferred when a major collection is deposited with, or acquired by, an institution and archives. In such cases, the recordings may be listened to only onsite. Wider access might be facilitated if rights holders could be persuaded that their intellectual property was not at risk. A respondent to one survey remarked, "It does not make sense to catalog anything until we are sure that we will be able to use it."[202]

Policies restricting access have broad implications for the publication and dissemination of research. Hearings conducted for this study revealed concern from representatives of the academic community as well as of the public. "What good is a book about music if you cannot hear the music?" remarked one scholar.[203] A written submission noted that doctoral work "is expected not only to be publishable, but indeed to be published." Academic presses often require that authors secure necessary rights; graduate students are unlikely to have the resources to secure them. "For this growing group of scholars, the result is a need to reconceptualize the [research] project, often in ways that dilute its academic merits and impact, as time and productivity pressures demand that something come from this work, and quickly."[204]

A survey of educators reported a consensus that "the music has to be heard repeatedly in the whole of the work, phrase by phrase, or note by note," and that researchers must be able to manipulate the sound with the ability to "stop and start, slow down and speed up and even divide the music into layers."[205] This same survey recommended creation of a "unified database of property rights associated with sound recordings to facilitate the location of rights holders."[206]

Some believe that rights holders should be required to register online to maintain protection of older sound recordings. U.S. and international laws have eliminated such formalities as a requirement

---

[201] Ibid., 54.

[202] Smith, Allen, and Allen 2004, 15.

[203] Testimony of Clifford Murphy, Ph.D. candidate in ethnomusicology, Brown University, "Copyright and Academic Research" session, National Recording Preservation Board public hearings, December 19, 2006, New York.

[204] Statement submitted to the National Recording Preservation Board by Thomas G. Porcello, associate professor, anthropology, and director, Media Studies Program, Vassar College.

[205] Nancy Davenport, "Obstacles to Access and Preservation of Recorded Sound." See Appendix C to this study, 157.

[206] Ibid., 160.

for copyright protection. However, a database of rights holders—even one in which inclusion is voluntary—could help users of historical recordings identify rights holders and conceivably reduce piracy by individuals who were unable to identify them. Such a database might be particularly useful in identifying rights holders of recordings made prior to 1972, for which no copyright registration database exists because such recordings were not eligible for federal protection.

Academics will argue that in most cases, the sound recordings of interest, despite their cultural significance, are of little economic value to the copyright owners. One witness at the hearings, a doctoral candidate in ethnomusicology engaged in the study of country music in New England, lamented that many regional recordings protected under copyright have not been reissued. These recordings, the witness noted, "are part of the historical and traditional fabric of our nation's regional cultures. Indeed, by choosing not to reissue regional recordings or vernacular musics, copyright holders are doing damage to regional culture and are essentially denying America's working class ... and ethnic communities access to their own expressive culture." He also noted that contemporary artists may have no knowledge whatsoever of the decades-long history of the vernacular style that accounts, in part, for their style of performance today; in effect, they are unaware of the tradition that has spawned them. Additionally, perceptions of the origins and geography of vernacular styles are shaped by what is commercially available. It is difficult to unravel this history if vernacular recordings are not available for study and listening. There are some fee-based online services that make accessible otherwise-unavailable recordings. Although these services could be useful to researchers, they are inaccessible to individuals who cannot afford to subscribe or who are not close to an institution that is a subscriber.[207]

As an alternative, audio files can be *streamed*, that is, made available for audition, but not downloading, over the Internet. Streaming could make collections accessible on campuses and to the public without the legal and licensing hurdles required to make a recording for sale, because listening to streamed files does not entail the creation of a personal copy for the user.[208] Under present law, a free streaming service of pre-1972 published recordings might be an efficient means to make holdings more accessible than they are at present. State laws restricting unauthorized use of pre-1972 recordings do not address streaming. However, if the underlying work of a recording (e.g., a musical composition) is protected by copyright, performance of that work, which streaming encompasses, might require licensing from the rights holder. In the case of radio broadcast and other unpublished recordings, rights holders might include not only music publishers, composers, and lyricists, but also scriptwriters, nonmusical talent, broadcast networks, sponsors, and members of

[207] Testimony of Clifford Murphy, December 19, 2006.

[208] Streamed files are written to discs as buffered copies and are temporary; some rights holders, however, have proposed that they are entitled to compensation for the creation of the temporary, buffer copies. The issue is not fully resolved.

professional unions contributing to the broadcast, such as members of the American Federation of Musicians.[209] June Besek addressed the copyright issues related to preservation and streaming of pre-1972 published and unpublished works in the two reports she wrote for the NRPB. It is recommended that these reports be read in conjunction with this study.[210]

Rights and Access: Impact on Fund-Raising for Audio Preservation

Testimony at the NRPB hearings indicated that expectations of access can help drive the selection of recordings to be preserved, but that this focus can be to the detriment of recordings with greater access restrictions. The perception that recordings held by institutions are unlikely to be accessible (even if properly stored and physically protected) discourages the deposit of collections with institutions and is detrimental to cultural conservation. Further testimony about rare recordings that are extant but not found in public archives revealed that "a vast number of these [very rare and culturally significant] recordings in fact are in private hands [only]. And one of the reasons they are in private hands is that those who hold them realize in many cases that once they go into an institutional setting, they will no longer be available or certainly no longer be freely available."[211]

For sound recordings in a specific collection that need preservation, there is no distinction between those that are legally accessible and those that are not: both are in jeopardy of being lost. Potential funders of recorded sound preservation projects may, however, draw a distinction. Collections in greater need of preservation may not receive funding support if they are to remain unavailable for off-site listening once preserved. A submission from Columbia University to the NRPB hearings describes access as absolutely crucial:

> For many libraries [sound preservation] is a very expensive proposal, and the only way to justify it (and/or get funding for it) is thanks to what I like to call the trump card of digital: greatly increased access. Severe copyright restrictions are the wrench that can derail the whole system, so materials are not digitized.[212]

Whether or not a collection will be broadly accessible, once digitized, may be the deciding factor for funding agencies that are interested in supporting that collection's preservation. As was noted in testimony before the NRPB

> with limited dollars to fund preservation work in ... a myriad of formats, if a given amount of money can fund the digitization

---

[209] "Rights issues for these things just make your head swim," remarked one participant at the preservation hearings.

[210] See footnotes 185 and 186 for citations.

[211] Testimony of Tim Brooks, "Copyright and Academic Research" session, NRPB public hearings, December 19, 2006, New York.

[212] Statement submitted to the National Recording Preservation Board by Marcos Sueiro Bal, Preservation Division, Columbia University Libraries. Available at www.loc.gov/rr/record/nrpb/pdf/bal.pdf.

> of a collection of public domain photographs from the 1920s that can be put online for millions of people to see and use, or to fund a dark archive of audio recordings that need preservation but can't be distributed online, the choice is clear. With limited funds, a greater impact can be made today by funding the preservation of materials that can be put online versus materials that would have to be listened to in the reading room of an archive or copied after securing permission from the copyright holder, [if even known]. … Ten years ago, researchers ... expected to have to travel [to repositories] and use the materials on-site. Today, online distribution is the norm for preservation projects. Increasingly, materials that are not online are going to be used less than other materials and use is largely the determining factor in what gets preserved.[213]

Preservation Issues and Section 108 of the Copyright Act

The Copyright Act of 1976, enacted in 1978, extends in Section 108, as amended in 1998, special privileges to libraries and archives related to the duplication of collections. These privileges make the creation of library and archival copies fully permissible in only the narrowest of environments. Yet even these narrow exemptions are not applicable to many sound recordings because federal copyright law does not cover pre-1972 sound recordings fixed in the United States. Section 108 applies to recordings that are protected by federal copyright, namely, U.S. recordings made after 1972 and most post-1923 foreign recordings. In addition, the provisions of the law can govern the use of works that are embodied in a sound recording. For example, while federal laws have no jurisdiction over a 1952 recording, if that recording includes a song or other musical or literary work under copyright, some provisions of Section 108 governing use of that recording could apply.[214]

Section 108 describes the circumstances under which a library or an archive may generate a replacement copy of published items and a preservation copy of unpublished items in its collections. The law permits institutions with audiovisual archives to make up to three copies of published and unpublished recordings for the purpose of preservation.[215] Section 108 reflects best preservation practices as they were understood in the mid-1970s and the late 1990s, when the legislation was enacted and amended, but the law has failed to keep

[213] Testimony of David Seubert, curator, Performing Arts Collection, Davison Library, University of California, Santa Barbara, "Copyright and Intellectual Property Issues" session, NRPB public hearings, November 29, 2006, Los Angeles.

[214] Copyright law as it relates to pre-1972 commercial sound recordings was examined in a report commissioned by the National Recording Preservation Board as part of this study. See June Besek 2005, *Copyright Issues Relevant to Digital Preservation and Dissemination of Pre-1972 Commercial Sound Recordings by Libraries and Archives*.

[215] The stipulations that permit making copies of published and unpublished recordings differ, as is subsequently described.

pace with best practices currently followed by the audio engineering and the federally and privately funded restoration communities.

In its submission to the NRPB, the Harry Ransom Center at the University of Texas commented:

> Although the Section 108 exemptions provide essential liberties to the Center and other qualifying libraries and archives, the limitations regarding the dissemination of copies in digital formats remain a significant hindrance. At this point in the development of recorded sound technology, digital formats are not only expected, but required by researchers and the general public. Restricting distribution copies to analog formats is unreasonable and impractical when cassette tapes are rapidly becoming obsolete and audio CDs and MP3s have become the commercial standard.[216]

In 2005 the Library of Congress convened a study group to examine Section 108 and preservation issues. The group was charged to "provide findings and recommendations on how to revise the copyright law in order to ensure an appropriate balance among the interests of creators and other copyright holders, libraries and archives in a manner that best serves the national interest." The group issued its final report on March 31, 2008. Included in that document are recommendations for changes to copyright statute.[217] The report identified several issues familiar to the preservation community; however, the compromise that the report reflects stops short of what is needed to ensure the preservation of and ready access to historical materials in a digital age.

The restrictions found in Section 108 on the copying and sharing of sound recording by libraries and archives raise the likelihood of redundant efforts and hence increase the total costs of preservation. The exclusion of most musical sound recordings from the loan provisions granted in Section 108 is difficult to defend when digital technology makes possible the easy sharing of print and visual media. Conforming the treatment of musical sound recordings under Section 108 with that of other forms of intellectual property would seem a sensible public policy option. (See "File Sharing Among Institutions" below for further discussion of this issue.)

---

[216] Written submission to NRPB by Mary Sue Neilson, manager, Technology and Digital Services, with assistance from Leanda Gahegan and Emma Saito Lincoln, submitted on behalf of the Harry Ransom Center at the University of Texas at Austin, (January 30, 2007), 4. Available at http://www.loc.gov/rr/record/nrpb/pdf/texasransom.pdf.

[217] United States Copyright Office and the National Digital Information Infrastructure and Preservation Program of the Library of Congress, *The Section 108 Study Group Report* (March 2008). Available at www.section108.gov/docs/Sec108StudyGroupReport.pdf. See also *Section 108 Study Group: Information for the March 2006 Public Roundtables and Request for Written Comments,* February 10, 2006, 3-4 (http://www.loc.gov/section108/docs/FRbackground2-10-06.pdf), and Mary Rasenberger and Chris Weston, *Overview of the Libraries and Archives Exception in the Copyright Act: Background, History, and Meaning,* April 14, 2005 (http://www.section108.gov/papers.html).

Authority to Make Replacement Copies of Sound Recordings

Section 108 of the Copyright Act contains provisions that allow libraries and archives to strike preservation copies of some unpublished sound recordings and replacement copies of some sound recordings of foreign and domestic origin. It is even possible to place online certain foreign nonmusical sound recordings. Unfortunately, however, the utility of these Section 108 provisions for the preservation community is limited by other provisions that govern the number of copies an institution may make of a work, the circumstances under which it may make the initial copy, and the scope of recordings to which the provisions apply.

Section 108 permits libraries and archives to make three copies of a published protected work for replacement purposes. These are usually designated as a *master copy*, a *service copy* (for everyday use), and *a submaster copy* from which service copies are generated. While reasonable for analog preservation, this model does not meet the objectives of best-practice preservation in the digital era. Application of digital preservation technologies can require producing multiple interim/buffer copies generated by the various computers, audio workstations, and servers involved in the digital preservation workflow. If the term *copies* is narrowly defined, adherence to best practices for even routine digital preservation is both illegal and impossible.

Organizers of the Section 108 Study Group observed that current law has no space for, and does not allow for, digital copies that are made in the course of preservation work.[218] Cataloging and storage of analog works do not require creation of copies. However, digital preservation requires the creation of multiple copies, some of which will be held temporarily. For example, when an audio engineer duplicates an analog recording for preservation, his or her first responsibility is to render as true a copy of the original as possible—a *preservation master.* It is standard archival practice to record that copy *flat*, that is, without any imposed equalization of the frequency range or use of restoration techniques to mitigate defects in the recording. However, because these techniques can dramatically improve the listening experience for the average person, the preservation workflow also often includes creating one or more access files that have been enhanced for listening. Some archives produce a high-resolution, enhanced master file from which lower-resolution access files can then be generated for various delivery methods, for example, burning CDs, using the Web for downloading, or streaming audio to a listening station. While the exact strategy for access files varies among archives, best practices for digital preservation and access clearly requires the ability to routinely produce files from an original source in excess of the three-copy limit mandated by the DMCA.

Indeed, archives may need to make more than three copies just to store digital files safely. For example, the LOCKSS (Lots of Copies Keep Stuff Safe) program, developed by Stanford University, uses

[218] *Section 108 Study Group Report*, 6.

open-source software to manage a network of Web archives where member libraries can store and access their digital content. In this program, copies of files exist on multiple servers that are geographically distributed and separately managed by each library. This is an economical and secure alternative to the centralized repository systems that are beyond the budgets of many smaller institutions. Under the restrictions of the DMCA, published audio could not legally be archived in LOCKSS or other similarly structured preservation environments.

In the case of published works, the three digital copies are not strictly preservation copies, but are designated as "replacement" copies. They can be made only under a specific set of conditions. Before a digital copy can be made, the original must be "damaged, deteriorating, lost, or stolen," or in an obsolete format for which "the machine or device necessary to render perceptible a work stored in that format is no longer manufactured or is no longer reasonably available in the commercial marketplace." In addition, "an unused replacement cannot be obtained at a fair price." The law provides no guidance for determining whether a work is reasonably available or establishing its fair price.[219]

The requirement in Section 108 that before a replacement copy may be made, a work must be "damaged, deteriorating, lost, or stolen" has a particularly negative impact on the preservation of sound recordings. A major tenet of preservation is to create copies *before* damage or deterioration compromises presentation or interpretation of the original work. Many deteriorating works made of paper, such as books, photographs, or maps, can be digitally reproduced without any loss to the integrity of their original content. Such is not the case with sound recordings. If, as the law requires, a recording must already be damaged or deteriorating when the preservation copy is made, the copy will reproduce those imperfections in an audible form. In effect, the law allows preservation of audio only when it is too late.[220]

In addition to the replacement provisions of Section 108(c), Section 108(h)(1) provides that libraries, archives, and nonprofit educational institutions may "reproduce, distribute, display, or perform in facsimile or digital form a copy" of a sound recording made during the past 20 years of "any term of copyright of a published work ... for purposes of preservation, scholarship, or research ... ." The exemption does not apply if the recording is in print or available at a reasonable price, or if the Register of Copyright has received notice from the copyright holder that one of these two conditions is currently met or soon will be satisfied through reissue or some other means. Tens of thousands of discs are available for sale through out-of-print

---

[219] 17 U.S.C. Section 108(c).

[220] *The Section 108 Study Group Report* recommends that "fragile" be added as one of the conditions under which a replacement copy may be struck. The recommendation defines a fragile copy as one that "exists in a medium that is delicate or easily destroyed or broken, and cannot be handled without risk of harm." The reference to "a medium that is delicate" implies a medium vulnerable to deterioration whether or not it is already manifest (p. v).

record dealers and online auction sites; these titles could not be digitized under Section 108(h). The requirement that the work be unavailable "at a reasonable price" therefore means that only the rarest recordings can be preserved using this section; the bulk of recorded sound heritage will still be at risk.

The number of sound recordings subject to the preservation opportunities in Section 108 is extremely limited. Because Section 108 applies only to works protected by federal copyright, the only sound recordings that fall under its provisions are those made in the United States on or after February 15, 1972, and foreign sound recordings. The practical effect is to sharply curtail the applicability of the law. The replacement-copy provisions, for example, would not apply to pre-1972 U.S. sound recordings because they do not have federal protection. An institution would not be able to use Section 108(h)(1) to digitize and provide access to a post-1972 recording until 2048, when the recording will enter its last 20 years of copyright protection. As of 2010, only foreign recordings made before 1936 may be made available under Section 108(h), if all applicable requirements were met.

The final report of the Section 108 Study Group expressed the belief that "pre-1972 U.S. sound recordings should be subject to the same kind of preservation-related activities as permitted under section 108 for federally copyrighted sound recordings." However, the study group questioned whether it would be "feasible to amend the Copyright Act without addressing the larger issue of the exclusion of pre-1972 sound recordings from federal copyright law."[221]

File Sharing among Institutions

The legal ability to share digital files among libraries is a means to make the most efficient use of funding for preservation. Section 108 of the law provides guidelines for the creation of copies of materials for use in another library or archive.[222] However, Section 108(i) excludes copyrighted musical works from such privileges. The consequence is that the privileges granted in the section are not extended to sound recordings of copyrighted music, which are the object of the most widespread interest to scholars, educators, and the public.

Given the limited resources for preservation, collaboration between institutions will minimize duplication of effort and will reinforce the respective missions of the library and university communities.[223] The language of Section 108(g) is intended to prevent the sharing of written materials or periodicals for the purpose of avoiding purchases and subscriptions. Besek writes that it is unclear how collaborations involving sound recordings could be conducted in a manner consistent with copyright law. The language of the law

[221] *Section 108 Study Group Report,* 129.

[222] Section 108(c)(2) states that the copies produced may not "be made available to the public in that [digital] format outside the premises of the library or archives in lawful possession of such copy."

[223] Samuel Brylawski, "Preservation of Digitally Recorded Sound," in *Building a National Strategy for Preservation: Issues in Digital Media Archiving* (Washington, DC: Council on Library and Information Resources and Library of Congress, 2002), 52–66.

permits reproduction and distribution of works only on random, unrelated occasions. Besek argues that the fair-use doctrine[224] would allow collaboration in the sharing of sound recordings under certain circumstances, but that the matter would likely be subject to prior review by the institution's counsel and the possibility of a conservative interpretation.

Educational Use, Fair Use, and Digital Rights Management

Much attention has been drawn to the effects that copyright law is having on the educational use of sound recordings. A white paper released in 2006 by the Berkman Center for Internet and Society at Harvard Law School argues that copyright law is "among the most important obstacles to realizing the potential of digital technology in education."[225]

The Berkman report outlines four copyright-related obstacles to the use of digital materials in education:

1. Unclear or inadequate copyright law relating to crucial provisions such as fair use and educational use
2. Extensive adoption of digital rights management (DRM) technology to lock up content
3. Practical difficulties obtaining rights to use content when licenses are necessary
4. Undue caution by gatekeepers such as publishers or educational administrators

Most universities have established internal, intranet, online services that provide classroom materials (including audio recordings) to students. The sites are password protected and available on, and sometimes off, campus. The services have redefined the library reserve system where curriculum-related readings and listening assignments are set aside for students. Several library professional associations have issued guidelines for such reserves, citing fair use in support of such activities.

While fair use is frequently invoked, there is little case law interpreting its application to specific situations. Some archivists believe the lack of applicable case law discourages institutional general counsels from authorizing preservation and access programs on the basis of fair use. Fair-use provisions in the copyright law (Section 107) permit use of excerpts of copyrighted materials, including recordings, for educational and scholarly purposes, for citation in news reporting and criticism, and for nonprofit activities. However, the

[224] 17 U.S.C. Section 107.

[225] William W. Fisher and William McGeveran, The Berkman Center for Internet and Society, *The Digital Learning Challenge: Obstacles to Educational Uses of Copyrighted Materials in the Digital Age.* Research Publication No. 2006-09 (August 10), 2. In their introduction, Fisher and McGeveran argue that the radical transformation wrought by digital technology, and observed in so many sectors, has not occurred in education owing to provisions of copyright law that govern the educational use of content. Available at http://cyber.law.harvard.edu/home/2006-09.

courts have interpreted fair use to be an affirmative defense. In other words, the burden is on the defendant to prove fair use; the plaintiff does not need to establish that the use falls outside fair use.[226] Besek further notes that "favored uses are not automatically deemed fair, and other uses are not automatically unfair. The determination depends on the facts of a particular case."[227]

Most witnesses at the hearings conducted in support of this study who were affiliated with educational institutions expressed a belief that copyright law as it applies to sound recordings is too complex to interpret easily, too restrictive, or both. Section 108, for example, which limits access to digital copies made available under that section to library premises, is too narrow to address all educational needs. One witness called for "premises" to be expanded to include network domain, in order to accommodate "the manner in which students and scholars use information in the current academic and scholarly environment. Increasingly, learning is occurring off-site, that is, at home, in the dorm or just anywhere on campus, in addition to the classroom and library."[228]

A major concern of educators consulted by the writers of the Berkman report was DRM (software encoded in digital works to impede unauthorized duplication). Today, few, if any, new sound recordings are encoded with DRM software. Yet as has been underscored in these pages, the ability to migrate the digital content is essential to preservation. Given that all digital content is stored in some physical medium and may eventually be rendered unreadable by software developments, digital content must be periodically copied, or transcoded, to new storage or a new storage format. Decoding DRM-encoded files will sometimes be necessary to produce these copies, yet circumventing access control measures is illegal under the DMCA (P.L 105-304) of 1998.

State laws, owing to their complexity, offer no remedy. A study commissioned by the NRPB that included examination of the provisions of copyright laws in selected states concluded that "given the amorphous nature of common law and the variations among states, considerable uncertainty about what is allowable under the civil law of the various states is likely to remain."[229]

One case in the state of New York drew considerable attention in 2005. In *Capitol Records, Inc. v. Naxos of America, Inc.*, the Second Circuit Court of Appeals to the New York Court of Appeals held that sound recordings made before February 15, 1972—the earliest date on which federal copyright protection extends to sound recordings—have common law copyright protection until federal preemption

---

[226] Joanna Demers, *Steal This Music: How Intellectual Property Law Affects Musical Creativity* (Athens, GA: University of Georgia Press, 2006), 120.

[227] Besek 2005, *Copyright Issues Relevant to Digital Preservation and Dissemination of Pre-1972 Commercial Sound Recordings by Libraries and Archives*, 9.

[228] Testimony of Gordon Theil, head of the Arts and Music Libraries, University of California, Los Angeles, "University Libraries, Research, Teaching, Digital File Management" session, NRPB, November 29, 2006, Los Angeles.

[229] Besek 2005, 43. Besek reviews California, Illinois, Michigan, New York, and Virginia.

of state law in 2067.[230] In his testimony before the NRPB, attorney David Levine observed that the *Naxos* decision suggested that the traditional federal law definition of fair use neither applies to New York common law copyright nor extends exemptions for preservation work by libraries and archives. The implications of the decision, argued Levine, were far-reaching, extending an absolute protection to all sound recordings made since the beginning of recorded sound in the 1890s. In practice, the *Naxos* decision precluded "noncommercial dissemination of pre-1972 sound recordings for scholarly purposes that long ago ceased to be of any commercial value. … The hurdles created by the overly restrictive New York copyright law," stated Levine, "create disincentives to move ahead with any mass efforts to preserve these recordings through digitization, and distribution of these recordings to the public for teaching, research, or scholarly endeavors." Archives would be tasked with securing permission from the various rights holders before initiating preservation and reformatting activity. "From a legal perspective," Levine added, "conducting archival and preservation activities is made effectively impossible."[231]

A subsequent ruling, in June 2008, by the United States District Court for the Southern District of New York State, in *EMI v. Premise PI*, established that fair use *does* apply to sound recordings protected under common law copyright.[232] Informal inquiries by the NRPB to ascertain whether the *Naxos* decision was influencing the conduct of New York residents and institutions, or was potentially affecting out-of-state parties, revealed little awareness of the New York court's ruling. While the NRPB's inquiry could hardly be considered conclusive, the very lack of anecdotal evidence that the decision was having any impact captures the bigger picture—that copyright law is often either ignored or not understood. One witness at the audio preservation hearings noted that the restrictions affecting pre-1972 have "impinged on legitimate cultural activities. They have also, frankly, undermined respect for copyright law."[233]

---

[230] See USCOA, 2 No. 30, *Capitol Records, Inc., Appellant, v. Naxos of America, Inc., Respondent*, 2005 NY Int. 27, April 5, 2005.

[231] Testimony of David S. Levine, resident fellow, Center for Internet and Society, Stanford University, "Copyright and Intellectual Property Issues" session, National Recording Preservation Board public hearings, November 29, 2006, Los Angeles.

[232] The record of decision is available at http://cyberlaw.stanford.edu/system/files/Order%20Denying%20Federal%20PI.pdf. The *Naxos* ruling raised some interesting implications for access. Had fair use not applied to sound recordings under common law, it might be argued that a non-resident of the state of New York, delivering a digitized sound recording to a New York State resident, could be in violation of New York State law—even if the delivered recording was for personal use in scholarly research. It would also have been unclear whether a non-resident receiving a sound file from a New York resident could be held culpable for receiving a copy that was illegal at its source.

[233] Testimony of Tim Brooks, December 19, 2006.

Copyright, Preservation, and the Public

The treatment of sound recordings under copyright law is exceptionally complex owing to the lack of uniformity between the treatment of sound recordings and that of other works, the consequent split between federal and state law, and the multiplicity of rights holders that may have some claim on an individual work. The public may have, at best, only surface impressions about the application of copyright and fair use to recorded sound from reports in the mainstream media about legal actions that have been taken against file-sharing Web sites, about individuals committing significant violations of the law, and about new models for distribution of music over the Internet.

Few would dispute that the public has developed high expectations about access to music—including the expectation to receive it at no, or negligible, cost. "The Internet has changed everything about the way we access information and think about preservation," reported one witness at the NRPB hearings.[234] Most acknowledge a need for some bulwark against infringement. But many of the situations described in these pages have been about the accessibility of older sound recordings for historical research and artistic interest. Some argue that rights holders should, at the very least, consider permitting access to protected material from Web sites that could be available at libraries and other educational institutions for streaming, if not also for downloading.

The Brooks study reveals a landscape in which decades of recordings—recordings that copyright holders have shown no interest in reissuing commercially—are unavailable legally. But efforts to make recordings available by following the law may be frustrated. Some independent labels seeking to release older recordings in compliance with copyright report that their expected sales of only 500 to 2,000 units have prevented them from obtaining licenses from rights holders. Major record labels have been unwilling to invest time to research rights and to negotiate a fee to license the historical recordings for such limited runs. Having made their intentions known, reissue producers report that rights holders often then advise them that continuing with the project without permission may put the reissue producer at risk of violating copyright. At the same time, many illegal reissues have reached the market. In some instances, these titles are released by labels with very small catalogs and small runs of their individual releases. But there have also been labels with modest runs but huge catalogs.[235]

[234] Testimony of David Seubert, November 29, 2006.

[235] The Document label, based in England, has exhaustively reissued American blues, gospel, and country music and has a catalog numbering well into the hundreds. Similarly, the Classics label, produced in France, has released hundreds of titles. While both labels have dropped some items from their catalogs, several hundred releases are available at any one time. In all likelihood, items are discontinued when stock is exhausted.

Remedies

A consequence of the experiences described in this section is that even well-meaning citizens may be dismissive of copyright law. More important, copyright statutes are imperiling preservation because the ability to make preserved sound broadly accessible to the public influences decisions concerning where limited resources are invested in preservation—decisions that can be entirely independent of the importance of the recordings or of the physical condition of the source material.

If the public expects ready access as a component of preservation, and laws prohibit this, what are the possible solutions? The first decade of the twenty-first century finds the record industry in turmoil. Older business models, dependent upon purchases of long-form physical, commercially packaged records (LPs, then CDs) from brick-and-mortar retailers, have eroded. Despite industry consolidation (there are now only four major record companies), professionals foresee little stability in the record business. Major record companies see a necessity to take aggressive actions to stop unauthorized duplication of their works by individuals while they work to reinvent their business models. In today's climate, it is not logical to expect record companies to relinquish exclusive publishing and distribution rights. However, the public discussion is not furthered by characterizing those who desire access to historical recordings before 2067, and licenses or laws that facilitate preservation, as part of a faction opposed to copyright protection.

Wider access to preserved recordings has the potential to create public interest in neglected recordings and to generate revenue to rights holders from back catalogs. Such revenue might help fund preservation projects. One witness at the preservation hearings observed, "We need to enable avenues for funding in business models to support preservation, enabling access to collections, allowing generation of revenue for preservation, and offering some reasonable safety mechanism from litigation. The benefits are clear. Access creates interest and awareness, which in turn creates potential for revenue and funding. We cannot expect that archives can survive in the funding environment that they traditionally have."[236]

The alternative to broad access to preserved recordings is what preservationists term *dark archives*, i.e., repositories with restricted use, or no use, permitted until copyrights expire. It will be difficult, if not impossible, to create business models for funding the preservation of recordings held in dark archives. One witness argued that federal and private organization funding of dark archiving, as well as public access projects, is essential if we are to assure the preservation of audio heritage: "Even if the copyright law is changed, there will still be millions of hours of deteriorating audio on lacquer discs or tape that have little to no economic value but tremendous cultural

[236] Testimony of Chris Lacinak, Audio-Visual Preservation Solutions, "Preservation Challenges and Practices at Archives and Libraries" session, NRPB public hearings, December 19, 2006, New York.

and historical importance that will need to be held in dark archives until their copyright term expires."[237]

Few would dispute the plea expressed by a Columbia University archivist: "We need laws that support long-term preservation of the digital versions and that support provision of access to them that is equitable for copyright holders but does not raise insuperable barriers to fair use. Preservation without access is pointless, and institutions hesitate to use scarce resources to preserve sound recordings when there is no assurance that anyone can have access to them."[238]

Michael Feinstein, a prominent recording artist with a significant collection of unpublished, privately made recordings and radio transcriptions, spoke at the NRPB hearings about the challenges in legally sharing these recordings. One obstacle he noted was obtaining rights from the artists who contributed to the recordings, who were often represented by professional trade unions. Hundreds of thousands of recordings have been made of broadcasts or live performances with no agreements in place for future use, or repurposing, of the recordings. "The cost of clearing the clip from the owner of the material and the cost of clearing the song ... is so extraordinarily prohibitive that nobody will ever [hear] it. ... The copyright holders would not take the pains to preserve it because it is not viable. And there has to be change in that ... I think the change has to come from the musicians' union. It has to come from everybody. It is the only way ... now with the Internet where so many things have been bootlegged ... I think that everybody is going to say, 'Well, we have to go along with because it basically is going to turn out to be that or nothing.'"[239]

Neil Portnow, president of the National Academy of Recording Arts and Sciences, suggested these issues might be resolved by a think tank.[240] There is little question that legal impediments to preservation and access will be overcome only if there is collaboration among all interests—legislators, consumers, rights holders, archivists, and the public—and commitment from these parties to saving our audio heritage efficiently and fairly. The link between preservation and access is an unforeseen consequence of the digital age, but it is clear that it is an irrevocable link—one that, if not acknowledged and addressed through law and/or licensing agreements, will generate lawlessness and jeopardize our national recorded sound heritage. As a copyright attorney noted in testimony

> we need to look at [access controversies] less from the [digital rights management] side and more from the broader perspective of what technology can do that does not impact the pecuniary

[237] Testimony of David Seubert, November 29, 2006.

[238] Testimony of Emily Holmes, on behalf of Janet Gertz, director of the Preservation Division, Columbia University Libraries, "Preservation Challenges and Practices at Archives and Libraries" session, NRPB public hearings, December 19, 2006, New York.

[239] Testimony of Michael Feinstein, recording artist and collector, NRPB public hearings, December 19, 2006, New York.

[240] Testimony of Neil Portnow, president, National Academy of Recording Arts and Sciences, NRPB public hearings, November 29, 2006, Los Angeles.

> concerns of individuals or groups and that there is a growing body of literature ... dealing with social sharing, ... how the sharing of information brings societies together. ... We all benefit as a society as we grow culturally from access to information … it does not necessarily destroy business, it does not kill off the creative spirit. If we alter the arrangements that currently exist, you can begin the discussion.[241]

Creation of new copyright laws or licensing procedures that acknowledge best practices in audio preservation and assure access to audio heritage is essential to ensure the preservation of that heritage and its understanding and appreciation by generations to come. Arguably, introducing efficiencies to licensing could also reduce digital theft. In the hearings conducted for this study, a variety of stakeholders in preservation and the audio industry suggested several solutions and recommendations. The Association for Recorded Sound Collections (ARSC), an organization of approximately 1,000 archivists, librarians, audio engineers and technicians, collectors, and historians, made five recommendations to the NRPB for changes to copyright law. Some or all of these recommendations have been endorsed by the American Library Association, the Music Library Association, the International Association of Jazz Record Collectors, the Society for American Music, the Society of American Archivists, and the Association of Moving Image Archivists.[242] To bring its recommendations under the auspices of a number of interested groups, ARSC, with the Music Library Association, established a Historical Recording Coalition for Access and Preservation in the fall of 2008.

The recommendations are as follows:

1. **Place pre-1972 U.S. recordings under a single, understandable national law by repealing section 301(c) of Title 17, U.S. Code, the provision that currently keeps pre-1972 recordings under state law until 2067.** Proponents of extending federal protection to pre-1972 recordings point out that, without such a change, any amendment to federal copyright law, including changes to the treatment of orphan works that have been an object of congressional attention, will have negligible effect on sound recordings. The absence of federal protection for pre-1972 recordings, ARSC argues, "has created massive confusion. Instead of a uniform and understandable national code, we are faced with a welter of state laws, ... all varying from each other, most based on ad-hoc common law rather than legislation, and none [appearing to directly address] the needs of recordings in the Internet age."[243]

   Toward that end, the FY2009 Omnibus Appropriations Act (P.L. 111-8) directs the U.S. Copyright Office to conduct a study on the "desirability of and means for bringing sound recordings

[241] Testimony of David Levine, November 29, 2006.

[242] See http://arsc-aaa.invisionzone.com/forums/index.php?showtopic=50 and www.recordingcopyright.org.

[243] Tim Brooks, Comments for a Hearing on the Current State of Recorded Sound Preservation. *ARSC Newsletter* 113 (Winter 2007). Available at http://www.timbrooks.net/PDFs/nrpb1219.pdf.

fixed before February 15, 1972, under federal jurisdiction." The study, to be delivered to Congress not later than two years from the enactment of the bill in March 2009, is to cover "the effect of federal coverage on the preservation of such sound recordings, the effect on public access to those recordings, and the economic impact of federal coverage on rights holders. The study is also to examine the means for accomplishing such coverage."[244]

2. **Harmonize the term of coverage for U.S. recordings with that of most foreign countries, i.e., a term of 50 to 75 years.** Debate continues in Europe on the term of copyright for sound recordings. In spring 2008, an industry-backed proposal was introduced in the EU to extend the copyright term for recordings from 50 to 95 years. In light of the previous defeat of a similar initiative in the United Kingdom, the EU proposal is less sweeping. As approved by the European Parliament on April 23, 2009, copyright in sound recordings would be extended to 70 years. However, the measure must be approved by the European Union Council of Ministers.[245] If approved, the extension would not be retroactive and would include a "use it or lose it" provision for future recordings once they become more than 50 years old.[246]
3. **Legalize the use of orphan recordings (i.e., those for which no owner can be located).** The amendment to federal copyright law affecting orphan works will not apply to pre-1972 recordings if they remain excluded from federal copyright protection. In the 110th Congress, orphan works legislation (S. 2913) passed the Senate by unanimous consent in late September 2008. Hearings were held in the House on similar legislation (H.R. 5889), but the bill did not reach the House floor before the end of the 110th Congress. As of the beginning of summer 2010, orphan works legislation had not been introduced or debated in the 111th Congress.
4. **Permit and encourage the reissue by third parties of abandoned recordings (i.e., those that remain out of print for extended periods), with appropriate compensation to the copyright owners.** The coalition argues that there should be a "compulsory license to allow public access to recordings that may still be under copyright but are not available from the rights holder, with reasonable compensation to the rights holder."[247]
5. **Change U.S. copyright laws to allow the use of current technology and best practices in the preservation of sound recordings**

[244] The directive appears in the "Explanatory Statement Submitted by David Obey, Chairman of the House Committee on Appropriations, Regarding H.R. 1105, Omnibus Appropriations Act of 2009." U.S. Congressional Record. House of Representatives, February 23, 2009, H2397.

[245] The Council consists of ministers from each EU member state. Owing to a complex weighted voting system, one analysis estimates that at least a 73.9% majority would be needed to pass the law. Whether a sufficient number of European states that had opposed an extension to 95 years will support an extension to 70 years is unclear. If the European Council does approve the proposal, EU member states will have two years to implement the extension into national law. See: http://www.simkins.co.uk/articles/ebpEUextension.aspx

[246] See www.soundcopyright.eu.

[247] Testimony of Tim Brooks, December 19, 2006.

by nonprofit institutions. Specifically, the coalition recommends lifting the restriction that allows striking copies only after the deterioration of the originals is advanced, eliminating the limit on the number of copies that can be made, and removing provisions that impede the sharing of files among institutions.

Conclusion

Copyright law is commonly acknowledged as lagging behind the technological advances, the changes in distribution practices, and the accelerated displacements of one media format for another that have characterized the past 30 years. Twice during the past century, the U.S. Congress has comprehensively amended the copyright law. It is not unusual for debate over major public policy issues, such as copyright, and proposed legislative remedies to extend over several sessions of Congress in order to allow adequate time for a consensus to develop.

Today we are witnessing a complex, protracted, and often-acrimonious struggle between creators, producers, distributors, and users of creative works, in response to which a number of laws have been proposed and enacted. The extraordinary developments of the past 25 years in digital audio technology, new media, and the ease of duplication and production, as well as changes in how consumers use recordings, have contributed to the perfect storm referenced earlier in this chapter. During these years, amendments to federal copyright law have been more narrowly focused. Although these changes have been fashioned to address issues bearing on sound recordings and to quiet that storm, the forecast remains far from tranquil. Many users allege that the more recent amendments to copyright law have approached protectionism for copyright holders; meanwhile, copyright holders contend that copyright law still falls well short of clamping down on piracy. Those desiring greater access to sound recordings also draw attention to the 95-year gap between the invention of the phonograph in 1877 and 1972, when audio recordings were first protected under federal copyright law. This provision of the law, as has been noted, is responsible for the absence of any public domain in sound recordings; it also fosters the dynamics that interfere with preservation and access, and may even generate distrust of copyright law. As also noted, a large community of archives, scholars, and librarians has been urging for a reassessment of the span of federal protection of sound recordings. This issue will be the subject of a two-year study by the U.S. Copyright Office called for by Congress pursuant to passage in early 2009 of omnibus spending legislation for fiscal 2010.

As hearings for this study confirmed, limitations on recorded sound preservation and on public access to sound recordings are a consequence of current law. Some of these obstacles are the result of the pace of technological developments. Policy makers did not intend for revision of copyright to create these problems; many would like to see the revisions lifted. Even recognizing the existing support for recorded sound preservation (because who, after all, could oppose it independent of their specific interests), developing a consensus among all stakeholders and reforming existing federal laws may be impossible without significant compromises by all the communities affected by the law. If one acknowledges that a universally acceptable reform of copyright law is most likely elusive at the moment, the question then becomes whether there are approaches to rights-inherent challenges to preservation and access that can be both compliant with copyright law and effective, even if only for an interim period.

Indeed, there have been some innovative responses that merit attention and that may offer models for others to adapt to individual circumstances, pending further developments at a national level. For example, some smaller services (primarily Webcasters) and nonprofit and public institutions have made great strides in providing access to an increasing variety of sound collections. New business models created by the recording industry and Webcasters' industries hold promise to make accessible to the public fields of recorded music and other sound recordings that have previously not been available. Doing so will be beneficial to generating support for preservation.

As another example, the Metropolitan Opera has established an entrepreneurial access pathway to its recent and historical broadcasts. Through its "Met Player" subscription service, the company has put in place the technology to deliver, on a subscription or a fee-per-use basis, "superior streaming of audio and video performances, including those shot in high-definition."[248] Met Player also provides access to historical radio broadcasts and television performances. This is an instance in which one of America's leading cultural organizations has taken the lead in digitally preserving and providing broad public access to its own history. Ownership of the copyrights related to the broadcasts in its archives was necessary, but not sufficient, for the Metropolitan to offer this service. The opera company had to negotiate with and obtain numerous licenses from representatives of those who contributed to their performances, including singers, instrumentalists, and technicians. Despite the challenges, this initiative proves that distribution of unpublished historical recordings can be achieved.

Not all archives are as fortunate as the Metropolitan Opera in being able to commercially distribute their holdings to the public. The Met has the advantage of being the producer of the performances and of having detailed documentation of the contributors to each performance, enabling the company to know exactly what parties have rights to each performance. This situation is the exception, not the norm. For example, hundreds of open-reel tape recordings by important country music artists, recorded during live performances of the late 1940s through the early 1970s, were recently rescued from a Pennsylvania barn. The discovery has been hailed for the rich cultural trove it holds. But even initial news coverage about the

[248] See http://www.metoperafamily.org/met_player/.

collection acknowledged how complex rights issues related to the collection will be if any of the performances are to be distributed.[249] Rights owners of unpublished recordings might include the producer of the concert, the venue, the recording engineer, the artists, the record companies with whom they were associated at the time of the performance, and others. If funding for the preservation of these tapes must come from revenue gained through sales of the recordings, a number of parties will have to be willing to enter into explicit, but creative, licensing agreements. All of the parties in such agreements will also need to temper expectations—financial compensation is likely to be minimal. Historical recordings reveal our rich heritage, but few have the potential to make heirs rich. Unless rights holders and preservationists are willing to work together, many valuable recordings risk being lost or becoming irretrievable.

As has been described in these pages, the dynamic between copyright law, preservation, and access surfaces in several communities of organizations and individuals who use sound recordings for a variety of personal, professional, and academic activities. In commissioning a national plan, the U.S. Congress directed the NRPB to "increase accessibility of sound recordings for educational purposes."[250] The Berkman study notes that "the regime governing educational use of content, like all of the [*sic*] copyright, requires balance. The system must encourage the development and dissemination of content as well as facilitate its use. Any changes must not destroy sufficient incentives for creators or distributors."

However, the Berkman study does not see amending U.S. copyright law as the sole solution. In addition to "reform of at least some problematic legal rules," the study notes the following "paths toward reform":

- greater reliance on technology to help users analyze the need to secure licenses for using content and to assist with rights clearances where necessary;
- agreements among educators concerning standards and best practices for their use of content, reliance on fair use, and deployment of DRM; and
- an increase in distribution of content under more-open licensing models, such as Creative Commons, thus enlarging the amount of content available for unencumbered educational use. [251]

In commissioning this study, the U.S. Congress requested "recommendations for changes in such laws and restrictions to enable the Library of Congress and other nonprofit institutions in the field of sound recording preservation to make their collections available to researchers in a digital format." The Congress also asked that the study "[take] into account the research and other activities carried

[249] Tristram Lozaw, "Country Discovery Is Reel Find," *Boston Globe* online, March 22, 2009. Available at http://www.boston.com/ae/music/articles/2009/03/22/country_discovery_is_reel_find/.

[250] National Recording Preservation Act of 2000 (P.L. 106-474), Sec. 111.

[251] Fisher and McGeveran, *The Digital Learning Challenge*, 90–91.

out by or on behalf of the National Audio Visual Conservation Center at Culpeper, Virginia." The Library of Congress holds the largest and most diverse collection of sound recordings in the United States at its Packard Campus in Culpeper. There, the Library is undertaking preservation of more than three million radio broadcasts, sound recordings, and moving-image items. With the authorization and support of Congress, the center is providing public access to sound recordings on the premises of the Library's Recorded Sound Reference Center, located 80 miles away in the James Madison Building on Capitol Hill, via a high-security fiber-optic communications link that transmits digital files of sound recordings that have been digitally preserved in the laboratories of the Packard Campus.

As Congress recognized in the legislation authorizing the NRPB and the present study, the technological and physical resources available at the Library's Packard Campus facility would enable the campus to share its audiovisual collections, including many unique recordings, with hundreds of libraries throughout the United States—if rights issues could be resolved. In addition to the constraints posed by copyright law, some collections at the Culpeper facility are governed by gift agreements that restrict their use to Library of Congress facilities in perpetuity, even though the Library is required to spend significant amounts of public money to catalog and reformat these materials. License agreements with donors and rights holders could be forged to provide research access by millions of people to the invaluable collections held entrusted to the nation.

The Library of Congress is but one of hundreds of libraries, archives, and museums in the United States that have developed or might develop working relationships with the broad range of sound recording producers, broadcasters, and others who are rights holders in audiovisual collections in need of preservation. Some of these relationships are already in place and involve complex collaborations, with licensing and access agreements that often serve the preservation and access interests of both parties. For example, in January 2009, the Library signed an agreement with Sony Music, Inc., that allows the Library to develop a Web site to provide public access, via streaming technology, to tens of thousands of pre-1925 acoustically recorded commercial sound recordings, many of which have been unavailable since the late 1920s. This "national jukebox" will be launched in the fall of 2010 with a planned initial offering of 10,000 selections recorded for Victor Records. Additional selections will come from both the Victor catalog and the Columbia label. Even though access is restricted to streaming, and most of the recordings would have been in the public domain if recordings were subject to the same federal laws as other property, the agreement and the jukebox break new ground in the collaboration between a publicly funded archive and a major record label.

From other examples—developed across a broad spectrum of public and private institutions—could emerge a core model applicable to a wide range of rights holders and publicly funded institutions that would broaden access and, in so doing, accelerate preservation efforts. However, model solutions based on bilateral agreements between specific rights holders and individual institutions must evolve beyond narrow project "silos" to become scalable models with the potential for broad impact on preservation and access. The OhioLINK agreements with two record companies, described in the first chapter of this study, may provide a model basis of such agreements.

However effective individual initiatives such as these may be, they will not resolve all the outstanding issues. Responsibility for cutting this Gordian knot lies in great part with the U.S. Congress. Congressional action is key to preserving America's recorded sound history, protecting ownership rights, and providing public access over the long term. Omnibus copyright legislation may have been sufficient for the print and analog age, but digital technology and the veritable explosion in digital delivery systems can render regulation and current practices anachronistic and have disproportionate effects on different stakeholders.

Copyright law reform, however important, is not the sole solution. If focused toward well-defined objectives, collaboration between archives and educational institutions, record industry executives, music publishers, and artists, composers, and producers who are participants in the music industry could lead to some loosening of restrictions, thereby facilitating access to historical or out-of-print sound recordings and resolving many of the current difficulties. A willingness on the part of the industry to make licensing sound recordings more efficient might encourage pirate labels to legitimize their releases, and produce income for rights holders from otherwise-dormant recordings.

One objective of the next phase of the National Recorded Sound Preservation Plan is to identify and weigh possible responses to the challenges outlined in these pages. The need is urgent to develop a set of realistic recommendations to address the concerns that divide the communities of stakeholders in recorded sound, all of whom recognize the incalculable benefits conferred on our future by preserving our past.

APPENDIX A

National Recorded Sound Preservation Study:

Announcement of Study and Public Hearing (November 2006)

The Librarian of Congress and the National Recording Preservation Board (NRPB) of the Library of Congress are conducting a study on the current state of recorded sound preservation and restoration in the United States. The study is intended to inform the drafting of a comprehensive plan for a national audio preservation program, as directed by Congress in the National Recording Preservation Act of 2000, P.L. 106-474.

To aid in completing the study, two public hearings are scheduled:

Los Angeles	November 29, 2006
New York City	December 19, 2006

Objectives and issues

Audio preservation today is not simply a matter of collecting and storing, or transferring endangered recordings to the digital domain. To achieve the objectives of long-term preservation requires a commitment to long-term processes (possibly with no discernible end) to maintain the quality of preserved materials and the ability to access them. Are the efforts and resources being invested in rescuing recordings today diverting attention from the sort of programs and resources that will be needed to support preservation through the decades? What will be needed to sustain long-term preservation and what sort of collaborative effort might help to achieve this?

The Library of Congress seeks comments and information that will assist the Librarian in understanding the issues involved in recorded sound preservation nationwide.

The preservation community

The Library is especially interested in comments from

- representatives of major and specialized sound archives, and institutional collections holding commercial and unpublished sound recordings

- major and independent record labels
- audio engineers affiliated with corporations or institutions, or who are self-employed
- scholarly and professional organizations involved with the production, study, use or preservation of recorded sound
- individuals with personal, often specialized collections of recorded sound, including published and unpublished materials
- the legal community and academic or other specialists in copyright, fair use, and intellectual property law as it pertains to preservation of, and access to, protected sound recordings.

Issues of interest to the Board

The questions listed below touch on matters of concern to us. We do not intend witnesses to treat these as a list to be answered individually and specifically; these questions are intended only as a guide. Neither do we believe this list to be exhaustive. Witnesses should speak to the concerns most important to them, and these may include experiences and issues that witnesses believe the Board has not identified or sufficiently emphasized.

- What drives prioritization of your preservation efforts, e.g., is it driven by assessment of the most vulnerable elements in your collections, or largely determined by projects or evaluation of the cultural value of specific recordings or other factors?
- Is your preservation program designed to be sustained for the long-term?
- Do you see potential opportunities for partnerships and collaborations within the public or private sectors to support preservation, or between the public and private sectors?
- What are the effects of U.S. law governing copyright and fair use on preservation and access, and what amendments or additional provisions would you recommend the U.S. Congress enact in this area?
- What creative solutions might overcome obstacles to preservation?
- What preservation issues are receiving insufficient attention?
- How can public consciousness be raised about the importance of dedicating public and private resources to recorded sound preservation?

Where

The November 29 Los Angeles hearing will take place at the Renaissance Hollywood Hotel, 1755 North Highland Avenue, Hollywood, California 90028, from 9:30 a.m. to 5:00 p.m. The December 19 hearing in New York will take place at The Princeton Club of New York, 15 West 43rd Street, (between 5th and 6th Avenues), New York, NY 10036, from 9:30 a.m. to 5:00 p.m.

For additional information on hearing locations and times, please refer to the website of the National Recording Preservation Board [http://www.loc.gov/rr/record/nrpb/].

To participate

Groups or individuals interested in participating in these public hearings should contact the Library of Congress about submitting oral and written comments. All requests to testify orally must be made no later than November 17, 2006, for the hearing in Los Angeles, and November 28, 2006, for the hearing to be held in New York. Requests should clearly identify the person and/or organization desiring to comment. Submission of testimony, or a preliminary summary of remarks, should be submitted with the request to testify. If your offer to appear in person is accepted, a copy of your complete testimony (preferably a file sent via email to rbamberger@crs.loc.gov or sleg@loc.gov) must be submitted by November 22, 2006 (Los Angeles) and December 12, 2006 (New York). Testimony for the hearing record will be accepted until the end of January 31, 2007.

Contacts

Steve Leggett, Library of Congress, M/B/RS Division, Washington, D.C. 20540. Telephone: 202/707-5912; Facsimile: 202/707-2371; email: sleg@loc.gov; or, Rob Bamberger, Consultant to the National Recording Preservation Board, Library of Congress, Washington, D.C. 20540. Telephone: (202) 707-1122; email: rbamberger@crs.loc.gov.

Testimony and comments sent by electronic mail or delivered by hand are strongly encouraged. Submissions sent through the U.S. mail are strongly discouraged owing to delays in delivery of surface mail owing to security procedures.

Electronic submissions should be directed to rbamberger@crs.loc.gov with a cc to sleg@loc.gov. (See file formats and information requirements below). Submissions delivered by hand should be brought to the Library of Congress, M/B/RS Division, James Madison Memorial Building, Room LM-336, 101 Independence Avenue, SE, Washington, DC 20540. (Those sent by regular mail should be addressed to Steve Leggett, Program Coordinator, National Recording Preservation Board, Library of Congress, M/B/RS Division, 336 James Madison Memorial Building, First and Independence Avenue, SE, Washington, DC 20540.)

Written submissions are also invited from persons or organizations unable to testify or attend the hearings. All written comments or supplementary information should be received, in camera-ready copy, by January 30, 2007.

File formats and required information

(A) If by electronic mail: Send to rbamberger@crs.loc.gov (with cc to sleg@loc.gov) a message containing the name of the person making the submission, his or her title and organization (if the submission is on behalf of an organization), mailing address, telephone number, telefax number (if any) and e-mail address. The document itself must be sent as a MIME attachment, and must be in a single file and in a recent, if not current, version of: (1) Adobe Portable

Document File (PDF) format (preferred); (2) Microsoft Word; (3) WordPerfect; or in (4) Rich Text File (RTF) or (5) ASCII text file formats.

(B) If by regular mail or hand delivery: Send, to the appropriate address listed above, two copies of the comment, each on a 3.5-inch write-protected diskette, labeled with the name of the person making the submission and, if applicable, his or her title and organization. Either the document itself or a cover letter must also include the name of the person making the submission, his or her title and organization (if the submission is on behalf of an organization), mailing address, telephone number, telefax number (if any), and e-mail address (if any). The document itself must be in a single file and in a recent, if not current, version of: (1) Adobe Portable Document File (PDF) format (preferred); (2) Microsoft Word; (3) WordPerfect; or in (4) Rich Text File (RTF) or (5) ASCII text file formats.

(C) If by print only: Anyone who is unable to submit a comment in electronic form should submit an original and two paper copies by hand or by mail to the appropriate address listed above. It may not be feasible to place these submissions on the Board's website and, as noted earlier, use of surface mail is strongly discouraged owing to the uncertainty of timely delivery.

Background on the preservation study and hearings

The National Recording Preservation Act of 2000 (Public Law 106-474) was signed into law by President Clinton on November 9, 2000. The law established a National Recording Registry in the Library of Congress to maintain and preserve sound recordings and collections of sound recordings that are culturally, historically, or aesthetically significant. It additionally requires the Librarian of Congress to implement a comprehensive national recording preservation program after soliciting the participation of, and taking into consideration the counsel of, other recording archivists, educators and historians, copyright owners, recording industry representatives, and others involved in activities related to recording preservation and with interests in making sound recordings more accessible for research and educational purposes. The law also established a National Recording Preservation Board that, among other activities, will study and report on the current state of sound recording preservation practices and activities in the United States. The authorities of the Act expire on September 30, 2008.

The legislation, in section 124(b) (2 USC 1724), charges the Librarian of Congress, in consultation with the National Recording Preservation Board, to conduct this study and after completion of the study, to develop a coordinated national sound recording preservation program. The objectives of this program are (1) to coordinate activities to ensure that efforts of archivists and copyright owners, and others in the public and private sector, are effective and complementary; (2) to generate public awareness and support for these activities; (3) to increase accessibility of sound recordings for educational purposes;

and (4) to undertake studies and investigations of sound recording preservation activities as needed, including the efficacy of new technologies, and recommend solutions to improve these practices.

The undertaking of the study and the conduct of these hearings coincides with the completion of the National Audiovisual Conservation Center (hereafter NAVCC) in Culpeper, Virginia, where the Library's collection of sound recordings, film, and video will be consolidated. One purpose of the NAVCC will be to conduct preservation of the ever-growing body of deteriorating published and unpublished sound recordings in the Library's collection that are, in effect, a history in sound of the nation's social, cultural, and historical record.

Through the development of a comprehensive national recording preservation program, the Library hopes to raise public and private recognition of the importance of recorded sound preservation and, in consultation with the National Recording Preservation Board, to identify initiatives to help solve the challenges faced by all stakeholders, recognizing the different environments in which universities and archives of all sizes, museums, libraries, record companies, e-commerce, and others operate.

These hearings are also intended to seek comment on potential public and private partnerships for significant accomplishment in furthering recorded sound preservation. The Librarian is also interested in comment on how to raise public awareness of the importance of sound recording preservation and a recognition of needs that must be met to achieve it.

The National Recording Preservation Board, appointed by the Librarian, consists of twenty-one members, seventeen of whom are drawn from institutions and organizations specified in the Act, and an additional four at-large members. These institutions and organizations are: The National Academy of Recording Arts and Sciences (NARAS); The Recording Industry Association of America (RIAA); The Association for Recorded Sound Collections (ARSC); The American Society of Composers, Authors and Publishers (ASCAP); Broadcast Music, Inc. (BMI); The Society of European Stage Authors and Composers (SESAC); The American Federation of Musicians (AF of M); The Music Library Association; The American Musicological Society; The National Archives and Records Administration; The National Association of Recording Merchandisers (NARM); The Society for Ethnomusicology; The American Folklore Society; The Country Music Foundation; The Audio Engineering Society (AES); The National Academy of Popular Music; and The Digital Media Association (DiMA).

* * *

In January 2007 the invitation to submit written statements on audio preservation was supplemented by a request for three types of information.

1) How are archives, libraries, and university libraries tracking what they have in their collections? If they don't know what they have,

what systems or models would they use to compile this information and what sort of support would they see as necessary to accomplish it?

2) In the absence of resources to process or preserve sound recordings, are institutions withholding information about what they have?
3) There's relative consensus on the percentage of motion pictures that have been lost, for whatever reason, and knowledge about specific losses. Can anyone provide to the board anecdotal, but verifiable, evidence or accounts of specific sound recordings of socio-cultural value that are already lost?

APPENDIX B

Report of a Task Force Discussion to Define Prerequisites, Core Knowledge, and Graduate Educational Directions for Sound Preservation Professionals, and to Review an Annotated Bibliography of Audio Preservation Resources

Prepared for the Library of Congress National Recording Preservation Board by The Kilgarlin Center for Preservation of the Cultural Record, The University of Texas at Austin School of Information

Prior Discussion, 2003–04

This task force meeting, held in late July 2006 at the University of Texas at Austin School of Information, was the third in a series of meetings that convened specialists and experts to address the complex challenges and issues facing recorded sound preservation.

In July 2003, the University of Texas at Austin School of Information, the Library of Congress, the National Recording Preservation Board, and the Association of Research Libraries sponsored *Sound Savings: Preserving Audio Collections*, in Austin, Texas. *Sound Savings* brought together practitioners, educators, and scholars whose work represented the current thinking in the field of audio preservation. In the symposium's final panel session, stakeholders agreed upon several immediate actions. The development of classroom and laboratory curricula in audio preservation was high on the agenda, based on enthusiastic consensus among panelists on the need for a core educational curriculum for audio preservation to be used in library schools and in preservation/conservation training programs. A number of core elements for a curriculum were articulated. To support academic curricula, institutions were encouraged to create fellowship and internship opportunities to allow students to build practical skills, knowledge, and ability.[1]

In 2004, a roundtable of specialists was convened by the Library of Congress and the Council on Library and Information Resources to recommend procedures for transferring analog audio tape and audio disc to digital output for preservation purposes. Resulting from this meeting was a series of recommendations for improving the practice of analog audio transfer for preservation. Of the 15 recommendations, the first was to "develop core competencies in audio preservation engineering," which roundtable participants began to flesh out. Roundtable participants emphasized the imperative role of

[1] Association of Research Libraries, *Sound Savings: Preserving Audio Collections* (Washington, DC.: Association of Research Libraries, 2004).

formal education in preparing professionals to address the preservation needs of audio collections.[2]

The 2006 Project

To progress on the immediate actions defined during the 2003 *Sound Savings* Symposium and in subsequent meetings, the Library of Congress, under the auspices of the National Recording Preservation Board (hereafter referred to as "the Board"), and the Kilgarlin Center for Preservation of the Cultural Record (hereafter referred to as "the Kilgarlin Center" or "the Center") discussed how they might collaborate to further the audio preservation education and research agenda. In fall 2005, the Board contracted with the Center for 10 months to accomplish the following:

- hire a professional active in the audio preservation field to perform a comprehensive review and critical evaluation of the literature on preservation of sound recordings, culminating in a bibliography to support educational initiatives and the field at large;
- compile a list of formal (undergraduate and graduate) national and international courses/programs of study offered in sound archives, engineering, and audio preservation; and
- convene a group of experts in the field of audio archiving, engineering, and preservation to review, discuss, and edit the literature bibliography; evaluate the educational offerings in sound archives and preservation; and define the core knowledge for three groups of professionals: audio archivists, audio preservation managers, and audio preservation engineers.

In November 2005, Sarah Cunningham was hired half-time to undertake a critical evaluation of the literature and to create a list of courses and programs of study in fields related to sound recording preservation. Cunningham, who holds an MLIS and a Certificate of Advanced Study in Preservation Administration from the University of Texas at Austin School of Information, has been working and participating actively both nationally and internationally in the field of sound recording preservation. A part-time lecturer to the University of Texas at Austin School of Information, she teaches the school's introductory and advanced courses in audio preservation and reformatting.

The Task Force

In late July 2006, a task force of 15 experts was convened for a two-day meeting at the University of Texas at Austin School of Information. Task force members were selected based on their knowledge of and expertise in specific aspects of audio preservation, including

---

[2] Council on Library and Information Resources and National Recording Preservation Board, *Capturing Analog Sound for Digital Preservation* (Washington, DC.: Council on Library and Information Resources, 2006). Available at www.clir.org/pubs/reports/pub137/pub137.pdf.

administration of sound archives and collections, audio engineering, copyright and intellectual property, library and archives preservation, graduate instruction in preservation, and conservation and conservation science. A list of task force participants is provided on pp. 154-155.

Before arriving in Austin, task force members received a draft of the audio preservation literature bibliography and were asked to prepare to discuss the following during the meeting:

- With the goal of drafting a master's curriculum for educating professionals who will manage and preserve recorded sound collections:
  - What is the body of knowledge required?
  - At what depth and breadth should topics be addressed?
- With the goal of producing a bibliographic resource on the philosophy, history, and current practice of preserving sound collections:
  - What is missing from the literature review, both in terms of overlooked topics and subjects currently unaddressed in the extant literature?
  - What is the best way to ensure that all relevant topics are covered?
  - Should the literature bibliography and review be made available via a Web or a monograph publication, or both?

Summary of Meeting Discussions

This section summarizes two days of intense discussion and debate on the defined topics. From the outset the task force agreed that, to ensure the future of the audio record, the field must have formally educated professionals at all levels (archivists, preservation managers, and engineers). Apprenticeships and workshop models alone cannot provide the education necessary to sow the field with knowledgeable professionals who can manage the preservation of our recorded sound heritage and anticipate the future needs of sound collections. Increasingly, much as in the conservation field, where conservators are educated and specialize in specific areas (e.g. paper, manuscripts, books, photographs, paintings, and textiles), the preservation challenges of audio carriers brought on by 125 years of constant innovation and obsolescence are such that institutions now seek preservation specialists to tend to the specific requirements of sound recording media. As with moving-image media, the complexities inherent in sound recordings deserve focused study if the fragile body of recorded sound that has been and will be produced is to survive as a record of human social, scientific, artistic, and personal endeavors.

Defining the Audio Preservation Field

The field of audio archiving, preservation, and engineering is vast and expanding; there can no longer be universal specialists. This said, the task force found it difficult to draw hard lines between the various types of work done and knowledge required by recorded sound professionals. Those who develop, catalog, and reference sound collections and those who manage their preservation have overlapping knowledge requirements. Likewise, audio preservation managers need to have a solid grounding in the work of audio preservation engineers. However, for the nation's vast store of small sound collections held in archives, libraries, and museums, one audio professional may need to know a good bit about all aspects of the field.

Premaster's Degree Requisite Knowledge and Experience

The question of premaster's requisite knowledge and experience was discussed. What types of skills and knowledge will best prepare a student to matriculate in master's programs that provide specializations in audio archives, audio preservation management, and audio preservation engineering? A number of task force members felt that, to provide a solid underpinning, graduate students require a combination of prerequisite education, including

- the hard sciences (math, chemistry and physics)
- perceptive psychology
- critical listening
- electrical acoustics
- psychoacoustics
- sound and acoustic technology
- relevant experiences in ethnomusicology, oral history, radio or music

The ability to listen critically and to communicate effectively was emphasized particularly as basic prerequisites for all students studying the field, denoting the union of technical and management skills required universally by audio practitioners. The task force acknowledged that some of the specified prerequisite knowledge and experience could be incorporated in the master's curriculum itself. As audio preservation management, audio archives, and audio preservation engineering mature as research and career paths, master's programs can begin to expect applicants to possess higher-level prerequisite knowledge and skills.

Defining the Profession

1. Audio Archivist

For the purposes of this report, we have chosen the term *audio archivist* to represent audio archivists, librarians, and curators.

The knowledge and skills required of an audio archivist are akin to those defined for an audiovisual archivist but are specific to recorded sound.[3] A combination of practical and theoretical education

[3] Ray Edmondson, *Audiovisual Archiving: Philosophy and Principles* (Paris: UNESCO, April 2004).

and training, and prerequisites that signal a broad and versatile background, should equip the audio archivist to administer and lead the work of a recorded sound archives. An historical background may be ideal in understanding and evaluating for collecting purposes the social significance of sound recordings. A certain level of technical knowledge will also be essential, though with the broadening of the field to include audio preservation management positions (defined below), the audio archivist will be relieved of some of the historical burden of knowing "everything."

The core knowledge and skill requirements for the audio archivist could be achieved as a study track within the requirements of a broad library and information sciences curriculum (for which the degree award is typically an MSIS, MLS, or MLIS).

Core Knowledge and Skills: The first three knowledge areas listed below represent core courses; the fourth category can be translated into two core courses. Directed studies and an internship requirement will be included in the curriculum.

Recorded Sound Foundations
- Recorded Sound History and Formats
- Material Science and Technology and Structure of Sound Carriers
- Basic Audio Properties

Preservation Foundations
- History, Philosophy, and Ethics
- Assessment of Collection Preservation Needs
- Environmental, Protective Enclosure, and Handling Requirements
- Disaster Planning and Preparedness

Preservation Reformatting of Audio
- Techniques for Preserving the Source Original
- Reformatting of Analog Carriers for Preservation (knowledge of processes and basic skills in)
- Technology Assessment

Collection Management
- Collection Management Philosophy, Principles, and Strategies
- Appraisal
- Archival Processing
- Intellectual Control
- Reference
- Copyright and Intellectual Property
- Digital Archiving
- Organizational Theory and Behavior
- Communication
- Policy for and Planning of Audio Archives
- Cost Analysis and Budgeting
- Performance Planning and Evaluation
- Project Management
- Human Resource Management

- Contracting for Services
- Quality Assurance
- Facilities Planning
- Marketing and Development
- Grant Writing

2. Audio Preservation Manager

The task force focused on defining the core knowledge requirements for a new type of audio/preservation specialist, an Audio Preservation Manager. The goal of a master's curriculum specifically tuned to teaching the preservation management of recorded sound would need to be well rounded and include courses in administration, materials science, and technology, preparing audio preservation managers to oversee decision making and work addressing the wide-ranging preservation needs of recorded sound collections. The audio preservation manager must develop the knowledge of and a basic skill level in transfer processes. Ideally, s/he will supervise an audio preservation engineer or will be responsible for contracting for transfer services and for overseeing the quality assurance of transfer products.

There was some discussion about which discipline provides the most logical home for a master's curriculum in audio preservation management, especially given the interdisciplinary requirements of such a program of study. There was agreement that the Library and Information Science (LIS) discipline is the intellectual home for the topic, given the history of library and archives preservation management as a subdiscipline of LIS and the rich nature of LIS study as a discipline. However, because a combination of humanities, hard science, and information-based knowledge is required, the task force emphasized that schools best positioned to fulfill the curricular requirements of an audio preservation management program would be those situated in robust academic communities where interdisciplinary research and study is possible and encouraged. Furthermore, schools in close proximity to recorded sound archives and collections staffed by audio preservation specialists are better positioned to fulfill the practical learning components of an audio preservation management curriculum.

Given the proposed nesting of a graduate curriculum in audio preservation management within a broad LIS curriculum, the task force discussed how to officially acknowledge concentrated study in audio preservation management. The task force felt that, in addition to an LIS master's, a certificate (e.g., a Certificate of Advanced Study) presents one good possibility, especially given that these certificates are already used to formally verify concentrated study in preservation and conservation in LIS and art conservation curricula. In the case of audio, the certificate would signify additional, advanced study in recorded sound preservation management, beyond the LIS master's requirements.

Core Knowledge and Skills: The task force envisioned the creation of a specialized Certificate of Advanced Study program composed of courses, directed study, and internship opportunities that would impart the following knowledge and skills. The certificate would be offered within a broad-based LIS master's curriculum that includes courses in collection management, archives, research methodology, and organization and description of information objects. The knowledge areas below represent core courses.

Recorded Sound Foundations
- Recorded Sound History and Formats
- Material Science and Technology and Structure of Sound Carriers
- Basic Audio Properties

Preservation Foundations
- History, Philosophy, and Ethics
- Assessment of Collection Preservation Needs
- Environmental, Protective Enclosure, and Handling Requirements
- Disaster Planning and Preparedness

Preservation and Reformatting of Audio
- Techniques for Preserving the Source Original
- Reformatting of Analog Carriers for Preservation (knowledge of and basic skills in processes)
- Administrative and Technical Metadata
- Copyright and Intellectual Property
- Technology Assessment
- Designing a Reformatting Lab

Digital Archiving
- Media Refreshment
- Conversion to Neutral Formats vs. Emulation to Retain Original Format Migration
- Significant Properties of Digital Objects and Their Importance for Preservation
- Format and Metadata Repositories
- Authenticity and Reauthentication
- Electronic Records Repository Construction, Use, and Administration

Preservation Management
- Organizational Theory and Behavior
- Communication
- Policy for and Planning of Preservation Programs
- Cost Analysis and Budgeting
- Performance Planning and Evaluation
- Project Management
- Human Resource Management
- Contracting for Services
- Facilities Planning
- Marketing and Development

- Grant Writing
- Quality Assurance

3. Audio Preservation Engineer

The task force defined this specialization to incorporate knowledge and skills derived from the engineering sciences, the fine arts, the humanities, and the information sciences, with the goal being production of professionals skilled in the art and science of transferring analog sound to digital for long-term preservation. This specialization requires in-depth knowledge and skills in audio engineering, the arm of audio science dealing with the recording and reproduction of sound through mechanical and electronic means, which itself draws on many disciplines, including electrical engineering, acoustics, psychoacoustics, and music. However, this specialization is not purely nor solely audio engineering; broader knowledge is required so that audio preservation engineers will be equipped to participate fully as professionals in the libraries, archives, and museums where they will be employed, as well as to add productively to the profession's development.

What the task force envisions is a master's-level curriculum that may best emerge through a joint degree program between the LIS and audio engineering disciplines. As is true for the audio preservation management curriculum, a program of study for the audio preservation engineer would be situated in robust academic communities where joint degrees and interdisciplinary research and study is possible and encouraged. Furthermore, schools in close proximity to recorded sound archives and collections staffed by audio preservation engineers are better positioned to fulfill the practical learning components of a curriculum.

Core Knowledge and Skills: The knowledge areas below represent core courses. The fourth core area, audio engineering, may require two or more courses. Directed studies and an internship requirement will be included in the curriculum.

Recorded Sound Foundations
- Recorded Sound History and Formats
- Material Science and Structure of Sound Carriers
- Advanced Audio Properties

Preservation Foundations
- History, Philosophy, and Ethics
- Assessment of Collection Preservation Needs
- Environmental, Protective Enclosure, and Handling Requirements
- Disaster Planning and Preparedness

Preservation and Reformatting of Audio
- Techniques for Preserving the Source Original
- Reformatting of Analog Carriers for Preservation (advanced knowledge of and skills in processes)

- Technology Assessment
- Designing a Reformatting Lab

Audio Engineering
- Audio Design
- Digital Audio
- Audio Postproduction
- Transducer Theory
- Real-Time Digital Signal Processing
- Engineering Acoustics
- Digital Speech and Audio Processing
- Quality Assurance

Digital Archiving
- Nature of Computer Data Files
- Reliability, Authenticity, and Custodianship
- Conversion, Migration, Emulation, and Reauthentication
- Digital Archaeology
- Ingest
- Metadata and Access
- Levels of Service

Information Retrieval Systems

Analog and Digital Playback and Production Equipment: Functioning, Repair, Maintenance, and Testing

Doctoral Studies

With the growing complexity of information objects and concomitant preservation and access concerns, preservation requires now, more than ever, good empirical and theoretical scholarship. Research universities must educate leaders to teach preservation in library and information science programs, to assume positions at upper administrative levels in libraries and archives, and to advocate for and promulgate policy to preserve the nation's documented heritage. To achieve these ends, library and information science must attract and support doctoral students in the field of preservation.

As a result, two institutions that have provided master's level education respectively in (1) library and archives preservation administration and conservation and (2) art conservation have recently introduced doctoral-level study. Likewise, for the field of sound recording preservation and archiving to fully mature, the LIS discipline must support doctoral study in this area. As with most doctoral research, the nature of study and research in audio preservation and archives will be interdisciplinary. The research topics discussed by the task force ranged broadly, from materials science to new media design to policy development, including
- Ingest Automation
- Nondestructive Testing of Media

- New Media Design
- Applied Nanotechnology
- Sensor Design
- Advanced Secure Network and Archives Structures
- Advanced Peer-to-Peer and Grid Computing
- Advanced Signal Processing
- Advanced Preservation and Restoration Technologies
- Synced Sound Preservation
- Advanced Encryption and Decryption Technologies
- Semantic Audio Retrieval
- Public Policy Development
- Patent Research

Defining the Literature of Audio Preservation

The task of defining the literature of recorded sound preservation brought to the fore the intertwining, interdisciplinary nature of research and study in this field. How do we organize the wildly varied yet overlapping subjects that comprise the literature related to audio preservation?

The template for the literature review was specifically created for this task and was based on literature review methodologies used in the humanities. By evaluating the articles, the experience and education of the authors, and the standards reflected in the articles, the bibliography reflects the top articles in the field. To best serve the evolving discipline, the top articles in each subject area were included in the bibliography as determined by the template.

Because this is a new field without an established body of literature, journal articles from many different disciplines were included in the review, including those of the Audio Engineering Society, the International Association of Sound Archives, the Association of Recorded Sound Collections, and the Institute of Electronic and Electronics Engineers. Standards for reformatting and the storage of digital files are evolving rapidly, making it imperative for sound recording professionals to stay current with the latest studies in the field.

The task force made a number of suggestions with regard to the addition of select papers and articles to, and the organization of, the substantial body of works represented in the bibliography. The task force suggested specifically, as much as possible, to organize the bibliography by topic and to provide brief annotations for select readings that require differentiation from similar titles. This proved to be a difficult intellectual challenge given the lack of a set terminology for the relatively young field of recorded sound preservation and the interdisciplinary nature of its knowledge base. The task force reiterated what had been noted in *Capturing Analog Sound for Digital Preservation*; audio preservation and its cognate fields must develop a common vocabulary.

The task force felt strongly that, to keep the bibliography up-to-date in a fast-changing field, it should be published in an online format. The Library of Congress will be hosting the bibliography on its Web site and adding new literature resources on a regular basis. The bibliography can be found at http://www.loc.gov/rr/record/nrpb/nrpb-clir.html.

Task Force Participants

Peter Alyea
Digital Conversion Specialist
Motion Picture, Broadcasting & Recorded Sound Division
Library of Congress

Robert Bamberger
Senior Policy Analyst, Congressional Research Service
Library of Congress

Samuel Brylawski
Editor, Encyclopedic Discography of Victor Recordings
University of California, Santa Barbara

Elizabeth A. Cohen
Cohen Acoustical, Inc.

Sarah Cunningham
Research Associate, Kilgarlin Center for Preservation of the Cultural Record
School of Information
University of Texas at Austin

Ellen Cunningham-Kruppa
Director, Kilgarlin Center for Preservation of the Cultural Record
School of Information
University of Texas at Austin

Eugene DeAnna
Head, Recorded Sound Section
Motion Picture, Broadcasting and Recorded Sound Division
Library of Congress

Jon Dunn
Libraries Senior Technology Advisor and Associate Director for Technology
Digital Library Program
University of Indiana Bloomington

Patricia Galloway
Assistant Professor
School of Information
University of Texas at Austin

Georgia Harper
Manager of the Intellectual Property Section, Office of General Counsel
University of Texas System

Gregory Lukow
National Recording Preservation Board
Chief, Motion Picture, Broadcasting and Recorded Sound Division
Library of Congress

George Massenburg
George Massenburg Labs

David Seubert
Curator of the Performing Arts Collection, Special Collections
Davidson Library
University of California

Sheila Fairbrass Siegler
Head of Paper Conservation
Nebraska State Historical Society, Gerald R. Ford Conservation Center

John Spencer
Bridge Media Solutions Inc.

APPENDIX C

Obstacles to Access and Preservation of Recorded Sound

by Nancy Davenport

We live everyday life surrounded by recorded sound, wanted and unwanted: the alarm-activated CD, a car radio, thumping bass beats leaking from a fellow bus rider's iPod, the elevator's special brand of music, the tune of the computer as it boots up, and hundreds of melodies used as ring tones on the ever-present cell phone. Given the pervasiveness of recorded sound, as well as the tools and opportunities to personalize sound to mood, task, function, or time of day, it may be surprising that there is a category of recorded sound much less accessible for casual listening, close study, or performance. Mixing metaphors, this class of recorded sound is often referred to as "out-of-print recorded sound." This report focuses on that niche of the recorded sound heritage: materials that are no longer commercially distributed but are not in the public domain; materials of primary interest to the scholarly and collecting communities that are not readily available and accessible to either group.

This report is based on interviews with members of the community concerned with recorded sound: curators of sound archives, music librarians, musicologists and music researchers, sound engineers, collectors, copyright specialists, rights owners and agents, and performers. The findings are based on interviewees' descriptions of obstacles to access or preservation that impede use of a body of work today and possibly in the future. The obstacles are found throughout the life cycle of curatorial care. Overcoming them will require commitment, significant financial resources, and trust and cooperation among all the sectors interested in recorded sound.

In *Capturing Sound: How Technology Has Changed Music*, Mark Katz writes:

> When performed, live musical sound is fleeting, evanescent. Recordings, however, capture these fugitive sounds, tangibly preserving them on physical media, whether wax cylinders or plastic CDs. Once music is reified—made into a thing—it becomes transportable, collectable, and manipulable in ways that had never before been possible. ... the distinctive aspects of recorded sound have encouraged new ways of listening to music,

> led performers to change their practices, and allowed entirely new musical genres to come into existence (Katz, 5).

The kind of listening that allows and supports scholarship such as that of Barbara Oakley Allen, whose dissertation was entitled "A Comparison and Critique of the Recorded Performances of Stravinsky's Concerto for Piano and Wind Instruments," is dependent on several factors. For example, the music has to be heard repeatedly in the whole of the work, phrase by phrase, or note by note. It must also be manipulable: the listener must have the power to stop and start, slow down and speed up, and even divide the music into layers.

The musicians and sound curators whom I interviewed for this report gave countless examples of the need for both the recording and the player to be under the control of the listener. *Deep listening*, or scholarly listening, may be pleasurable; however, it primarily involves listening for content, in note, performance, mood, texture, and technology. The sound recordings that scholars want are housed in archives and libraries around the world. This paper focuses solely on U.S.-based institutions and interviewees' recommendations for making recorded sound more accessible and more permanent.

Discovery

Interviewees often talked about their frustration in locating sound recordings. The sources of this frustration range from finding no reference to the location of a particular recording to finding insufficient specific information. Many of these recordings are part of library collections (usually kept in the special or non-book collection), but because of work backlogs they have not yet been described in the library's catalog. Moreover, when a library or an archives catalogs large collections, its choices may not meet the needs of the researcher in search of a particular recording. For example, a collection might be named for its donor, its label, or the artist. There may be a brief note indicating the number of discs in the collection but no item-level description of each recording. Some catalogs carry detailed information on the better-known materials in the collection but pay little attention to the rest. This situation fails to meet the needs of researchers, who may require details such as the place and date of performance, the names of the musicians, the recording studio and engineer, or even the matrix number. Whether the researcher is comparing multiple interpretations or searching for one exemplar, specific attributes are needed.

Another problem with discovery derives from the ease and convenience of Internet searching as contrasted with the difficulty of searching hundreds of library or archive catalogs that may have differing search protocols. Today's researchers rightfully expect that sound archives should be able to combine their descriptive holdings information into a single data set available to the scholar's desktop.

Access

Once a researcher has discovered a recording, the next step is to listen to it. To do so, he or she usually must travel to the holding archive. While travel was once considered a standard part of the research process, it may not necessarily remain so. Consider the teaching faculty member who can travel only during intersessions or spring and summer breaks. Added to the cost of travel and lodging is the fact that many special collection sections are open only during standard business hours, not in the evenings or on weekends or holidays—the very times the researcher might be most available.

After overcoming the next potential obstacle—complying with increasing security demands for identification and personal authentication—the researcher confronts a new set of problems that relate to the facility and the fragility of the material. The first hurdle the researcher encounters are donor- or owner-imposed restrictions on the collection. An institution may have physical possession, and even physical ownership, of a collection and yet be subject to donor- or owner-imposed restrictions on its use. Although these restrictions impede access, libraries and archives agree to them because most have expiration dates after which the material will be more freely available. To circumvent the restrictions takes time, and the response to a request to use the materials can be idiosyncratic and based largely on the requester and the purpose of the request.

Still another obstacle relates to unique nature of the researcher's listening requirements. Rarely does a researcher want to hear a recording only once. Most researchers need to listen to the same passage over and over to hear the bowing technique of the violinist, to transcribe a jazz riff, to compare the interpretations of several artists performing the same piece, or to note the changes in an artist's performance over time. The interviewees recounted multiple instances in which they were not permitted to listen to a recording multiple times. They might be told, "The library's policy is to allow each listener only one complete playing of the material," or "The material you have requested is fragile; because of preservation concerns you may only listen to it once." Other facilities, while not bound by policy restrictions, do not have the staff to help multiple researchers, each of whom needs to have a needle dropped in a particular spot on a disc every 10 seconds. Underlying the frustration, much of the material is truly fragile and could be damaged by repetitive needle drops in the same spot. Another impediment is that some facilities that have recordings have no playback machines and will not lend the materials to an individual or an institution that does possess suitable playback devices and trained staff.

Some archives have solved some of these problems for their users. For example, one institution, at 24 hours' notice, will burn a CD with the passage the researcher wants to hear again and again. The disc is placed into a locked CD player, and the researcher can hit the repeat button as often as desired. At another institution, researchers who request a passage of a full recording are given a non-return CD with the passage burned. The CD can be used in a classroom, a laboratory, or a dormitory. The institution finds this method of providing access to be low cost and relatively risk-free.

The scholar who desires to incorporate such materials into a curriculum or to publish a book with an accompanying CD confronts still another set of obstacles. The right to use much of the material for activities beyond solitary scholarship often requires securing legal permission. Incorporating sound recordings into classrooms is difficult, but easier than securing publishing or performing permission. Most higher education institutions use a course-management system to distribute syllabi and associated class materials to registered students. The course-management system serves as an electronic gatekeeper, allowing access to registered students while denying access to others. Faculty members at schools without a course-management system, however, have a more difficult time. Creating password-protected, limited-duration Web sites that parallel the lecture plan is one approach, but some faculty members worry about leaving the site "live" for a whole semester and thus have a hard time teaching comparative music classes. They ask, "Is making the sound available on the Web 'publishing'?" They fear that a Web crawler that identifies their Web site could cause the semester to end in litigation. While many scholars expressed such concerns, others took the opposite view, saying they are reluctant to always ask permission because they believe that the traditional right to assert fair use of the material will be weakened if they do not assert it regularly.

The problem is not limited to the classroom. Scholars who want to share materials with their peers from inside or outside their institutions cannot do so through a course-management system. Some have resorted to posting the sound bite on a personal Web site for a limited period, having previously alerted their colleagues about the window of availability.

Scholars who want to illustrate research findings with samples of the sound face yet another challenge: determining who owns the rights. Interviewees described in detail the time, level of effort, and cost of securing rights. In the absence of a master registry that is updated as rights change hands, scholars must assume responsibility for tracking down the owners. Some owners are unsure of their rights for works created years ago; they may respond with a casual "It's OK with me, if I'm the one to tell you OK." Such a response leaves the scholar unsure how, or even whether, to proceed. Other scholars, certain they have found the rights holder and made the request with the proper level of specificity, find their queries go unanswered; perhaps, they surmise, because their work was not intended as a commercial enterprise and responding was not worth the effort to the company. Scholars appreciate companies that respond promptly, even if their request is turned down. Multiple interviewees described having to conduct many rounds of rights searches to secure needed permissions.

Solutions Proposed

Each interviewee was asked, "If you were chosen to solve the problems that you identify as obstacles to access or preservation of recorded sound, what would be your solution?" Their proposed solutions are summarized below. Not all the solutions are congruent, and not all would be acceptable to the entire range of sectors interested in recorded sound. To implement them would require some guarantees to the "consumer or scholarly" side of the equation, guarantees much like those Mark Katz offers for resolving peer-to-peer file-sharing problems and that are adapted as follows (Katz, 183). Katz maintains that systems designed to resolve users' issues must be:

- *Easy*—There must be a single site and simple, intuitive searching, as well as sophisticated scholarly interrogation.
- *Reliable*—Information must be up-to-date, accurate, treated as a part of cultural heritage, and available to all as a public good.
- *Legal*—The scholar should be able to depend on the information contained in the rights owner's database and to proceed without additional checking.
- *Permanent*—The data files must be maintained permanently. (Many interviewees think this task is so important that it should be entrusted only to an institution such as the Library of Congress.)

Interviewees proposed the following solutions:

1. **Create a unified database of sound recordings held by libraries and archives, as well as by individual collectors, to address problems of discovery**. Many interviewees suggested that a national recorded sound database be developed, and that libraries and archives be strongly encouraged to deposit records of their holdings in it. While the goal is an identification system rich in detail about the performance and artist, with information about the recording's manufacture, institutions should begin to participate with the records currently available about their holdings. Serious individual collectors should be encouraged to deposit information about their collections into this database.
2. **Create a unified database of property rights associated with sound recordings to facilitate the location of rights holders**. Scholars, performers, curators, and publishers related in detail their efforts to locate names and addresses of rights owners. The interviewees called for a new system to replace the current patchwork approach. This recommendation seeks to develop a voluntary cooperative that would be available to all segments of the recorded sound community.
3. **Rewrite the copyright laws to mandate online registration.** The copyright law should require online registration of works owned, sold, or renewed. While the goal of this recommendation is identical to that of the unified database outlined in recommendation 2, the mechanism for its creation and participation would be legally mandated, rather than voluntary. To strengthen this recommendation, some interviewees suggested that it specify that works not

registered would automatically fall into the public domain.

4. **Rewrite the copyright law to compel rights owners to permit use of their work.** Researchers who made this recommendation believe that it is in keeping with the spirit of copyright as it appears in the U.S. Constitution, permitting exclusive use for a short period of time followed by wide availability for the diffusion of knowledge.
5. **Affiliate the Library of Congress with at least one library in each state so that the Library's sound recording holdings could be more broadly available**. With the ability of digital technology to transfer sound recordings to geographically disparate locations, the Library's collections could be made available for use in every state, minimizing the need for long-distance travel. Each state would have to create facilities for deep, repetitive, and manipulative listening.
6. **Create a massive, distributed jukebox of sound**. iTunes and other commercial entities have tested and proved a business model that enables users to download a wide assortment of sound recordings at a reasonable price. Interviewees recommended development of a noncommercial variant that would provide better tools for discovery, access, incorporation, and use for casual users as well as scholars. Structured fees would be tied to the level of use—casual use at one fee and performance at a different, presumably higher, fee. The purchase of the material would include the purchase of the rights, and no additional rights clearance would be required.

   In this model, no institution would relinquish its ownership or physical possession of the underlying recording. As digital copies were made, information about them would be posted to the jukebox. The only centralized organization and enterprise created would be the jukebox Web site and the business and financial operations. Two analogous representations of this model are eBay, a site through which the transactions take place but where the "content" is distributed throughout the selling community, and AbeBooks, which operates as a centralized point of discovery, access, and business transactions for many out-of-print book dealers.
7. **Train librarians and archivists in copyright law**. Many of the interviewees described situations in which they had tried to use materials in a library or an archive and been told that the rights to those materials were unclear. In most such cases, the librarian or archivist refused to serve the material, even for listening purposes. The individuals who refused to grant permission generally noted that they were afraid that they or their institutions might be the target of an infringement lawsuit if they complied with the request. Scholars think that some curators have become so wary about possible infringement that they are ignoring fair use of the material for scholarly purposes.

Preservation Obstacles

Many of the reasons cited by interviewees regarding the difficulty of preserving recorded sound have a corollary in access issues. They include staff shortages, lack of staff expertise in preservation techniques and modalities, lack of equipment and space, fragility of the materials, uncertain rights ownership, large backlogs of material to be treated, slowness of technology, and lack of financial resources. In spite of the often-sad state of affairs in libraries and archives, the scholars have learned they cannot rely on corporate sound recording archives for purposes of their research. "Corporate archives were only as good as the corporations' motivations. Beyond a certain point, companies lacked a compelling reason to preserve recordings that did not hold commercial promise, and if a company went out of business, its archive would not necessarily be maintained, and the continued preservation of the recordings housed therein became more a matter of accident than of intention" (Sterne, 327).

A Heritage Health Index published in 2005 revealed that 46.4 million collection items of recorded sound were housed within the institutions that participated in a baseline cultural heritage study. Of these items, about 40 percent were described in "unknown condition" and another 20 percent were in need of preservation (Heritage Preservation, 2005).

Two of the case studies featured in the nationwide review include audio materials: the Carl Sandburg Collection held by the library at the University of Illinois at Urbana-Champaign; and the Media Library and Archives of WGBH, Boston's public radio and television outlet. The WGBH case study notes that "WGBH Media Library and Archives today faces the same daunting challenge shared by all moving image and sound archives: audio and video media are fragile, susceptible to chemical and physical decay, and have a short life expectancy. These factors, coupled with the obsolescence of playback equipment, require that such materials be routinely migrated to new formats."

For the Carl Sandburg collection the study says:

> The University of Illinois has been committed to preserving and providing access to this uniquely American collection; yet, the resources to properly care for such an important resource were unattainable within normal funding strictures. The primary threat to the roughly 300,000 leaves of Sandburg's literary manuscripts, galley proofs, correspondence, and associated papers is their acidic content. A secondary threat to the collection centers on issues of media obsolescence and the deterioration of magnetic and photographic media. This portion of the collection consists of more than 3,000 photographs, 613 recordings, and 12 motion pictures. While these items constitute a small portion of the collection, they provide the contemporary researcher with insight into Carl Sandburg as he was in life, both through his persona when reading prepared materials and through the more candid moments captured in the snapshots and included within his photograph collection.

The problems revealed by the Heritage Health Index are typical of those that libraries and archives face daily. When libraries and archives do not have enough staff to handle all of their operations, they typically choose to favor public service areas, on the assumption that satisfied patrons and users can be called upon to add voice and credibility to budget requests and to forestall complaints. Since preservationists often know the collection thoroughly, they can easily substitute for serving the client, but the reverse is rarely true. Preservation requires knowledge not only of the content and condition of a collection but also of materials science and of chemistry; it requires an ability to use specialized equipment and technologies and years of training or apprenticeship in the handling of fragile materials. When an institution invests in recruiting and training preservation staff, it hopes to retain the staff and amortize this investment over several years.

As recording technology and media have changed over the years so has the equipment needed to play successive formats, and much of the equipment has become scarce to rare. Curators tell stories of preservationists who have rebuilt machines by cannibalizing other devices or by reconstructing pieces. These skills are usually self-taught and are akin to those of a mechanical engineer or surgeon. Creating a digital surrogate to use as a service copy or for preservation is a slow process. In March 2006, the Library of Congress convened an Audio Engineers' Roundtable to explore ways to speed the process of analog to digital conversion so that more recordings can be digitized without loss of content.[1]

Making digital copies requires yet another labor-intensive process: creating metadata. Metadata—or data about data—communicates with the computer about file size, file format, and other technical details that, taken together, make the digital recording sound the same as the original. While the digital file may be regarded as a preservation format, its very creation starts another media life cycle of curatorial care—one that inevitably leads to preservation.

The lack of space and, more important, of environmentally controlled space, is a common problem for archives and libraries. Storing collections for optimal preservation requires a vastly larger footprint than storing them efficiently does. Weight considerations frequently dictate that recording discs be stored on the lower levels of buildings, where they are more often subject to water leaks and flooding. If a collection arrives with a donor restriction that the contents must be permanently housed together as they were when in the donor's possession, the collection will take more space than it would if sorted by format.

Institutions often hold recordings, or collections of recordings, for which the rights to access or use are uncertain. Administrators may defer investments in preserving such materials and instead

[1] The Library of Congress also convened a meeting in March 2004 on digitizing analog sound. A report of that meeting is available in *Capturing Analog Sound for Digital Preservation: Report of a Roundtable Discussion of Best Practices for Transferring Analog Discs and Tapes* (Washington, DC: Council on Library and Information Resources and Library of Congress, 2006).

preserve those with clearly defined usage rights. And the very nature of assembling a collection, whether local, regional, or national in scope, means that preservation care is meted out through a triage system. Managers must weigh the costs of preserving fragile sound recordings against the costs of preserving collections overall, and must demonstrate efficiency and effectiveness in terms of number of items preserved. Amidst these tradeoffs, cultural heritage hangs in the balance.

Works Cited

Heritage Preservation. 2005. *A Public Trust at Risk: The Heritage Health Index Report on the State of America's Collections*. Washington, DC: Heritage Preservation and Institute of Museum and Library Services. Available at http://www.heritagepreservation.org/HHI/index.html.

Katz, Mark. 2004. *Capturing Sound: How Technology Has Changed Music*. Berkeley, CA: University of California Press.

Sterne, Jonathan. 2003. *The Audible Past: Cultural Origins of Sound Reproduction*. Durham, NC: Duke University Press.

Acknowledgments

The Council on Library and Information Resources is grateful to the many people who made themselves available for interviews. While interviews were scheduled for 30 minutes, they often lasted an hour or more, and included lively and thought-provoking conversations about how the "problem" could be solved. Particular thanks go to the following individuals:

Bonna Boettcher, Cornell University
Jose Bowen, University of Miami, Ohio
Tim Brooks
Gary Churgin and Lisa Jacobson, Harry Fox Agency
Stan Cornyn
Stephen Davison
Tim Fabrizio
James Farrington, University of Rochester
Patrick Feaster, University of Indiana
Michael Feinstein
Mark Katz, Peabody Conservatory, Johns Hopkins University
William Howland Kenney
Lawrence Lessig
Jeffery Magee, University of Illinois, Urbana-Champaign
Judy McCulloh, University of Illinois Press
Peter McDonald, Syracuse University
Daniel Morgenstern
David Sanjek, BMI
Anthony Seeger
William Shurk, Bowling Green University

APPENDIX D

Folk Collections in Crisis Report: Concluding Discussion and Recommendations

The following text is taken from Folk Heritage Collections in Crisis *(Washington, DC: Council on Library and Information Resources, 2001), 51-55. The publication reports on a meeting convened by the American Folklore Society and the American Folklife Center at the Library of Congress on December 1-2, 2000. The purpose of the meeting was to formulate recommendations for the preservation of and access to America's folk heritage sound collections. The full report is available at http://www.clir.org/pubs/abstract/pub96abst.html.*

The salient innovation of the symposium was the gathering of many experts who have few or no opportunities to talk and develop collaborations. Despite the participants' diversity of experience and interest, consensus emerged about the nature of the problem, which extended far beyond preservation, and the solutions, which extended far beyond technological fixes bought with additional funding. It was clear that each sector that was represented, from archives to the law, holds part of the solution, and that only collaboration will achieve lasting progress. The way to engender collaboration and achieve scalable results depends urgently on continuing the dialogues that began at the symposium.

The diversity of the group attending the symposium was itself a common topic, and most discussions revealed a general lack of coordination in need of immediate remedy. Suggestions for organized coordination included the formation of interdisciplinary committees that could pool resources and information and develop standards, and the formation of advocacy groups to create new partnerships, raise funds, and generate public interest. Enlisting the new executive director of the American Folklore Society as a general coordinator was also proposed.

Each group that developed strategies for improved access, preservation, and rights management agreed on the need to

- develop a Web portal to provide links to resources and reference materials and to facilitate the coordination of the efforts of diverse communities;
- increase public awareness about heritage collections and the crises they face;
- develop best-practices guidelines and standards;

- develop better education and training opportunities for researchers, archivists, audio engineers, and community members;
- develop partnerships among the technology, corporate, and entertainment sectors;
- extend the reach of expertise and resources to regional and local levels in ways that include but also go beyond the Web portal;
- create and fund teams of experts who could work as consultants, traveling to different sites to lead workshops, provide expertise, provide services, etc.; and
- establish regional centers for preservation and distributed access when appropriate.

Specific recommendations for access, preservation, and rights management follow, along with the names of the organizations best positioned to play leading roles in each area.

Access

1. *Develop an interdisciplinary online portal.*
   Develop an interdisciplinary online portal that will provide access to existing materials and resources for sound archives [Society of Ethnomusicology in collaboration with Harvard University].
2. *Create an ethnographic thesaurus.*
   Convene the Ethnographic Thesaurus Working Group to develop a proposal for submission to the National Endowment for the Humanities for the July 2001 deadline. The proposal will provide planning grant funds to shape this project with a clear scope of work, budget, and an institutional home [American Folklife Center, American Folklore Society, May 2001].
3. *Develop metadata schemes.*
   Investigate and develop the use of Dublin Core or other relevant metadata schemes to facilitate the creation and sharing of descriptions and indexes of unpublished ethnographic recordings [University of Washington, Harvard University, Library of Congress, Michigan State University, American Folklore Society, Society of Ethnomusicologists, and others].
4. *Develop regional facilities for local access.*
   Explore the designation of regional facilities that might provide data-migration and other resources to small and midsize archives [Library of Congress; Indiana University; Harvard University; University of California, Los Angeles; and others].
5. *Disseminate information about the symposium results.*
   Urge participants to include a link to the symposium Web site and sound preservation information [all].

Preservation

1. *Develop an urgency matrix.*
   Develop and post on the symposium Web site an urgency matrix

and best-practices preservation guidelines for small to midsize archives. This document will not be comprehensive but should include recommendations for affordable and reasonable preservation of the most common recording media (e.g., reel-to-reel tape, audio cassettes, video cassettes, digital audiotape) with cost models for treatment and equipment recommendations [Association for Recorded Sound Collections, Audio Engineering Society].

2. *Develop a magnetic media manual.*
   Ensure that the Research Libraries Group magnetic media manual is translated into simple language to be useful for folklorists, ethnomusicologists, collectors, and others with sound collections. Have a link from Research Libraries Group site to the symposium Web site [Research Libraries Group].
3. *Develop guidelines and best practices for capture.*
   Develop and publish a set of guidelines and best practices for information capture, metadata, etc., to cover all sound media by 2002 [Audio Engineering Society, Library of Congress, Association for Recorded Sound Collections].
4. *Publicize standards developed for audiovisual facilities.*
   Publicize standards developed by the Library of Congress for its Culpeper facility to be a model for handling cultural legacy audio and visual materials and update national standards as needed [Library of Congress].
5. *Develop scalable models for digital preservation.*
   Provide expert service and production facilities to small and midsize archives for digital preservation and data migration [Library of Congress, Digital Library Federation].
6. *Develop a vendor registry.*
   Develop a list of reputable vendors of equipment and services for sound preservation, especially firms able to handle legacy formats [Library of Congress, Association for Recorded Sound Collections].
7. *Recruit and train technicians.*
   Encourage technical and engineering schools to train the next generation of expert technicians for audio preservation and include legacy format competency [Audio Engineering Society, Library of Congress, Association for Recorded Sound Collections].
8. *Disseminate collections survey results.*
   Disseminate collections survey results from the symposium and provide this information to organizations that perform similar surveys, such as the National Recording Preservation Board at the Library of Congress, to ensure that small and midsize archives are included in national statistics [Council on Library and Information Resources, American Folklife Center].
9. *Develop a registry of recordings.*
   Track the existence and location of preserved audio recordings with machine-readable records and online registries to guard against duplication of effort and maximize preservation of unique recordings.

10. *Develop training workshops.*
    Develop a series of workshops where national and large university archives can provide training and guidance to small and midsize archives on sound preservation. This could be a "SWAT team" approach, with several experts who might be called on as needed, perhaps to approach the National Endowment for the Humanities for funding through the Preservation Assistance Grants category [Association of Recorded Sound Collections in collaboration with the American Folklife Center; the Library of Congress; Harvard University; Indiana University; University of California, Los Angeles; and others].

Intellectual Property Rights

1. *Establish a listserv.*
   Establish a listserv to continue the conversations of the relevant symposia [American Folklife Center, American Folklore Society, January 2001].
2. *Develop ethical guidelines for dissemination.*
   Convene a larger group to discuss and develop ethical guidelines for publication and online presentation of audio recordings from ethnographic archives. Include ethicists, artists, and community members. The group should consider the application of intellectual property and copyright law as it applies to ethnographic field recordings. The group should also map relationships for materials already collected and investigate the standards used by local communities, tribal groups, and artists for the issues surrounding intellectual property rights [National Endowment for the Humanities, Library of Congress, Recording Industry Association of America, American Society of Composers, Authors and Publishers (ASCAP), Broadcast Music, Inc. (BMI)].
3. *Develop model contracts.*
   Develop model agreements and issue lists for institutions to access and consult on the issue of intellectual property rights vis-à-vis the collector, the artist or tradition bearer, and the archive or institution. Post these model agreements online through the Federal Communications Commission symposium Web site [Library of Congress; Smithsonian Institution; Indiana University; Harvard University; University of California, Los Angeles].
4. *Renegotiate existing contracts if they are inadequate.*
   Encourage archivists and collectors to renegotiate inadequate contracts and agreements for clear rights protection [all].
5. *Create a database of public domain materials.*
   Create and maintain a database of materials in the public domain and digitize these materials on a priority basis [all].
6. *Establish a liaison to industry.*
   Establish a liaison to the commercial music industry to facilitate access to back catalogs and out-of-print recordings held in commercial vaults [National Academy of Recording Arts and Sciences, Recording Industry Association of America, institutional repositories].

7. *Provide rights training.*
   Provide archival employees with ongoing training on rights issues [all].
8. *Publish a guide to rights.*
   Develop an online and print publication on the basic intellectual property rights issues and use of archival collections, and disseminate this publication to sound archives. Perhaps model this on the publication *Working with Folk Materials in New York State* [New York Folklore Society, American Folklore Society, Society of Ethnomusicology].
9. *Update existing fieldwork handbooks.*
   Update existing fieldwork handbooks to include training and guidelines on rights and issues of privacy, along with advice on not depositing materials that may be too problematic [all].
10. *Offer continuing education.*
    Offer continuing education at professional meetings on intellectual property rights, privacy in metadata, and other issues [American Folklore Society, Society of Ethnomusicology, Association for Recorded Sound Collections, American Library Association].
11. *Represent copyright interests to lawmakers.*
    Form a committee to address copyright law. Explore increasing access to out-of-print recordings through compulsory licensing [Library of Congress, Recording Industry Association of America, BMI, Music Library Association, American Library Association, American Folklore Society, Association for Recorded Sound Collections].
12. *Update interlibrary loan regulations.*
    Update interlibrary loan regulations in the copyright law, work toward compulsory licensing of music that companies withhold because of uncertain rights, and encourage Congress to conduct oversight hearings addressing fair-use issues [all].